THE
SABIAN
SYMBOLS

TO WRITE TO THE AUTHOR

If you wish to contact the author or would like more information about this book, please write to the author in care of Llewellyn Worldwide and we will forward your request. Both the author and publisher appreciate hearing from you and learning of your enjoyment of this book and how it has helped you. Llewellyn Worldwide cannot guarantee that every letter written to the author can be answered, but all will be forwarded. Please write to:

Blain Bovee
℅ Llewellyn Worldwide
P.O. Box 64383, Dept. 0-7387-0530-6
St. Paul, MN 55164-0383, U.S.A.
Please enclose a self-addressed stamped envelope for reply,
or $1.00 to cover costs. If outside U.S.A., enclose
international postal reply coupon.

Many of Llewellyn's authors have websites with
additional information and resources.
For more information, please visit our website at
http://www.llewellyn.com

THE
SABIAN
SYMBOLS
&
ASTROLOGICAL
ANALYSIS

The original symbols fully revealed

Blain Bovee

Llewellyn Publications
Saint Paul, Minnesota

First Edition
First Printing, 2004

Background cover painting © 2004, Julie Condon / SuperStock
Cover design by Gavin Dayton Duffy
Edited by Andrea Neff

The chart wheel was produced by the Kepler program by permission of Cosmic Patterns Software, Inc. (www.AstroSoftware.com)

Library of Congress Cataloging-in-Publication Data

Bovee, Blain, 1950–
    The Sabian symbols & astrological analysis : the original symbols fully revealed / Blain Bovee.
        p.   cm.
    Includes bibliographical references.
    ISBN 0-7387-0530-6
    1. Astrology. 2. Zodiac. 3. Signs and symbols—Miscellanea.   I. Title: Sabian symbols and astrological analysis.   II. Title
    BF1711.B68 2004
    133.5—dc22   2004057752

Llewellyn Publications
A Division of Llewellyn Worldwide, Ltd.
P.O. Box 64383, Dept. 0-7387-0530-6
St. Paul, MN 55164-0383, U.S.A.
www.llewellyn.com

Printed in the United States of America

acknowledgments

The opportunity to write a book on the Sabian Symbols has been an extraordinary honor. I would like to thank the many people who made this project possible, who helped it to take shape, and who assisted in so many ways as to make adequate acknowledgment nearly impossible.

To Noel Tyl, a giant of a man in mind and spirit, whose generosity, wisdom, and encouragement exceed all reasonable expectation, I give my most heartfelt thanks.

To Diana Roche, whose gracious and kind words of encouragement helped me reach crucial realizations about the wonderful gift Marc Edmund Jones brought to the world, I most gratefully offer my deep appreciation. I can only hope that my work echoes Diana's deep respect for the original authenticity and genius of the Sabian Symbols.

For the indispensable guidance and supportive counsel of Stephanie Clement, and the ever kind Andrea Neff, I am very grateful.

I thank all of my friends who played a role in my understanding the Sabian Symbols: Dale O'Brien, who introduced me to the Sabian Symbols at the start of my astrological journey, and whose insights first revealed the magic and range of sense of the Sabian Symbols; Lynda Hill, whose generous enthusiasm naturally inspires many fruitful reflections; and the kindness of many others, through whose communications I have drawn much encouragement and insight, especially Antonio Pinto, my dear Portuguese friend, I give my thanks.

Most of all, I thank my wife, Clare, whose unswerving support and dedication fills my heart with love and wonder.

May this book be received in the spirit of honoring the words and genius of Marc Edmund Jones.

Dedication

Words are magic

Dipped in the wisdom
Of our ancestors
Words pluck strings reaching far through time
Ringing accordance with the heavens
Revealing the time we call "Now."

Honor the words.

CONTENTS

FOREWORD

Turn on your flashlight in a dark room: you discover something out of the blackness; was it there before you illuminated it?

We all know phrases of music—just four, five, six notes—that stop us in our tracks when we hear them, because we respond to them so personally. Where were those notes, where was that wisp of melody before the composer captured it? Why do we resonate with it so strongly?

Does knowledge exist independently of our knowing? Is it all out there waiting for us to discover it?

These are familiar existential gambits, reminding us of sentient miracles . . . and they apply strongly to our experience of the Sabian Symbols.

In a park some eighty years ago, a simple woman with psychic sensitivity and an astrologer/occultist sat together in a car under a tree in San Diego. They spent the whole day together divining symbolic images for every degree in the zodiac! THAT'S discovery out of the dark; that's capturing significant melodies; that's knowledge brought into being for us to know.

We can prove why there are 360 degree-units in the circle, and that proof is some three thousand years old! But why and how does each one of those units have something to say about life and how we live it? The answer is within us already, and that's why the Sabian Symbols are revelations indeed.

At first, face to face with something coming out of the dark, we can be intimidated. What is unknown, what is inscrutable, carries with it a fear of the negative. We are afraid of portents that may threaten us somehow.

This is where interpretation comes in. Symbols, by definition, require interpretation. Symbols represent something and they must be molded to fit our understanding, our reality experience.

For example: the Sabian symbol for the sixth degree of Taurus is "A bridge being built across a gorge," with the opposite degree (6 Scorpio) symbolizing "A gold rush." Although there is extremely telling and introspectively deep discussion tied to these two symbols—and we are led throughout this book into those rich libraries of thought by inspired astrologer Blain Bovee—we can feel that bridging a gorge suggests "making it, getting to another level." We can also appreciate that "making connections" can come into high focus supportively.

"A gold rush" can initially point the way to the reward, to "making it," to benefiting from reception by others.

Now this sixth degree of Taurus-Scorpio is on the Ascendant of mass murderer Charles Manson (erstwhile songwriter and singer trying to make it into show business, trying to cross the gorge from his dismal life start-up situation). This Ascendant is in high, high focus within Manson's horoscope; it could be called an obsessive point of focus, and the Sabian Symbol pair illuminates its substance significantly.

But that degree also holds my Uranus, the planet very important in my horoscope, within everything I do, an intense focus of creativity, individuation, and international exposure. In my careers as communicator (opera singer, advertising director, astrologer-therapist, author of thirty books, lecturer throughout twenty-six countries), I have constantly tried to build "across a gorge," to share knowledge, to make connections and be rewarded for it. I rush to the gold of evaluation, appreciation, acceptance, applause. I am entirely comfortable with those images. They explain much about me, why I am alive.

Bovee expands this to involve the concept of "taking life by the throat." So many times in younger years, I was recognized for ambition, conspicuous drive, and courage to make things happen. With Manson, it is not difficult to see the frustrated collapse into the gorge related to this image as well. He didn't make it across, and the reasons why are articulated elsewhere in his horoscope, with different themes illuminating the situation.

Top golfer Tiger Woods has the twenty-fourth degree of Gemini on his Midheaven, his focus of career and father. The Sabian symbol is "Children skating on ice," with the complementary opposite (24 Sagittarius) being "A bluebird standing at the door of the house." Ready to throw up your hands?

Besides guiding us carefully through the etymological backdrop of words, fine-tuning the incredible references that came out of the dark to Elsie Wheeler and Marc Edmund Jones, Bovee shows a style of relating symbolisms to personal awareness. For the "Children skating on ice" image, we are led through the child experience being crucial to gaining confidence on ice sometimes thin, slippery, dangerous. We know that the young Tiger Woods was demonstrating his golf swing on television at age two-and-a-half! We know that his father drilled the child constantly for some twenty years! And the bluebird image at the door of the house tells us to anticipate the happiness in fulfillment "out there" in the world.

For Tiger Woods, this Midheaven degree is obsessively focused and crucially exploited. He was born to be taught to make it! And he did.

We are learning the adroit skill of interpretation. We can not be put off by the new experience; by following Bovee's lead-in, we learn large gulps of knowledge with every symbolism we study. It quickly becomes our nature to identify life endeavors with the insight of the Sabian Symbols.

Imagine yourself in conversation with Pope John Paul II. You know his Sun is in the twenty-eighth degree of Taurus (with the complement being the twenty-eighth degree of Scorpio). The Sabian Symbols are "A woman pursued by mature romance"!!! and "The king of the fairies approaching his domain."

How can this be the focus for the leader of world Catholicism? If we introduce sensitivity to explain "a woman" and idealization to explain "romance," suddenly we understand more. The idea of "pursuing" is sensitively and unflaggingly interpreted to be his reach for the ideal. Aha!

And with "king of the fairies," Bovee shows us the symbolic reference to a realm charged with mystery and rarified energy: "an unreal reality." This is indeed the birthright of John Paul II.

I have worked with Bovee's manuscript many times to help refine what astrologers call rectification, adjusting an unknown or unsure birth time to workable accuracy at the Ascendant, at the Midheaven. It is uncanny how the Sabian Symbol can provide the polishing touch in such work, how the symbology can spark the thought that then ignites all the other measurement guidelines of the horoscope.

Bovee writes nobly, with deepest respect for the art of words and images. He abets illumination. Once we see his images of the original Sabian Symbols, we recognize them in a primal way, and we know they can be with us forever.

Bovee lights the dark and captures personally significant melody.

This enriching book takes its place with the classic Sabian Symbol literature by Marc Edmund Jones and Dane Rudhyar.

—Noel Tyl

INTRODUCTION

The Sabian Symbols are a set of 360 symbols corresponding to the degrees of the zodiac. Created in 1925 by Marc Edmund Jones with the help of a medium, Elsie Wheeler, the symbols were noted in pencil on notecards in an extraordinary one-day session in San Diego, California. Over the years, the Sabian Symbols have filtered into the astrological community, creating a swell of interest, especially among practicing astrologers.

Research on the Sabian Symbols has produced some wonderful work, that of Dane Rudhyar, for example, in his *An Astrological Mandala: The Cycle of Transformation and Its 360 Symbolic Phases*. Marc Edmund Jones published his work *The Sabian Symbols in Astrology* in 1953, culminating over thirty years of research. In addition to these two classics on the Sabian Symbols, there have been many new "versions" presented to the public. It is important to note that, somehow, as time has gone by, authors have had the tendency to change the words, introduce new phrasing, edit, and "tidy up" the originals. Even Dane Rudhyar considered the Sabian Symbols to be in need of "reformulation."

The version of the Sabian Symbols used in this book is that of the original penciled notations of Marc Edmund Jones. Diana Roche, in her wonderful book *The Sabian Symbols: A Screen of Prophecy,* has done the world of Sabian Symbol research a tremendous service by supplying images of the actual hand-penciled symbols from the original notecards. This has cleared up so much confusion resulting from years of manipulating the words used, sometimes adding words that Marc Edmund Jones never wrote, and often adding additional phrasing in an attempt to clarify.

In my own research on the Sabian Symbols, I began with a rather cavalier approach to how the Symbols actually read, giving nicknames such as the "Samson degree" to 28 Virgo, which originally read "A bald-headed man." But following Marc Edmund Jones' own stated sense of why he chose Elsie Wheeler to be the "medium" for the Sabian Symbols, and appreciating Diana Roche's contribution to this matter, I am fully committed to using Jones' words, and only his words.

I have discovered that the Sabian Symbols are richer and more internally consistent when the original wording is honored. The fact that Elsie Wheeler was relatively inexperienced in worldly matters and education only enhanced the freshness and purity of the images for which she was the medium. Marc Edmund Jones recorded his words in the intensity of the procedure, perhaps disabling the analytical mind in the haste to quickly capture in words the images that Elsie Wheeler relayed. Consequently, we find expressions that may not be politically correct in contemporary society, but that express an honest insight that transcends niggling questions of ingrained bias. Why anyone should distrust this, why anyone should feel the need to second-guess the words chosen, begs a serious question.

A case in point: the twelfth degree of Cancer and Capricorn read: "A Chinese servant nursing a baby with a message" and "A student of nature lecturing." This degree-pair expresses a fundamental motif of bringing a message, nurturing the potential to bring a message, of information of the world as seen through fresh eyes. This is precisely the reason Marc Edmund Jones chose Elsie Wheeler over the more sophisticated and worldly Zoe Wells. Jones thought the relatively fresh and intuitive mind of Elsie Wheeler would be less likely to distort her intuitions through an educated opinion. Jones' view on this is obviously a contentious assumption. The point remains, however, that there is no need whatsoever to change the words Jones used to express the image pictures of Elsie Wheeler, for that is the much more contentious and questionable assumption: that one can correct, enhance, or expand on the originals.

Correcting, expanding, interpretively enhancing, is exactly what the so-called mimeograph version attempts to do. The mimeograph version handed out to the students of Marc Edmund Jones attempted to expand on the original cryptic penciled notes. For example, the mimeograph version reads for the twelfth degree of Cancer: "A slant-eyed Chinese woman is nursing a baby, and all about the child is the glorious nimbus of divine incarnation." Leaving aside the somewhat surprising phrase "a slant-eyed Chinese woman," even Dane Rudhyar strongly addresses the tendency to overemphasize the messianic tone. Rudhyar writes: "This symbol has been unduly glamorized: there is no particular reference here to an avatar or messiah, except in the sense that every man is potentially the avatar or manifestation of a Soul that has a definite and relatively unique function in the vast field of activity we call Earth."[1] Curiously, even after making this astute observation, Rudhyar offers this interpretation for the same symbol: "A Chinese woman nursing a baby whose aura reveals him to be the reincarnation of a great teacher."[2]

It must be asked: What do we presume to be doing when we alter the original words and insights of the Sabian Symbols? That Marc Edmund Jones wrote in a way that today would be considered somewhat politically incorrect is not a real issue. In each and every case, the originals yield insights that, in my view, far exceed any existing variations. Any alteration whatsoever risks deflecting the original genius of the Sabian Symbols; risks distorting, through interpretive assumptions, the intuitive integrity of how the Sabian Symbols came to be. This can be said of any attempt to interpret the meaning of the Sabian Symbols, including this one. That is, however, as it should be, since furthering understanding of the Sabian Symbols for practical application must, of necessity, be an ongoing process. The approach in this work will be, therefore, one of strict adherence to, and honoring of, the integrity of the original version of the Sabian Symbols.

THE INTERNAL ORGANIZATION OF THE SABIAN SYMBOLS

From early on in the exploration of the Sabian Symbols, it was recognized that the full cycle of symbols exhibited internal structures that augmented their understanding and the depth and range of significance. Dane Rudhyar considered the Sabian Symbols to be a modern American I Ching, that is, a comprehensive set of symbols organized in terms of a time mandala that exhibited a similar inexhaustible resource of sense for all human situations, and that "spoke" in a modern language rooted in American sensibilities. The I Ching is the Chinese classic of time and change, also known as The Book of Changes. This great text remains one of the classic extant books of wisdom used all over the world, despite being firmly rooted in ancient Chinese sensibilities. The language of the I Ching is difficult to penetrate with understanding and consequently seems out of reach to many. Rudhyar's cogent appreciation of the Sabian Symbols, which, like the cryptic images found in the I Ching, form an intricate system of images based on the astrological mandala of space and time, lies at the crux of all future Sabian Symbol research.

There are, however, several key points about the symbolic language, the words used in the Sabian Symbols, that call for serious consideration. First, the words of Marc Edmund Jones were written on the original notecards in 1925. In the ensuing years, language, communication, and information systems underwent an explosion of development in North America and the world. As a consequence, many of the Symbols, as they were written, appear to be already out of date. This has led most writers on the Sabian Symbols to change words and modernize expressions in an attempt to make the meaning of the Sabian Symbols more accessible. This is an approach, as already noted, that I do not support.

Secondly, Rudhyar's depiction of the Sabian Symbols as an American I Ching may be misleading. It might be presumed that the internal sense of the Sabian Symbols is accessible only to English-speaking peoples. My own research, in this book, has proved otherwise. By adhering strictly to the words of Marc Edmund Jones, rich veins of sense can be traced to almost every world tradition from a vast array of historical periods. Simple etymological research reveals reservoirs of meaning that reach the world over, tapping into every major language, expressing universal themes of the human collective throughout time. Changing words and adding phrases may mislead interpretive understanding, directing thought along pathways that are not necessarily central to the original symbols. One of the greatest challenges in this work was to limit the scope of research into a manageable form. The reader may reliably understand that when there is a specific reference to a culture or religious tradition, the story does not end there. I have attempted to choose only the references that seem to most succinctly express the sense of the symbol motifs. In terms of Sabian Symbol research, this can only be a beginning.

OPPOSING DEGREE SYMBOLS

In his culminating work, *The Sabian Symbols in Astrology*, Marc Edmund Jones presented the opposing symbols organized on facing pages. Thus the first degree of Aries faced the first degree of Libra. His insight was that symbols that oppose one another, 180 degrees apart on the zodiacal circle, actually mirror the sense of each other; they work together in a meaningful way. Unfortunately, Jones' explanatory text makes it difficult to appreciate this insight regarding the reflection of sense in opposing degree symbols. Dane Rudhyar flatly stated that he found it difficult to recognize the complementary thematics of opposing degrees. In this work, I have taken up the challenge of the oppositional approach again, with the format difference of writing about the symbol pairs within the same text, thus inviting the reader to experience the interweaving of themes and motifs every time a particular symbol is referenced.

The implication of this approach is simple: for astrological application, one must think in terms of degree-pairs. To have a planetary placement in a degree, the first degree of Aries, for example, does not restrict, and should never restrict, the astrologer to the Sabian Symbol for the first degree of Aries. It is, in each case, best interpreted with and through the opposing symbol of the first degree of Libra. The cases are innumerable where someone does not resonate with the specific symbol for an important planetary placement but recognizes vividly the sense of the opposing symbol. Consequently, in preparing a horoscope, it is necessary to note both symbols, the oppositional pair, for each planetary and point placement. The rewards are immediately apparent.

Marc Edmund Jones was concerned with the so-called reverse symbols, symbols that seem to lend themselves to negative interpretations, using words like "failure" and phrases like "a large disappointed audience," "an airplane falling," and so on. There are those who tend to jump on any negative possibility available. This is not, however, the nature of symbols. Symbols, in and of themselves, are neither positive nor negative. A symbol can resonate with sense only in relation to the lived reality of the individual or to an actual situation. In life, as with symbols, the most dire circumstance can prove to be a very positive event. The opposing-degree approach in this book dispels any need to be upset due to assumptions about "negative" meanings.

THE FIVE-DEGREE CYCLE

The fivefold cycle of degrees has been noted in earlier works on the Sabian Symbols. It is a useful organizational principle that, for astrological purposes, allows the reader to understand an internal development of sense. The fivefold cycle corresponds to five aspect relationships in astrology: conjunction, opposition, trine, square, and quintile. Through these qualitative orientations, one can easily detect an unfolding story, an unfolding of general themes throughout the text of consecutive degree-pairs.

The first degree of each cycle of five, the conjunction, brings energy to a new situation. It illuminates, and infuses an energetic thrust into life and the world. There can be a simple naiveté about beginnings, or a sense of simple, innocent first steps into a new and fresh situation. Corresponding to the conjunction aspect, the first degree of every five-degree cycle is therefore a new focus.

The second degree brings awareness of "otherness." A fundamental split is more clearly thrust upon the situation: self and other; this and that. After bursting through the door with an energy to manifest something with the first degree, or conjunction, there arises a sharp pulling up to consider an element or factor that had not been initially considered. Hence the underlying theme is an "awareness of" something else, not a general pervasive awareness of space, but one intentionally organized which thrusts contrasting energies into the situation.

The third degree addresses situations that flow easily, embellishing awareness, refining self-definition, exploring within relatively safe and protected circumstances. The third-degree symbols suggest working with existing circumstances: building out of the reigning conditions of one's situation or the situation and established conditions that define, perhaps even dominate, individual efforts to build. Corresponding to the trine aspect, each third degree of the cycle attempts to manage or maintain a position, hold on to what has been initiated, attempting to stabilize developments. This can manifest in a negative sense as being in a rut with no desire or energy to change things, or it can be characterized as having a groove that is comfortable and therefore calls for energy to maintain it.

The fourth degree presents a challenge: the energy to build, construct, perhaps even to consummate developments of the preceding degrees in a human manifestation. Working with one's situation, a challenge motivates self-application to work on both weak and promising potentials. There is always an element of discomfort within the fourth degree of each series, which has the feel of struggling to fit in. For example, an individual may be torn between individuality and social expectations, or between something desired now, but for which one has to wait or for which one must work. The internal tension generates energy to work on the situation depicted, and therefore is potentially very creative, albeit with a struggle.

The fifth degree, corresponding to the quintile, the 72-degree aspect, brings a flare of creativity that seems to resolve the thrust of the issues in the preceding four degree-pairs. In a sense, the fifth degree is a culmination marked by ease and achievement, insight, and a capacity to naturally manifest in a manner that is comfortably true to oneself. The struggles of the preceding fourth phase are integrated. The stabilizing energy of the third phase is elevated to a higher manifestation. The split awareness of unforeseen factors of the second phase is resolved in a higher awareness. The original thrust of the first phase finds an expression that exhibits genius and creativity.

The fifth phase of unfolding has a feel of completion, yet is never entirely complete. The consummation gives way to yet another forward thrust expressed in the succeeding first degree of the next fivefold cycle, and thus, the unfolding of time and situation continues in the wheel of all 360 degrees, all 180 degree-pairs.

PRECEDING AND SUCCEEDING SYMBOLS

As the fivefold organization demonstrates, the sense of any particular Sabian Symbol is woven with those before and those that follow. A planetary placement in a specific degree always draws upon and arises out of the previous situation, the previous Sabian Symbol theme. It also flows on to the following symbolic expression as a natural development, growing into the next degree symbol as the individual integrates, individuates, and matures through life experience.

The reader is strongly encouraged to read the story as it unfolds rather than insist on the quick fix of a specific placement meaning one specific thing. Symbols do not operate that way: the fast-food approach will not a satisfying meal make.

Marc Edmund Jones writes: "There are unlimited ways in which these Sabian Symbols can be interpreted; and the practiced student or professional astrologer need not confine himself to any one mode of approach."[3] To this statement might be added that every approach to symbols in general is interpretive in nature. To be true to the sense of symbols requires an openness to ever more sense, to further interpretation. It is a process on its way, a work in progress, and therefore calls for a deep trust and appreciation of the rich resource to continually reward mature and sincere investigation in new ways.

APPLYING THE SABIAN SYMBOLS

To illustrate how one might explore the meaning of the Sabian Symbols, and in particular, apply a particular symbol or symbol pairing, consider the sixteenth degree of Cancer/Capricorn: "A man before a square with a manuscript scroll before him" (16 Cancer) and "Boys and girls in gymnasium suits" (16 Capricorn). The sixteenth degree of Cancer is the degree within which my Midheaven lies. (Please note that when searching for the pertinent Sabian Symbol, each degree placement of a planet or point is to be rounded up.) The Midheaven is the point in a horoscope signifying the highest point to which one strives in life, suggesting career potentials, vocation, and a sense of the gift one seeks to bring out into the world through one's life. On another level, the Midheaven represents one's conscious awareness of oneself: who you think you are in the world. With an accurate birth time, the Midheaven can be precisely ascertained, yielding a reliable point around which one's aspirations can be understood.

"A man before a square with a manuscript scroll before him" is an image of a search for meaning through interpretive means. The "square" is a symbol of a four-sided mandala, itself a symbolic representation of the whole, of life, the cosmos, the human world. Looking at a mandala while holding a manuscript scroll suggests having a secondary document as an aid to interpret and understand the square symbol. In my life, I have spent many long hours literally doing just that: years of studying Tibetan and Chinese manuscripts with dictionaries piled around my desk while in graduate school; years of reading German and Greek philosophic texts, again with dictionaries and resource books ever in hand. I can say that when occupied in this manner, I feel very much myself.

One of the key motifs within this degree symbol is that of a "code book." To illustrate, let me take a scene from one of my favorite movie moments, a scene from the Marx Brothers' film *A Day at the Races*. I should perhaps add that I love horse racing, especially the intense process of deciphering the voluminous information contained in the past performance pages of the racing form. A visit to any racetrack in the world will provide one with the same sight over and over again: throngs of individuals poring over immense amounts of detailed information attempting to get a read on the race.

In the film *A Day at the Races,* there is the famous "Tuttsie-Fruitsie Ice Cream" scene. Groucho is at a betting window at a racetrack trying to lay down a win bet on the horse of his choice. Chico, who is out of money, is pushing an ice cream cart around calling out for customers, "Tuttsie-Fruitsie! Get your Tuttsie-Fruitsie ice cream!" Chico sees Groucho and, sensing an easy mark, convinces him to ignore his choice in the race and to buy a code book to decipher the real winner. Groucho buys the book but can't understand it, since the code book is written in an indecipherable code of its own. Groucho complains to Chico, who in turn convinces Groucho to buy another code book to decipher the code book. After a process of selling several more code books to Groucho (all of which come from inside the ice cream cart, and which now are stacked high in Groucho's arms), Chico takes Groucho's money to the betting window and puts a win bet on Groucho's original pick. Groucho gets shut out at the betting window altogether and has to listen to the race call without having wagered. Of course, Groucho's original pick comes home a winner. Chico cashes his winning ticket with a big smile and runs away, leaving Groucho with the ice cream cart and a mountain of code books.

Horoscopes are mandalas. The art of interpretation lies in the analysis and articulation of symbols synthesized and expressed in time and space. Following the downside of the Marx Brothers' tale, overinterpreting, overmeasuring, overanalyzing with an armload of code books, like this one I might add, can be one's downfall. Simple intuition and natural intelligence applied on the basis of solid principles of analysis are often all one really needs. That is an important point when it comes to deciphering the Sabian Symbols.

The Sabian Symbol for the sixteenth degree of Cancer seems to depict a situation that says: "There it is all laid out before you. Now read this and see what you can make of it." This symbol will manifest in many ways: for any interpretive work involving texts or language, blueprints, maps organization or design of any kind, and productive, deeper "readings" (hermeneutics) of something that is symbolic of a whole, and of course, code books. As a practicing astrologer, I work with the horoscope mandala on a daily basis, my prized reference and code books always near at hand. My home is adorned with Tibetan mandalas on the walls. I tend naturally to interpret everything in my life through a mandala principle. I love books of wisdom that do the same, like the Chinese classic, the I Ching.

The opposing degree, "Boys and girls in gymnasium suits" (16 Capricorn), also reflects recognizable elements in my life. I literally have coached girls' basketball teams, track teams, and soccer teams. I have a woeful tendency to dress in what is only slightly short of a uniform, rarely departing from the comfort of blue jeans and a black T-shirt. I have loved, in younger years, team sports, paying special attention to having the proper dress for each activity. I love the team spirit, especially complimenting the talents of others in order to help them show their best. It is apparent that the Sabian Symbols reflect an almost literal sense that is easily recognized in my life.

Literal manifestations of the Sabian Symbols are not uncommon, however it must be pointed out that they are by no means the rule. I have found that older people who have done well at integrating their potentials in life tend to be literally living their pertinent Sabian Symbols. On occasion, this is so striking that I can hardly tell the client anything new, so familiar and at ease are they with their own horoscope and Sabian Symbol potentials. More often, clients are still on the way to realizing their personal potential. The Sabian Symbols in these cases can be exhilarating in their revelations. "Literalism" is not at all the equivalent of literal manifestation. Literalism kills symbolic sense, deadens rich resonance, reduces sense possibilities to lifeless stickers.

For example, a man with a Sun placement in a degree with the Sabian Symbol referring to a young naked girl would, out of literalism, assume the symbol can have no applicable sense for him: he is not a little girl. One might strive to force a number symbolism with little result, for example: "Three old masters hanging in a gallery" or "Three mounds of knowledge on a philosopher's head." Non-Jewish people might assume that the "rabbi" degree symbol can have little meaning for them. Such approaches are missing the point of Sabian Symbol application. I have attempted, through the combining of opposing symbols, to offer enough resource for fruitful reflection about applicable sense. One must take any interpretation of the Sabian Symbols as a starting point for creative, insightful, and imaginative exploration.

SABIAN SYMBOLS IN LITERAL MANIFESTATION

Literal manifestations of the Sabian Symbols in people's lives do occur, however, and can be a great source of revelation, humor, and surprise. Here are some examples:

- George W. Leppert: May 9, 1849 (Schaffenburg, Germany, 8:42 PM): the three-legged man who walked on all three legs until age sixteen. He had Uranus at 23°45' Aries. Sabian Symbol pair: "An open window and a net curtain blowing into a cornucopia" (24 Aries) and "A third wing on the left side of a butterfly" (24 Libra). Here is a perfect example of how important it is to work with the opposing symbol pairs. Just looking at the Aries degree seems to miss this extraordinary manifestation of a "third wing"!

- Anna Nicole Smith: November 28, 1967 (Mexia, Texas, 7:08:50 AM): famous for winning a huge estate settlement from her second husband, oil tycoon J. H. Marshall II. Her first husband was a fry cook. Anna has both the Sun and Ascendant at 5°36' Sagittarius. Sabian Symbol pair: "Drilling for oil" (6 Gemini) and "A game of cricket" (6 Sagittarius).

- The Avro Arrow: October 4, 1957 (Winnipeg, Canada, 12:00 PM): Canadian-engineered jet far ahead of its time, which promised to revolutionize the aeronautics industry. Although the test models excelled in performance, the project was "killed" by the government after only six planes were produced, and just before testing a new engine so advanced that it is still a legend within the world of aeronautic engineering. Saturn is at 9°54' Sagittarius. Sabian Symbol pair: "An aeroplane falling" (10 Gemini) and "A golden-haired goddess of opportunity" (10 Sagittarius). Note the opposing degree symbol again almost literally tells the story, however the Canadian air industry has yet to fully recover after missing that golden opportunity.

Using the same Sabian Symbol pair, consider Antoine de Saint-Exupéry: June 29, 1900 (Lyon, France, 9:15 FROT). The famous author of *The Little Prince* died in a plane crash in 1944. He had Uranus at 9°23' Sagittarius and his North Node at 9°39' Sagittarius.

Consider John Baird, the inventor of television in 1926. Much of Baird's research was conducted at his home where he worked with the equipment available to him at the time. John Baird had Mars in the thirteenth degree of Scorpio: "An inventor experimenting." In chapter 2, the amplification of this symbol, "An inventor experimenting," is an image of tinkering with possible better ways. "Invention" is an ingenious creation or devising something new, something discovered or innovative. "Experimenting" means to try out. Experiments try and test new inventions for their usefulness or effectiveness. One might tinker with an array of apparatus, attempting to make something invented work, working with whatever one can get one's hands on. Imagine an eccentric inventor in a garage cluttered with all manner of saved gadgets, parts of discarded items, and supplies, many of which are pieced together in some new, inventive way. Tinkering with "stuff" depends largely on what is at hand to work with: an improved mousetrap; a better flush apparatus for the toilet. Sometimes inventions aren't worth a "tinker's dam": the disposable plug used to stop up a hole in a pot while the tinker repairs it.

Benjamin Franklin, with Saturn in the thirteenth degree of Taurus, is also remembered as a scientist and inventor in addition to his responsibilities as an historically significant statesman. The famous image of Franklin flying a kite with a key attached in order to attract lightning resonates with the inventor experimenting degree, even though it is the Taurus placement that his Saturn occupies. The added sense of carrying Saturnine responsibilities is only amplified when the symbol opposition is considered: "A man handling baggage" (13 Taurus) and "An inventor experimenting" (13 Scorpio).

Literal manifestations are common, but not always the case. Often one must work with the internal motifs of the symbols to see how they apply. Having a good resource book that reliably sets out an abundant range of meanings is indispensable. The reader will note that each entry in this book lays a solid foundation of meaning for the exact words of Marc Edmund Jones, outlines a central thrust of sense for each degree, provides situational illustrations of the combined symbol sense, and provides concise and insightful suggestions for application and further reflection.

FAMOUS EXAMPLES SHARING A SABIAN SYMBOL

Another approach to illustrate the use of the Sabian Symbols is to look at the degree-pair first, and then offer examples of famous people in order to demonstrate the range of sense application. Two degree-pair examples follow:

"A jewelry shop" (23 Taurus)
and "A bunny metamorphosed into a fairy" (23 Scorpio)

Aspect: Trine.
Quality: Maintaining.
Shared motifs: 'The ethereal glow that evokes other realms,'
'mirth and reality,' 'less is more, more or less.'

This degree-pair speaks to the question of authenticity, of the thin line between reality and imagination, between coarse and rarified appearances. A jewelry shop houses an array of gems and gold, trinkets and adornments, which create an aura of all-a-glitter. But all that glitters is not gold. "Bunny" is an endearing nickname for a rabbit. Even to contemplate a bunny metamorphosing into a fairy spirit evokes a sense of a rarification of the ordinary, the common, into the extraordinary. Such experiences evoke questions of where the reality lies. One may be shocked or surprised to perceive that something is not real, yet the emotional experience is very real until such time that the perception is proved real or just an illusion. Taken together, the symbols suggest heightened sensitivities, special awareness of other realities, rarified realms of experience. With these thoughts in mind, consider the following examples of famous people:

- Prince Charles: Sun in Taurus: may wear "crown jewels" someday and is known for his interest in "energies" outside the "ordinary," such as holistic health techniques, organic farming, and a passionate interest in architecture, where he publicly attacks modern architectural designs and fights to protect buildings exemplifying classical architectural features.

- Joseph McCarthy: Sun in Scorpio: famous for the "witch hunts" in the early 1950s. "McCarthyism" was the excessive tendency to see "reds" and "commies" behind every rock and tree.

- Marshall Applewhite: Moon in Taurus: Heaven's Gate cult leader; believed a UFO hidden in the Hale-Bopp comet was coming for the cult members. His cult believed that humans are entities cloned by extraterrestrials. Members committed mass suicide so that their souls could be reunited with the aliens within the Hale-Bopp comet. Note that the following degree-pair contains a direct reference to comets, illustrating how the significance of the Sabian Symbols carries over into preceding and succeeding degree-pairs.

- Michael Jackson: Mars in Taurus. The superstar is arguably better known for the transformation of his appearance over the years through plastic surgery.

- Robert Ripley: Jupiter in Taurus: created "Ripley's Believe It or Not!®"

- Carlos Castaneda: Saturn in Scorpio: author of books based on the shamanic teachings of Don Juan, which deal with numinous powers that lie behind the appearances of things.

"A Spaniard serenading his senorita" (26 Taurus)
and "Indians making camp" (26 Scorpio)

Aspect: Conjunction.
Quality: Focus.
Shared motif: 'Finding one's new place out in the world.'

This degree-pair suggests the ways in which one might find one's new place in the world. The serenader seeks through serene song a place in the heart of the beloved. Itinerate Indians make a camp after a long day's journey. Both symbols evoke awareness of evening activity. Both suggest taking one's place in a temporary location: below the beloved's window, in a good camping area with water and protection, near promising hunting grounds. A group may sing camp songs around the fire at their campsite, or a serenader may inject humor into a song to effect a smile and endearment in the one being serenaded. Both situations suggest an element of unselfconscious fun. There is also a sense of belonging to a camp, taking a stance on some issue, and pitching one's case. With these themes in mind, consider the following well-known examples:

- Liberace: Sun in Taurus: flamboyant entertainer who blended humor and prodigious musical talent.
- Cleo Lane: Mercury in Scorpio: singer; five-octave range; hit highest note by a human voice ever recorded.
- Sir Arthur Sullivan: Mercury in Taurus: composer; "Gilbert and Sullivan."
- Groucho Marx: Venus in Scorpio: of the Marx Brothers, was known to sing a campy tune or two. Note that Groucho's Mercury placement is in the fourth degree of Libra: "A group around a campfire."
- Victor Borge: Mars in Scorpio: pianist, composer, humorist. "Comedy in Music" was Borge's Broadway hit, and he is remembered for his wonderful concert performances filled with puns, slapstick, marvelous piano playing, and his outrageous use of the "double entendre." Victor Borge significantly also has his Venus placement in the degree-pair expressing the use of the double entendre: "Two Dutch children talking" (15 Gemini) and "The groundhog looking at his shadow" (15 Sagittarius).
- Mao Tse Tung: Mars in Scorpio: leader and founder of the People's Republic of China.
- Joseph Stalin: Pluto in Scorpio: dictator who found ways to send many to camps. Clearly, the manifestation of the sense of "camp" takes a serious turn when citing the examples of Mao Tse Tung and Joseph Stalin, but demonstrates the vibrancy of sense conveyed by the Sabian Symbols. The planetary influence has much to do with how the symbol is manifested within the person's reality, hence Joseph Stalin's Pluto placement brings an ominous tone to what appeared in others as the lighthearted fun of "campy" songs.

ROBIN WILLIAMS: A SABIAN ANALYSIS

Robin Williams (July 21, 1951, Chicago, Illinois, 1:34 PM CDT) is well-known to most people for his amazing comedic skills, quick wit, and zany energy. Assessing his horoscope using the Sabian Symbols amplifies the impression of his considerable talents in dramatically illustrative ways. An astrological assessment of Robin Williams' horoscope also reveals much that can be recognized in his public personality.

An Astrological Overview

First, here are some astrological observations of Robin Williams' horoscope in order to provide a backdrop against which his Sabian Symbols shine.

Robin Williams has a Cancer Sun, Pisces Moon, and Scorpio Ascendant. This is a blend of energy, need, and self-projection that is extremely emotionally sensitive. The emotional flow is everything: sensitive and responsive to every change in the emotional weather; shifting with extraordinary ease in response to the reactions of others. We would expect an intense need to read situations intuitively, to adapt within a split second and perhaps surprise others regarding the intensity of his self-expression, but almost always in a manner that is extraordinarily pleasant and likable.

The horoscope exhibits a strong maternal imprint—Moon conjunct North Node, Venus conjunct South Node—and Robin has affirmed this many times publicly, saying his sense of humor comes directly from his mother. Mercury and Pluto conjunct in Leo and positioned in the public eye of the tenth house, dramatically emphasize his need to express himself in ways that will win deep public admiration and recognition. A compelling use of verbal skills in colorful and attention-grabbing ways is certain to be the vehicle for professional pursuits. Mars conjunct Uranus in Cancer combine action and eccentricity, innovation and deeds, in ways that, although surprising and out of the blue, seem safe: there is little about the public thrust of these energies that seems threatening.

Note the strong aspect relationships that exert developmental tension: Jupiter opposed Neptune, squared by the Mars-Uranus conjunction, forming a powerful T-square. This dynamic underlines the need for an outlet for talents, an outlet for the overactive mind and imagination, such as movies and television. Neptune in Libra and the twelfth house reinforces an affinity for television and film and provides an appropriate outlet for Mars-Uranus, the innovative and improvisational expression of intellect and wit. Jupiter in Aries augments the need to express himself in big ways, with speed and immediacy. Much of the fun in watching Robin Williams comes from witnessing the futile attempts of interviewers to control the conversation: there is little doubt who is number one when Robin Williams is being interviewed.

Robin's Moon is quindecile Mercury. The quindecile is an aspect of 165 degrees that is reliably understood to be expressed through obsession or compulsion. The Moon quindecile Mercury can manifest through a driven need to express how one feels; through feelings driving the thought processes; through sensitivities and intuitions that work well with others, with the public; and possibly as a *puer aeternis* complex: an eternal boy exemplified by his role as the grownup Peter Pan in the movie *Hook*.

Robin also has Jupiter quindecile Saturn: a tendency to overdo things, to push something too far, possibly, in Robin's case, because his father is not as supportive as his mother regarding his choice of profession, and therefore exacerbates the need to win appreciation and approval from the father or authority figures in general. Assuming the responsibilities of parenthood would help greatly to anchor the overall sense of being at the mercy of any wind that blows.

Sabian Symbols Amplifying the Public Impression of Robin Williams

Robin's Sun is in the twenty-ninth degree of Cancer: "A muse weighing twins" (29 Cancer) and "A woman reading tea leaves" (29 Capricorn). The energy to create security takes on an inspired quality, as if having a muse that guides the thrust to assess identity, in Robin's case, in amusing ways. The opposing Sabian Symbol lends a sense of continually reading between the lines while assessing the impressions made on others. The challenge is managed by way of his capacity to make a "quick read" of the atmosphere.

Robin's Moon is in the ninth degree of Pisces: "A man making a futuristic drawing" (9 Virgo) and "A jockey" (9 Pisces). The ultrasensitive Pisces Moon manifests a need to understand impressions and work with the intangible in innovative ways that spur others on. The shared motifs for the ninth degree of Virgo/Pisces read: 'Personal innovation,' 'drawing off the edge of the social page,' 'spurring on.' Both the "jockey" and the "futuristic artist" rely on inner resources and cunning instincts that deftly and quickly maneuver to effect the desired result, usually with a strong flourish

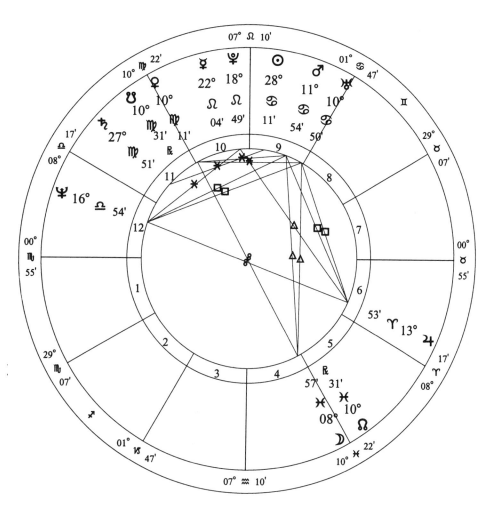

Robin Williams
July 21, 1951, 1:34 PM CDT, Chicago, Illinois
Placidus Houses

at the finish. Social intercourse is fueled by the need to push the boundaries, disturb contemporary paradigms, while drawing out a response from others and drawing others in to an atmosphere of emotional rapport. We would expect a sense of intimacy and flourish while going beyond the lines of social niceties: being outrageous yet so pleasant and agreeable at the same time as to win approval.

The Sun/Moon midpoint lies in the nineteenth degree of Taurus: "A newly formed continent" (19 Taurus) and "A parrot listening, then talking" (19 Scorpio). The text for this degree-pair reads in part: "Apply this degree-pair with a mind for stories that reach far, are far-reaching; stretch reality; cover a large territory. Listen for continuous chatter; scraps of information; drifting bits of misinformation. Consider mimicry; the Peter Pan syndrome; repeating words of others for protection; disdain for old ways of saying things; throwing stones." There is a strong suggestion that, as the symbols for the Sun/Moon blend suggest, Robin Williams has a need to break away from a large influence in his life, perhaps an inherited past, perhaps an expectation of social position or a demeanor associated with a social status, in order to become his own person. It is obvious that his verbal skills for parody and cutting wit would be the means by which he would achieve his independence.

Mercury is in the twenty-third degree of Leo: "A bareback rider" (23 Leo) and "A big bear sitting down and waving all its paws" (23 Aquarius). Mercury in Leo seeks recognition through communication, intellect, or mental capacities. The "bareback rider" is a symbol expressing riding without a saddle, like a trapeze artist flying without a net, free from being saddled with any constraints, protective or otherwise. The "big bear" symbol often manifests in physical traits of being stout or burly, often with abundant and unruly body hair. There is a performance sense to this degree-pair: a circus bear; a bareback circus rider. A lack of grace when handling delicate matters is managed with grace anyway: bringing grace to raw instinctual power. Notably, the impression given is one of possessing powerful arms, yet appearing harmless.

Venus is in the eleventh degree of Virgo: "A boy molded in his mother's aspiration for him" (11 Virgo) and "Men seeking illumination" (11 Pisces). As already noted, the maternal impression has been definitive for Robin Williams. The symbol "being molded by one's mother's aspirations" clearly expresses a desire to emulate his mother's aspirations for him, to enjoy the fulfillment of those aspirations, and to be liked, to be found attractive through a creative display of exacting insight. Since Robin's Moon is opposed to his natal Venus, the need for these two dynamics to work together effectively is greatly amplified.

Robin has Mars in the twelfth degree of Cancer: "A Chinese woman nursing a baby with a message" (12 Cancer) and "A student of nature lecturing" (12 Capricorn) are better understood together with Uranus in the eleventh degree of Cancer: "A clown making grimaces" (11 Cancer) and "A large group of pheasants" (11 Capricorn). Taken together, these symbols suggest a drive to manifest through the innovational and improvisational artistry of clowning. Consider the following motifs taken from the entries for these degree-pairs: "a knack for understanding incomprehensible mixtures of languages; getting right to the point while distorting the usual perspective; innocent innovations that convey meaning and insight; a rubber face; mimicry; having an impact on others that uplifts; having a felt understanding of the sharp edges of reality, of the inner emotional impact of brilliant ideas; a knack for infusing cold thought, pristine ideals, with a human element: the artistry of the wise fool." Add to this the use of strange elements, especially through a facility for foreign accents and exaggeration to get one's point across, and a portrait of the "zany" character of Robin Williams is clearly painted.

Jupiter is in the fourteenth degree of Aries: "A serpent coiling near a man and a woman" (14 Aries) and "A noon siesta" (14 Libra). Jupiter in Aries usually manifests as "big and quick." In Robin Williams' horoscope, Jupiter is strongly tied in, with an opposition to Neptune and a square relationship with the Mars-Uranus conjunction in Cancer, thus forming part of a dominating T-square, which "fires" through the improvisational Mars and Uranus. The fiery nature of Jupiter in Aries speeds up the delivery of quick wit, a rapid-fire and overblown capacity to expand on a theme: speaking without thinking. The "serpent coiling" symbol introduces sexual themes into the comedic routines, perhaps occasionally going a little too far, too quick, regarding off-color remarks. Every comedian tends to deliver "blue" comedy when performing in contained situations, such as standup routines in a nightclub. Robin is unlikely to be any different in this regard.

Robin has Neptune in the seventeenth degree of Libra: "Two prim spinsters" (17 Aries) and "A retired sea captain" (17 Libra). This symbol placement expresses a capacity for creative storytelling: spinning yarns; weaving magic having an effect like that of a spinning top. From the entry for the seventeenth degree of Aries/Libra: "stories that reinvent the past; spin around a central point. Listen for rollicking story-telling that picks up extra threads to add spice; two (or more) versions of one story. Watch for prim facial expressions; tightly drawn lips (recall Mrs. Doubtfire); salty takes on comings and goings; picking up loose threads until the tale is complete; pointed stories that take a while to come to a point."

Saturn is in the twenty-eighth degree of Virgo: "A bald-headed man " (28 Virgo) and "A fertile garden under the full moon" (28 Pisces). So often this degree-pair combines to focus on a great concern with matters of hair. The "Samson" degree symbols, as I have come to nickname them, are about personal power: the loss of power through something symbolic, like the cutting off of one's hair; and the return of power, because, like a fertile garden, hair grows back. Robin Williams is not, to my knowledge, bald, but he most certainly possesses a fertile mind from which he has been able to secure, through an abundance of personal accomplishments, the respect and admiration of others.

In conclusion, I will cite the symbols that apply to Robin Williams' nodal axis. One of my favorite Robin Williams' films is *The Fisher King,* a retelling of the Fisher King story from the Grail legend of Arthurian lore.

North Node in the thirteenth degree of Pisces: "A strong hand supplanting political hysteria" (13 Virgo) and "A sword in a museum" (13 Pisces). The lunar nodes are said to suggest a sense of purpose in one's life, to suggest an idea of direction for the attainment of personal fulfillment throughout one's lifetime. The Sabian Symbols for the thirteenth degree of Virgo/Pisces echo the Sword in the Stone motif of the Arthurian legend: drawing one's power as one would draw a sword from a stone. Think of a sense of balanced awareness: when to diffuse unruly situations with humor; when to rein in chaos with authoritative power. The thrust of this degree-pair lies in an ability to bring order to a situation that has gotten out of hand. Despite his well-known manner of injecting hilarious, larger-than-life chaos through his comedic forays, Robin Williams seems to project a sense of there being "a method to his madness," an ability to bring order to the chaos he so delights in creating. I would have to think that *The Fisher King* was a very important creative project for Robin Williams. It certainly is suggested in his horoscope through the mirroring sense of the Sabian Symbols.

SUGGESTED APPROACHES FOR ASTROLOGICAL APPLICATION

The practicing astrologer has an enormous amount of preparation to do with every horoscope. However, the Sabian Symbols are a wonderful addition to the creative astrologer's arsenal of interpretive tools. How one goes about using the Sabian Symbols is a matter of personal preference and style; however, I will offer the following suggestions based on my own use of the Sabian Symbols in the context of an astrological counseling practice.

First, print a hub-style horoscope, leaving enough room around the page borders to make notes. Then, using the reference chart found in the back of this book, write out the Sabian Symbols beside all planetary placements and points. Write both the symbol specific to the degree placement and the opposing degree symbol, remembering always to round up; for example, 12 degrees 13 minutes of arc equals the thirteenth degree in Sabian application. I suggest using two pens of different colors in a consistent manner: for example, the specific degree symbol always in blue; the opposing degree symbol always in black. The process takes only a few minutes, but it allows one to proceed with the astrological preparation, determining the important themes in assessing the horoscope, after which one can return to reflect on the horoscope as a whole with its Sabian Symbol background. Apply the Sabian Symbols to all of the planets: Sun, Moon, Mercury, Venus, Mars, Jupiter, Uranus, Neptune, and Pluto. I, personally, apply the Sabian Symbols to Chiron and the four major asteroids, Vesta, Pallas Athena, Ceres, and Juno, with very satisfactory results. Include the Ascendant, Midheaven, Descendant, and Nadir: the "four angles" crucial to horoscope delineation. Also determine the Sabian Symbols for the Sun/Moon midpoint.

Pay attention to the opposing degree-pair of Sabian Symbols for:

- Each planetary placement.
- The angles: Midheaven, Nadir; Ascendant, Descendant.
- The Sun /Moon midpoint.

Give special attention to special influences such as:

- Peregrine planets: any planet not in Ptolemaic aspect with any other body in the horoscope, i.e., conjunction, sextile, square, trine, or opposition.
- Any planet or point lying within the Aries point: within two degrees of all zero degree points of cardinal signs: Aries, Cancer, Libra, or Capricorn.

During the consultation conversation, one's eyes are constantly scanning the horoscope and the Sabian Symbols. You will find insights emerging through the symbols as the conversation unfolds and reveals important themes. Occasionally, I will ask a "research question," drawing on a particular Sabian Symbol, in order to explore an unclear area within the horoscope. Sometimes this works with surprising revelations; sometimes it does not resonate with anything for the client. The question, however, allows one to explore, and share with the client, something that potentially can be extremely rewarding.

THE WHEEL OF LIFE

The greatest reward of the full cycle of the Sabian Symbols lies in reading the whole story. One will begin to deeply appreciate the threads of sense as they weave from degree symbol to degree symbol, from sign expression to sign expression. Like the I Ching, the Sabian Symbols turn in an inexhaustible "Wheel of Life," which turns back into itself. Reading the entire cycle reveals an incredible story that unfolds in surprising, revelatory ways. The themes and motifs are universal and recognizable, and give a rich context to appreciate time and life situations. Resisting the urge only to look up specific symbols, but rather reading the text as a whole as an unfolding story, will give the practicing astrologer, and anyone interested in the collective wisdom of life expressed symbolically, a profound and inspiring appreciation for the significance of the Sabian Symbols. The full cycle of Sabian Symbols is like a poetic touchstone, a resource of riches we have only begun to tap.

The Sabian Symbols are not just for astrologers. Anyone who delights in contemplative thought will recognize the intricate weaving of sense that runs through all manifestations of human life. From the beginnings of life, through the individuation process as life unfolds, to the temporal finality of human existence, the Sabian Symbols touch on every compelling motif of the human journey. The rich array of motifs covers relationship, socialization, political elements, cultural dynamics, spiritual pursuits, and the relationship with the sacred. As each symbol unfolds into the next, textures and tones emerge, historical themes weave archaic sensibilities with contemporary issues; the tapestry of life emerges. By following the root origins of the words used in the Sabian Symbols, a vibrant sense of world cultures begins to be uncovered from what perhaps seemed at first to be very culturally specific. The true nature of symbols is to yield ever more sense.

It is my hope that this work may serve as a source of creative inspiration for turning the pages as one would mindfully turn the wheel of life. May this book convey my toil of love and delight with the Sabian Symbols. May it move you to learn, explore, and be enriched with insight and confidence to better help your clients, to better understand yourself. May it bring to light the wonderful gift that is the Sabian Symbols.

---

1. Dane Rudhyar, *An Astrological Mandala* (New York: Vintage Books, 1974) p. 117.

2. Ibid.

3. Marc Edmund Jones, *The Sabian Symbols in Astrology* (Santa Fe, NM: Aurora Press, 1993) p. 137.

The following interpretations for the Sabian Symbols are presented in degree-pairs, matching the mirroring sense of zodiacal degree oppositions. Please note that when searching for the pertinent Sabian Symbol, each degree placement of planet or point is to be rounded up: thus 2 degrees Taurus 1 minute of arc (2°1' Taurus) corresponds to the third degree of Taurus; and 29 degrees Pisces 58 minutes of arc is the thirtieth degree of Pisces; but 23 degrees Leo 00 minutes of arc is to be read as the twenty-third degree of Leo.

I have presented new keywords for each symbol pair as "Shared motifs," which are offered to augment the keywords of other authors, especially Marc Edmund Jones (see the appendices for Marc Edmund Jones' keywords and their amplification).

CHAPTER ONE

ARIES-LIBRA

"A woman rises out of water, a seal rises and embraces her" (1 Aries)
and "A butterfly made perfect by a dart through it" (1 Libra)

Aspect: Conjunction.
Quality: Focus.
Shared motifs: 'A fluid emerging moment,'
'a pinpoint of light capturing a tender moment.'

"A woman rises out of water, a seal rises and embraces her" is an image of accepting tender emotional impressions at the moment of emerging into life. A "seal" is a sea mammal often noted for its human characteristics, especially forearms that can be imagined to have an embracing capacity. "Seal" is also an impression used to close something, or to leave an impression as a mark of identity. The selkie fairy and folk tales of the North Atlantic tell of the seal-woman shedding her skin before coming on shore in human form. A seal skin is suggestive of swaddling clothes wrapped tightly around an infant child. The image is closely related to birthing, where the child is wrapped tight within the womb, as if in a seal skin, emerging all wrinkled with seal-like folds of skin, to stretch its limbs. Crucial at this moment is the embrace: a tender gesture of acceptance echoing the mother-child bonding after the first moments of birth.

"A butterfly made perfect by a dart through it" is an image of beauty and fragility caught in a perfect moment of precision. A "dart" is a thin, pointed object like a missile for throwing, or a pin for mounting specimens of butterflies on a display board.

The "butterfly" is renowned for its transformative life cycle: larva, cocoon, butterfly. Handling butterflies so as not to damage their fragile beauty is a delicate matter. One might capture a butterfly perfectly when a dart of sunlight breaks through a thick canopy of tropical vegetation, illuminating the beautiful butterfly in a picture-perfect moment.

The birth moment is one of exquisite, tender emotion. After emerging from the womb, the infant child yearns for unconditional love and acceptance: the warm, accepting embrace of the mother. The emotional impressions left at that moment might well last a lifetime. Such is the love, hope, and promise of the newborn child. One may want to preserve the moment forever, like preserving a butterfly in perfect form with embalming fluids, or capturing the event in a photograph. A "photograph" is a frozen visual image of time requiring developing fluids, like the amniotic fluids of the womb, in order to bring the image clearly into the world. Regardless of almost any circumstances, it is common for parents to celebrate the birth of their newborn child as perfect.

Apply this initial degree-pair with a mind to emergent moments that initiate a new life cycle; tender moments of raw emotion that leave lasting impressions. Watch for photographic moments; the desire to capture something in the perfect light, to show oneself in the perfect way. Be alert to the tendency to freeze the moment; to capture the time; to preserve an image as if it were a pinned specimen for display. Consider the fragrance of embalming fluids; the smell of newborn babies; fragrances that preserve a memory or impression; wrinkled skin; balms to treat wrinkles; affinities for garments that wrap around; adeptness on land and in water.

"A comedian entertains a group" (2 Aries) and "Light of the sixth race transmuted to the seventh" (2 Libra)

Aspect: Opposition.
Quality: Awareness of.
Shared motifs: 'Uplifting,' 'natural humors that shift the air.'

"A comedian entertains a group" is an image of a natural ability to uplift situations through endearing humor. A "comedian" is one who through actions, words, and expressions brings a light sense of amusement or joyful laughter to others. Imagine a baby making faces, blowing bubbles, or cooing while a group stands around adoringly, showing their delight. While telling jokes is the stock and trade of a comedian, an infant child is a natural comic, causing delight without intention. Even as the child develops a self-awareness and intentionally performs for adults, there is a youthful charm that entertains, bringing smiles to all around. "Humor," the quality of being funny, derives from the Latin *umere,* to be moist, as in fresh from the sea. Natural-born entertainers, like children still wet behind the ears, bring laughter and joy to an all-too-serious adult world.

"Light of the sixth race transmuted to the seventh" is an image of a shifting in the quality of light energy into a higher, accelerated frequency. "Race" can be a dicey topic if approached in a less than enlightened manner. Understood collectively as the gene pool of all mankind, race can seem a confusing mix of currents that accelerate development. Visible light, for example, is composed of elements of color, each having a measurable frequency; violet, the seventh in the color spectrum, having the highest frequency. "Transmutation" is a change in the nature or quality of energy or matter. Understood as an evolutionary phase of the race of mankind as a whole, transmutation would seem to be a natural progression; however, mutations often yield surprising results. In esoteric philosophy, transmutation from the sixth to the seventh ray is the movement from a path of devotion to a path of ceremonial magic that realizes the unity of all things, as well as open-mindedness, gentleness, and love.

"Dice" are two six-sided cubes inscribed with the numbers one through six. Throwing the dice in a game of chance in order to get a six and a seven may have one at sixes and sevens, since the outcome is impossible, hence confusing or humorous. Once the die is cast, the outcome is irrevocable, or so it appears. Every human being tacitly recognizes an uplifting shift in energy. Musically, a song is taken to a higher key, not just a key change, but an uplifting shift in the dramatic musical unfolding: harmonics open an awareness to new acoustic worlds; one leaves a stirring symphonic performance feeling uplifted. While one assumes inherited traits to be evident, sometimes unexpected traits come out of the mix. One has to entertain all possibilities, even the impossible or the impossibly funny.

Apply this degree-pair with a mind to the awareness of all uplifting shifts within experience; of darkness to light, cold to warm, coarse to sublime; confusing changes; seemingly impossible results. Watch for natural comics who use humor to lighten the air; natural presences that uplift the quality; the wisdom of childlike behavior. Consider ultrafine sensibilities; ultralight tenderness; imperceptible impressions; a knack for shifting gears in midstream; the release from a good laugh; humor as a means to deflect disappointment.

"A cameo profile of a man in the outline of his country" (3 Aries) and "Dawn of a new day, everything changed" (3 Libra)

Aspect: Trine.
Quality: Maintaining.
Shared motif: 'Choosing between first impressions
or fresh takes.'

"A cameo profile of a man in the outline of his country" is an image of a side-view relief of a man that carries an impression of national identity. A "cameo" is a small piece of hard stone, often of differing colored layers with an image carved in relief against a background of a different color. "Cameo" is perhaps akin to "camera," a light-proof chamber from which the apparatus for taking photographs developed. "In camera" is hidden from public view; "camera obscura" and "camera lucida" are devices used to project an image in natural colors for tracing; a "cameo appearance" is a bit part played by a distinguished performer. One gets the impression that a cameo profile shows a one-sided image like the profile of a Roman ruler on a gold coin, suggesting something more on the flip side.

"Dawn of a new day, everything changed" is an image of awakening to the fact that past impressions were misleading, incomplete, or just false. "Dawn" suggests a time of day when, after having slept on a matter, everything has changed. Imagine meeting someone who had left one with a less than favorable impression. After a time, in a new light, or after turning it over in one's mind, that impression may be entirely changed. One-sided impressions both shed light and obscure: it might be a relief to know there is more to a person than their appearance. The "bicameral" nature of the human brain suggests that, in addition to sense perceptions, there is a capacity to receive extrasensory impressions about someone or something.

Think of the growth of identity awareness in developmental psychological terms. A child begins to develop a defined sense of identity derived predominately from the family imprint, the determinate factors of social, ethnic, and national origin. As the identity emerges in relief from all conditioning factors, a hint of unique individuality begins to emerge. It is not exactly like the two sides of a coin. A right-brained personality may have a creative, highly suggestive impression about someone, only to have their embellished image reduced to a more realistic, defined image on a new day. A left-brained personality may have a well-defined, stereotyped impression only to find there is much more to the picture when seen in a different light.

Apply this degree-pair with a mind to the tendencies to seek stabilizing images of oneself, others, and the world; to stereotype others at the expense of their full individuality; to highlight only the prominent features. Think of the creative aspects of obscurations; the genuine identity being in camera; the blinding aspects of briefly illumined features. Watch for identifying facial profiles; the tendency to make things in the shape of one's country, one's state: a Texas-shaped putting green; a pool shaped like Barbados. Consider confusion about not being like the image projected; not being the image projected by others; the child who looks like a parent, but is not like the parent; or who looks nothing like a parent, but is like the parent.

"Two lovers strolling through a secluded walk" (4 Aries) and "A group around a campfire" (4 Libra)

Aspect: Square.
Quality: Challenge.
Shared motifs: 'Wandering away from group identity,'
'finding one's social circle.'

"Two lovers strolling through a secluded walk" is an image of a mutual attraction that opens the possibility of revealing the self while wandering separated from the group identity. "Two lovers" suggests an explorative time involving a couple mutually open to showing more of themselves and knowing more about the other. The lovers' attraction fuels the urge to wander beyond familiar and familial paths. "Seclusion" separates one from the group identity; frees up the possibility to be oneself apart from the imprint of family, ethnic, and national identity. "Strolling" derives from the Greek *strollen,* meaning to wander like a vagabond: one who has no settled home, aimlessly exploring the world.

"A group around a campfire" is an image of a gathering of people organized around an inward-looking spirit of identity. A "campfire" is a center of focus around which people gather to share in its warmth and fiery spirit. The fire arrests their gaze such that individuality is transcended in a constructive awareness of social order. Gathering around a campfire emphasizes the group as equals while deemphasizing hierarchical organization. The sense of individual identity becomes smaller in order for it to become richer and wider, through the social identity.

Developing social awareness follows two primary pathways: gathering around a communal focal point, reinforcing a sense of group identity; and wandering into the unfamiliar territory of developing a personal and intimate relationship. Paradoxically, each dynamic involves surrendering individuality while developing a greater sense of self. Lovers open themselves to know and be known while the fires of intimacy urge them along a path of, perhaps, awkward discovery. A campfire group gathers openly to know and be known through the common spirit that brings them together in fellowship. The path is not always easy. One may feel excluded from the group or unable to find oneself through the group identity. One may find that a relationship asks for too much self-surrender or is overly exclusive. The task is to explore both paths in order to find one's self.

Apply this degree-pair with a mind to the challenge of finding one's self in social circles and relationship; revealing more of who one is while giving up a defined sense of identity; wandering on unfamiliar paths away from the home fires. Watch for struggles to be included; the tendency to exclude others; the desire to belong; the need to pair off before daring to go it alone. Be alert to tentative steps while exploring social dynamics; feeling out of place in one's social circle; a tendency to orbit around what the group thinks. Consider early stages of awareness of being more than who you think you are; private realities of shared intimacy; a focused sense of tribal identity; the spirit to conform; secret paths of the nonconformist.

"A triangle with wings" (5 Aries) and "A man teaching the true inner knowledge" (5 Libra)

Aspect: Quintile.
Quality: Creative genius.
Shared motifs: 'Ease expressing one's inner self,'
'authentically surpassing limiting impressions.'

"A triangle with wings" is an image of an idealized form of transcendence. A "triangle" is a geometric form consisting of three straight sides. "Wings" are extendable, moveable limbs for the capacity of flight. Deriving from a root kinship with "wind," fast-moving air, "wings" has a poetic sense of moving swiftly through the air, wandering everywhere, soaring upward. While geometric principles precisely define what it is to be a triangle, psychodynamics of individuation add something more: a transcending capacity that, like wings that soar, goes beyond the hard and fast rules of definition.

"A man teaching the true inner knowledge" is an image of giving guidance from an inner source of authentic realization. "Teaching" is an action of showing or guiding another about something. "Inner knowledge" suggests knowledge derived from personal experience, synthesized within personal consciousness, as opposed to information. "True inner knowledge" is not about what is correct, certain, or clearly evident, in the objective sense, but rather authentic knowing: genuine awareness of one's self.

Imagine after having been around the block a few times in secluded relationships, and around a few campfires of this social group or that, that one comes to a place of knowing one's self in a way that is true to deep personal affinities. An inner authentic sense of self emerges and fearlessly takes wing, flying beyond rigid, confining definitions of identity. It is not enough that one be stereotyped within social, ethnic, and national definitions of identity. That would be like saying a photograph of oneself is one's self. The pinnacle of identity cannot be measured nor defined with precision, but rather is a creative transcending of self-awareness. "Know thyself" and "To thine own self be true" are not mere abstract idealizations.

Apply this degree-pair with a mind to a creative ease with which personal affinities rise to express one's true self; getting to know who one really is; integrating one's words, thoughts, and deeds, one's body, speech, and mind. Watch for a natural show of self not ruled by others; guiding others, not dominating them; bringing ideals to life; an inner marriage of poetry and precision. Consider being comfortable about not quite being in the social picture; a wakeful sense of self; a refined sense of personal and social harmonics; an understanding of the difference between guiding principles and rigid absolute truths; a knack for being oneself and getting away with it.

"A square brightly lighted on one side" (6 Aries)
and "The ideals of a man abundantly crystalized" (6 Libra)

Aspect: Conjunction.
Quality: Focus.
Shared motif: 'Seeing the world in a grain of sand,'
'accentuation.'

"A square brightly lighted on one side" is an image of a fundamental organizing principle with focused emphasis on one side. A "square" is a four-sided geometric shape expressive of the mandala principle: the principle of a quadrated circle expressing the structure of life, cosmos, and the human psyche. A mandala is a complete expression of the whole. For example, a "square meal" is one that is an honest, completely satisfying, well-balanced, and well-proportioned meal. A "town square" is the center around which the town is built. When one side of a square is brightly illuminated, it gains emphasis: one portion of the meal is larger than the rest; one side of the town square is busier, more brightly illumined.

"The ideals of a man abundantly crystalized" is an image of the full expression of ideals brought into clear, definite form. "Ideals" are principles of high standard, complete and satisfactory unto themselves, which exist in conception only. "Abundance" suggests fullness, plenitude, richness. To be "crystalized" is to become clear and definitely formed, like water freezing into ice. One's approach to life takes shape through the inner process of crystalizing one's views. "Crystalization" can carry a positive sense of clarity and richness born out of appreciative awareness, or it can refer to a hardened set of beliefs difficult to live up to or realize in life.

Consider the view of the human psyche, which sees the self as a unified whole, a circle, having an inner fourfold structure of primary, deep, archetypal structures. Each individual human being is organized primarily around one of these structures: for the thinker, the magician; the artist, the lover; the man of action, the warrior; the leader, the king/queen. The ideal human being would be well-balanced in all these capacities. A one-sided perspective may harden, crystalizing into mere narrow-mindedness, or it may refract an understanding of the whole through a single facet of the jewel of wisdom. Illumination of one side may lead to a bunch of unconnected, scattered ideas about life and reality, or it may shine upon an abundance of brilliant realizations.

Apply this degree-pair with a mind to almost compelling personal affinities that form a basis for individuation, realization, and idealization; a perspective that is a lens for viewing the whole. Think of abundance initiated through personal crystalized ideals. Watch for hardened ideals unable or unwilling to see other points of view; special awareness leading to a full array of unconnected ideas; seeing the world in a grain of sand, seeing through a lens or filter that magnifies the whole. Consider inner visions; being satisfied in the mind but frustrated in the world; working with lenses and filters; feeling self-satisfied while only getting something partly right.

**"A man successfully expressing himself in two realms at once" (7 Aries)
and "A woman feeding chickens and protecting them from the hawks" (7 Libra)**

Aspect: Opposition.
Quality: Awareness of.
Shared motifs: 'Simultaneous awareness of two realms,'
'conscious words and deeds.'

"A man successfully expresses himself in two realms at once" is an image of communication that integrates inner intention with outer expression. A "realm" is a domain such as a kingdom over which there is a range of power or influence. To "express" is literally "to press out." A successful expression is one that successfully presses out of one realm into another in a satisfactory way. Expressing oneself in two realms is "successful" only with an awareness that integrates two realms of "reality" through one's words or actions. An expression that harmoniously integrates two realms at once suggests a degree of mastery or an awareness of the pressing need to marry, for example, idea and word, word and deed.

"A woman feeding chickens and protecting them from the hawks" is an image of an action that actualizes awareness of two areas of concern at once. "Feeding" is nurturing: supplying sufficient sustenance to that which is under one's care. "Protecting" is to supply a shield or defense from harmful attack such as a sheltering cover of a home providing safety and security. "Hawks" are predators that hover in the sky, seeking their prey. "Chickens" are domestic fowl that are defenseless and confined to the ground. The woman's awareness is split between nurturing those under her protection while keeping an eye out for potential danger from another realm. She integrates nurturing, maternal actions with savvy warrior, protector energy.

Imagine having an idea crystal clear in your mind and struggling to find the right way to express it such that others might also clearly understand. One might take an image in the realm of imagination and accomplish its full expression in the world as a book, painting, or movie. One might aptly express the absolute and relative truth of a matter: maintain an awareness of two different perspectives at once. The woman feeding chickens expresses herself through actions rather than words or ideas. Her awareness weds two fundamentally different aspects of reality in a single expression of alertness.

Apply this degree-pair with a mind to mastering a split awareness; feeling at home in two worlds; translating two languages into a harmony of meaning. Watch for people who can do two things at once; who are more effective doing so; who are at ease in foreign territories. Be alert for a wide array of two realms: inner and outer;

possible and probable; higher and lower; harmful and nurturing; secular and sacred. Consider protective self-interest; paranoia about possible threats; gradual mastery of two aspects of some thing, idea, or action; showing hawkishness without while being a chicken within; appearing defenseless while being vigilant and powerful within.

"A large hat with streamers flying, facing east" (8 Aries) and "A blazing fireplace in a deserted home" (8 Libra)

Aspect: Trine.
Quality: Maintaining.
Shared motifs: 'Far-reaching implications'
'Where there is smoke, there is fire.'

"A large hat with streamers flying, facing east" is an image of a protective covering under an influence of a specific yet far-reaching nature. A "hat" is worn on the head, covering the culminating or chief part of a body, covering the seat of awareness. "Streamers" are ribbons or kerchiefs that adorn a hat. "East" is the direction associated with birth, dawn, spring: the advent of new life. Facing an easterly wind would cause hat streamers to fly in all other directions such as a new idea that has implications or a range of influence carrying over into others areas or realms. "Facing east" suggests looking for a fresh breath of life, anticipating, honoring something new, or perhaps waiting for something to blow your way: an Easter bonnet.

"A blazing fireplace in a deserted home" is an image of a warm, centering hearth without inhabitants. "A fireplace" is a structure built within a home specifically for containing combustion with a chimney in order to allow smoke to escape and blow away. A "blazing fireplace" is one in which a roaring fire burns, one that surely signals to the outside, through the smell and sight of streaming smoke, that there is a warm hearth inside. A "deserted home" is one that has been abandoned, or one to which inhabitants have yet to arrive. "Home" might be considered as the fifth direction, the center of the cardinal directions, the home fires around which life turns.

Smoke streams from a chimney the way streamers blow in the wind. Each originates from a chief place: head and hearth. A hat without a head is like a new idea that hasn't found a home in which to fully ignite. A home without inhabitants is a center to depart from or return to. "A large hat" suggests a sense of style and attention to appearance embellished by streamers flying: a special flare responsive and naturally flowing with every breeze that blows. Imagine waiting to see how far a big idea will go; waiting to gather all the implications of a core idea. The home is a human expression of a central organizing principle; the head, an expression of ever facing in one direction. There is ever a twofold sense of arriving and departing; advent of the new, leaving of the old; anticipating change, awaiting arrival.

Apply this degree-pair with a mind to the importance of a steadying influence for adventurous ideas; finding a warm center for far-reaching thoughts and speculations; anticipating the marriage of hearth and head, heart and mind. Watch for minds that sense the possible implications of core ideas; that sense a need for protection while entertaining foreign exploration; that watch to see if the ideas touch all the bases; that look to see where the original idea came from. Consider a tendency to be always waiting for something to happen, something to arrive, something to change; ideas that blow every which way but never land home; flying possibilities that have yet to come to a head; ideas that fulfill the promise of the maxim "Where there is smoke, there is fire."

"A crystal gazer" (9 Aries)
and " Three old masters hanging in an art gallery" (9 Libra)

Aspect: Square.
Quality: Challenge.
Shared motif: 'Penetrating insight and the suspension
of the time of recognition.'

"A crystal gazer" is an image of penetrating vision into a clear manifestation of the whole. "A crystal gazer" is one who looks into a round crystal ball. "Roundness" suggests completeness in all worldly dimensions: more depth than a flat surface; no fragmenting facets emphasizing some part over the whole. "Crystal" derives from the Greek word for ice, a clear solid resembling frozen water. "Crystals" such as quartz crystal are homogeneous solid bodies exhibiting a definite and symmetrical internal pattern. To "gaze" is to look steadily with relaxed, unfocused awareness as opposed to staring intently with focused attention on a single point. "Gazing into the future," as by looking into a crystal ball, is to penetrate with unfocused awareness into a realm of time yet to emerge.

"Three old masters hanging in an art gallery" is an image of culminating works of excellence suspended in a room for public viewing. "Old masters" are exemplars of a past time recognized for being the leading, culminating expressions of art, the influence of which lasts for long periods of time. "Hanging in an art gallery" is to be suspended in a room or building designed to preserve and display great works of art. Few past masters of art were recognized as masters in their own time. Their genius seems to be ahead of their time regarding the expression of artistic ideas and techniques. "Three masters" suggests the introduction of a third element having to do with finding a home that suitably honors their influence, much like finding a home in which to hang one's hat.

Imagine looking into a crystal ball, gazing into the realm of what is yet to come. One might have a sense that someday your works, ideas, and achievements will be recognized. If the crystal ball is cloudy, one's future is unclear, indistinct. Looking back in time to those who are the standards of admiration might clear one's view of the future. Crystal gazers and old masters share the aspect of not being recognized in their own time. The challenge of having a burning vision of one's ideals lies in the obscure likelihood of having that vision recognized.

Apply this degree-pair with a mind to the challenge of finding a home where one's creative visions can be hung; admiring a past in order to project a future; creating something new out of the same old stuff; a regard for past standards of creative expression that continue to excel in contemporary times. Think of recognition issues: not being seen or appreciated in one's own time; being regarded as having obscure or little influence; needing clear glasses to see. Consider clairvoyance, polishing or clarifying processes; preservation techniques; looking into internal structures; having the sense that something is about to happen when it already has happened.

"A man teaching new forms for old symbols" (10 Aries)
and "A canoe approaching safety through dangerous waters" (10 Libra)

Aspect: Quintile.
Quality: Creative genius.
Shared motifs: 'Digging into old symbols to float safe and
sound sense,' 'new territory in an archaic boat.'

"A man teaching new forms for old symbols" is an image of a mastery of the inner sense of symbols, past and future. Ancient symbols present creative genius of long-standing tradition that, like the great works of past masters, may have lost some luster through the years. "New forms" suggests refashioning the internal, invisible structures of sense within symbols. The only purpose of refashioning old forms into new ones is to bring the sense of a symbol alive again. Merely changing the external form of a symbol does not guarantee a reinvigorated appreciation of its meaning. It could be like a new shape for a coke bottle; a new dress for an old horse; a sanitized fairy tale for modern sensibilities; a kitsch veneer on an ancient treasure.

"A canoe approaching safety through dangerous waters" is an image of navigating turbulent situations in a fragile vessel within sight of calm, safe waters. A "canoe" is a water vessel that was originally a dugout, a tree trunk dug into and hollowed out, or a frame over which the bark of a tree was stretched. Noted for their maneuverability, canoes can be navigated into otherwise inaccessible areas. Canoes are not at their best in dangerous, turbulent waters. "Turbulence" is itself a condition that stirs up possibility. The split-second decisions and maneuvers required to paddle through rough waters require a deft touch. One might say that turbulence is a creative time out of which safety emerges for the voyager.

Symbols might be considered to be vessels that carry sense through time. Symbols may become, through time, hollow, as if their sense has been completely dug out, exhausted: a mere shell of their former richness. "Danger" is derived from dominion, a realm of power in which peril and possible harm are present. "Safety" is wholeness, soundness, and health: the absence of danger. Navigating dangerous waters toward safety and calm suggests that symbols, like canoes, can sometimes be channeled into narrow passageways that dangerously distort their original form and sense. This is not an impossible situation to navigate, but one demanding great skill, devotion, and adaptability.

Apply this degree-pair with a mind to the ingenious ability to make the unworkable work again; to make the unmanageable manageable; to make the hollow sound whole and true. Watch for on-the-fly repair jobs; arriving somewhere new and fresh, safe and sound; a know-how that gets somewhere. Think of shooting the rapids, reinventing the wheel. Consider emotional turbulence and splashes of crazy wisdom; choosing to stay in confusion rather than moving on to more stable and safe conditions; a heads-up approach; strokes of genius.

"The president of the country" (11 Aries)
and "A professor peering over his glasses" (11 Libra)

Aspect: Conjunction.
Quality: Focus.
Shared motif: 'Overseeing.'

"The president of the country" is an image of the pinnacle of political power, a societal expression of the most elevated stature. From the heights of political power, there is a responsibility for the welfare of all of the country's people. This is not a monarchy where "kingship" implies an accordance with the divine. A president is chosen in some manner of political process to manage the affairs of state. It is important to note that what it means to govern has historically shifted from "divine stewardship" to mundane management, yet still implies self-sacrifice for the welfare of the population. Whether the ruler is a benefactor or a malefactor of the country remains an open question.

"A professor peering over his glasses" is an image of an effort by one of authoritative knowledge to see clearly. A "professor" derives from the Latin word for public teacher, one who publicly avows something, and is the designation of the highest rank of teaching in institutions of higher learning. "Peering" is to look searchingly as in "peering over the horizon" in an attempt to see clearly what is there. "Peering over glasses" suggests looking over reading glasses, perhaps at students, or at one's peers, one's equals. "Glasses" are optical instruments that aid vision. "Peering over glasses" suggests a moment of distraction, or an attempt to see something else more clearly.

Every student is familiar with "the look": the arresting gaze of a professor that can convey many meanings. An unruly student can be set in place with "the look." One might experience uneasiness wondering whether "the look" is one of fault-finding disdain, curious surprise, or benevolent intrigue. "The look" creates a moment of suspense, the resolution of which can lead to outcomes spanning from intimidation to humor. A president looks out for his country. As the leader of a nation, the president is peerless, without equal, excepting leaders of other nations. President and professor are charged with the responsibility for others, their general welfare or their education. As with all leaders and teachers, one can only hope for a sense of wise vision.

Apply this degree-pair with a mind to having one's attention diverted away from personal concerns toward others; suspending self-welfare to assess the needs of others; a look of consideration in order to see clearly. Think of a gaze that catches others; attempting to see beyond implications of ideas for oneself only; lifting one's gaze to take the wider world into view. Watch for the transmission of power through one's look, through one's eyes; communication through the eyes; gestures suggesting an inward pause for deliberation. Consider overseeing; looking down upon; looking over or looking through someone or something; attempting to see beyond, over the horizon. Any way you look at it, the "eyes" have it.

"A flock of white geese" (12 Aries) and "Miners emerge from a mine" (12 Libra)

Aspect: Opposition.
Quality: Awareness of.
Shared motifs: 'Sounds that uplift,' 'departure to the south,' 'an instinct for working with others.'

"A flock of white geese" is an image of an instinctive sense of where one is going.[1] "Geese" are renowned for their V-shaped, chevron flight formation. No one goose stays at the head of the formation. There is a continuous rotation of the lead bird because the lead position is the most difficult: breaking the air like the prow of a boat moving through water in order that the others may draft behind. It is an expression of a group structure that most efficiently can make headway toward instinctive goals. Within the world of geese, loud honking announces the departing flight. Prevailing social hierarchies are set aside for effective realization of the the migratory destination.

"Miners emerge from a mine" is an image of making it back to home ground, back into fresh air. A "mine" is an excavation dug into the earth to obtain valuable ores, coal, or precious stones. "Miners" are those who work underground in the mines, or, in the case of insects, those who burrow into plants to feed upon a rich resource of nutrition. "Miners emerge" from the mine when their shift is over, by walking or riding a lift or train to the surface, not returning until the next rotation. They may emerge in no particular order, or perhaps, echoing the Pied Piper, the first in shall be last out; the last in shall be first to emerge. When the whistle blows, their shift is over. Canaries were used in the past to alert miners to the presence of dangerous methane gas. If the whistle doesn't blow, that is, if the canary dies, it is time to get out of the mine fast. Emerging from the mine must also be emerging into daylight, into fresh air, into the world.

White geese instinctively fly their migratory paths with an unerring sense of direction. Miners leave their underground world of toil with a natural sense of emerging into the light of day. Both miners and geese know where they are going, what direction they are headed in: there is no question of turning back. Larvae tunnel their way out of a tree, not returning until it is time to lay their eggs. There are common themes of paying a price for leading the way out: the lead bird fatigues; the plant dies; the miners can't breathe or even escape. A worthwhile resource motivates awareness of group cooperation to successfully reach the goal.

Apply this degree-pair with a mind to the awareness of a dependence on others for full realization; self-sacrifice in order that others may be free (the Bodhisattva vow). Think of childbirth; homing instincts; respiratory issues such as the first breath; gasping for air; clearing the air passageways; a strong wind that takes your breath away. Watch for emerging into the light; homing in; a honking good nose for where to go. Consider egoless leadership or issues about being first; moving from dark to light, from pure white to coal black, from underground into the world, from autumn toward spring; instinctual sensibilities regarding dramatically illuminating shifts.

"An unsuccessful bomb explosion" (13 Aries) and "Children blowing soap bubbles" (13 Libra)

Aspect: Trine.
Quality: Maintaining.
Shared motifs: 'Encasement,' 'blowing up,'
'little matters that become big deals.'

"An unsuccessful bomb explosion" is an image of a potentially powerful threat of danger that turns out to be hollow. "Bomb" is derived from the Greek for a loud, hollow sound. An "explosive bomb" is a hollow receptacle in which explosive, incendiary material is contained. When a bomb does not blow up, it may be a dud, or it may be a successfully contained explosion that does no harm. Consider one of the most significant modern inventions: the internal combustion engine. The motor of a car, for example, is a bomb designed to channel the energy of multiple explosions to make the wheels go around, to be productive or to get somewhere. The hollow encasement is crucial to the effects of the explosion. If the encasement were bubble-thin, its bursting could have damaging effects.

"Children blowing soap bubbles" is an image of breathing air into thin encasements with very short-lived results. "Soap bubbles" are formed by a thin film of soapy liquid infused with air or gas. "Blowing" is the action of breath moving air, but can also mean to fail, as in blowing an opportunity, to spend, to emit, or to burst like a tire. When children blow bubbles, there is laughter floating with the bubbles in the air. The object of the children's play is to float the bubbles for as long as possible. A bubble, like children's laughter, bursts easily: unpredictably, since it is not engineered to last.

Imagine the innocent, innocuous play of children blowing bubbles. Even adults cheer on successful, long-lasting orbs in the air. Popping bubbles seems to be of particular delight, especially if it is someone else's bubble. In the midst of the playfulness, a bomb may be dropped in your backyard, fail to explode, but thereby create a sense of dread or impending doom. Bomb squads, which attempt to defuse the potential danger, represent one of the most dangerous lines of employment possible. Literally, you just don't know when the bubble, and possibly your life, is going to burst. It is like walking on eggshells.

Apply this degree-pair with a mind to attempting to contain delicate but explosive situations; attempting to stabilize unstable situations. Listen for loud, hollow sounds; bubbling sounds; innocent remarks that blow up in your face; hollow threats. Watch for being adept at defusing tense situations; bursting the bubble of the overinflated, overly serious; extreme expressions of gaiety and doom, frivolity and seriousness. Think of a big show for a little result; a big result for something that shows little. Consider being out of puff, short of air; wartime experience with dud bombs. Managed delicately, there is a right time and place for both the success and failure of explosions and bubbles.

"A serpent coiling near a man and a woman" (14 Aries) and "A noon siesta" (14 Libra)

Aspect: Square.
Quality: Challenge.
Shared motifs: 'Intensity and rest,' 'napping through one's moment in the sun.'

"A serpent coiling near a man and a woman" is an image of the spiraling energies between a man and a woman. A "serpent" is a legless reptile that moves by creeping and gliding over surfaces. Long a symbol in many cultures for sexual energy, the serpent has many distinctive characteristics: shedding its entire skin; lazing in the hot sun; burrowing into the earth or under rocks; the amazing ease by which it coils like a rope gathered into a ring. Kundalini practices refer to the upward spiraling motion of life energy, often initiated in the coiling physical, sexual embrace of a man and a woman. The potential is one of a higher spiritual awareness; the challenge lies in the easy temptation to remain on a mere physical level.

"A noon siesta" is an image of taking a time of rest when the heat of the day is at its peak. A "siesta" derives from the Spanish for the sixth hour, the working day equivalent of noon. It harkens from a culture and climate that recognizes the appropriateness of a time out from the hottest part of the day. Productivity is greatly reduced in the heat of the noonday sun. It is even dangerous to remain active at such a time: heatstroke; sunburn; dehydration. The noonday sun in a hot climate brings a burning intensity to the situation, one that might have one shedding clothes or lying around. The paradox is that resting at noon in such conditions actually improves productivity.

Imagine an intensely hot day when the full light of the sun shines everywhere, illuminating everything: the time of the least shadow. At the sixth hour, the sun is at its highest position in the sky, a time associated with seeing all things clearly since it is at this peak time of illumination that there are the fewest obscurations. The potential with this time of day reaches to a fully awakened consciousness of the forms of reality, yet, paradoxically, it is during this time that one tends to want to sleep. Imagine the intense passions that draw a man and a woman together, coiling around them as it were, in intimate awareness of the powerful energies that bind them. It is paradoxical that at this time of the greatest awareness of each other, sleep overtakes the lovers.

Apply this degree-pair with a mind to the challenge of awakening to the highest potentials; of rising in full illumination or being all wrapped up in temporary pleasures; of drawing close to one's moment in the sun but retreating into the shade. Think of clinging to one another to cover a primal embarrassment of raw, naked energies; hesitation or lack of trust about the nature of powerful personal energies; always having an out when things become intense. Consider choosing lust over love; base over sublime energies; knowing when to knock off for a few hours; good sense about not getting burned; forfeiting one's possibilities to play it safe; childlike playfulness circling around mature potentials; sleeping potentials.

"An Indian weaving a blanket" (15 Aries)
and "Circular paths" (15 Libra)

Aspect: Quintile.
Quality: Creative genius.
Shared motif: 'The warp and woof of all cycles of life.'

"An Indian weaving a blanket" is an image of ingenious skills that weave protective coverings together with life possibilities as a whole. A "blanket" is a fabric that covers, hides, or protects in a uniform, unbroken fashion. "Blanket" derives from the Old French word for white, *blanc,* originally referring to a solid white woolen cloth. "Weaving" is an action that produces a whole by interlacing threads or yarns in a loom. In Greek mythology, the three Fates were depicted as weavers: Clotho spinning the thread of life, Lachesis measuring it, and Atropos cutting the thread. The Indian term "Tantra" literally means thread, implying a conception where every thread of life is interwoven together.

"Circular paths" is an image of continuous cycles of life ever returning in full potential. To be "circular" means that completion always returns to the beginning. A circle can be started at any point just as a new resolve about one's existence can begin at each and every moment. "Paths" are the many courses in life or the way upon which one walks. "Circular paths" may suggest going around and around, never getting anywhere; however, paths may be thought of as being on different levels yet folding into one another as an expression of the whole. Consider this temporal metaphor: life, daily activity, like individual threads woven to "build" upon the construction of a blanket; death, the blanket wears out; and transformative time and space, the creative potency of energy that awakens awareness of the whole.

The Buddhist conception of the Wheel of Life depicts life as a recurring cycle of entanglements, like being caught in a web from which it is difficult to escape. Ultimately there is no difference between the tangled states of life and consummate enlightened awareness: there is an ever present possibility for waking up. Imagine the recurring cycle of excitement and passion about one's possibilities and the consequent sense of frustration and disappointment when one's full potentials fail to be realized: a promising relationship fails to work out; an opportunity for success and happiness slips by; a favorite blanket becomes worn and must be tossed out. Since all threads of life touch each other in a comprehensive whole, there is no blame: even the smallest thread of life is an occasion for supreme success; even the tightest web has gaps between the threads.

Apply this degree-pair with a mind to a sense of innate genius to connect a single thread to the whole of life; an appreciation of weaving the differing dimensions of existence into a whole; a deep understanding that human failure is ultimately an illusion. Watch for monotonous tedium as in a resignation to piecework; repetitious frustration arising from a failure to learn from experience; a tendency to blame oneself for being caught in a web of suffering. Look for bright attitudes that celebrate the unique occasion of life; take joy in making what is hollow full, what is full empty; a resilient capacity to get back on the path.

"Brownies dancing in the setting sun" (16 Aries) and "A boat landing washed away" (16 Libra)

Aspect: Conjunction.
Quality: Focus.
Shared motifs: 'Repair,' 'celebrating the dance of life.'

"Brownies dancing in the setting sun" is an image of celebration at the end of the day. A "brownie" is a member of the fairy or elf family said to be benevolent in nature and associated with doing work for humans at nighttime. Recall the fairy tales about the shoemaker whose shoe commissions are completed at night by elves, or the tailor who is assisted by elves performing the fine stitching work while he sleeps. The "setting sun" is an image of day's end, twilight. Associated with harvest time, the gathering of the fruits of one's labors, this is a time of gathering with one's family to share an evening meal in joy. While humans prepare for their rest, the unseen natural spirits begin their work, bringing aid and renewal for the return of day.

"A boat landing washed away" is an image of natural forces sweeping away human constructs, calling for repair and renewal. To "wash" is to cleanse, as in washing clothes in order to prepare them for use again. "Washing away" implies the power of waves which carry off that which cannot withstand their force. A "boat landing" is a human construct for receiving ships from sea, or for securing vessels in safety from powerful tides. Ships cannot dock while the harbor is damaged or under repair, but this is not necessarily a bad thing, nor one for which one should feel blame or misfortune. Consider the repair of the well from the I Ching: "The well is being lined. No blame." Just as a well cannot be used while it is under repair, there are times when one must put oneself in order, repair, heal, enhance personal power through inner work, so as to be of greater benefit to others later on.

Imagine, having been outside all day, that one has a sunburn from the intense rays of the sun. As evening falls, one seeks a means to soothe the burn with a cooling salve. It is not a time of being at one's full power, ready for fully effective actions. It is a time to rest, heal, and salvage what you can from the results of the day. The healing process unfolds in its own time, imperceptibly and in a manner that requires patient waiting, allowing one's own healing capacities to perform their magic. After times of great crisis in life, one must repair, a process that cannot be hurried by an insistent mind.

Apply this degree-pair with a mind to repair, healing, and a personal relationship with unseen powers of nature. Think of responsive sensitivities to natural forces; the tendency to be disengaged from the world while waiting for renewal; waiting for one's ship to come in. Watch for cheerfulness while not being at one's best; finding salvation in patience; a knack for applying healing salves; an almost mystical sense of where and how inner work and repair occurs. Consider washing sounds; feeling washed out; being swept away by powerful forces; a strong sense of inner renewal; a positive attitude about the approaching new day.

"Two prim spinsters" (17 Aries) and "A retired sea captain" (17 Libra)

Aspect: Opposition.
Quality: Awareness of.
Shared motifs: 'Yarns that reinforce personal history,'
'stuck in a story's web.'

"Two prim spinsters" is an image of two unmarried proper ladies spinning yarns of mutually reinforced personal realities. "Spinsters" are mature, unmarried women and/or women who spin thread, twisting it into yarn. "Spin" derives from "span," to pull or draw something along, as in drawing a thread that is spun into a ball on a spindle, a narrow needle-shaped object used in hand spinning. "Prim" derives from "prime," the first or earliest, and has come to mean precise or neat in a stiff or fussy way. "Two prim spinsters" evokes an image of a well-rehearsed manner of maintaining things in the same proper way over years of shared experience. It is a reality spun out of a need to compensate for what didn't happen. The sustaining energies turn inwardly, toward each other, withdrawn from the wider world of experience.

"A retired sea captain" is an image of long experience with the tides of life, retired, but never tiring of spinning tales of the sea. "Retire" means to withdraw from public life, to take one's rest after long days of work. Literally meaning to draw back, "retire" is akin to "tirade," a prolonged outpouring pulled from pent-up energies. A "retired sea captain" might well look back on a life at sea, spinning stories over and over again. These tales would be a highly personal accounting, salted with individual flare and spiced with adventures of youth.

The spinsters may be retired as well. However, their retirement is an insular reality borne out of having never being married. We can easily imagine the gossipy conversation while knitting scarves for their nephews about whom a censorious tirade ensues. Perhaps for the spinsters, it is more often than not an internal dialogue or an icy silence tinged with prim expressions of bitterness. There may be two versions regarding the same point. The sea captain might spin yarns or windy tales of woe betiding a life at sea. Imagine watching the tides come and go while a boat dock is undergoing repairs. The sea captain may miss his life of being in command at sea, or resent being in dry dock. The story is sure to be turned around and around in his mind like being a fish out of water, or having something that silently needles one.

Apply this degree-pair with a mind to stories that reinvent the past; that maintain a precision about a shared experience; that spin around a central point. Listen for aloof censure; rollicking storytelling that picks up extra threads to spice things up; two versions of one story. Watch for prim facial expressions; tightly drawn lips; a fine touch with thread, cloth, yarn. Think of internal dialogues with a touch of solitary sadness: being alone together; empty silence even in company; salty takes on comings and goings. Consider silent awareness of backgrounds or past history, picking up loose threads until the tale is complete; pointed stories that take a while to come to a point; idiosyncratic self-absorption or a wizened regard for life all around.

"An empty hammock" (18 Aries)
and "Two men placed under arrest" (18 Libra)

Aspect: Trine.
Quality: Maintaining.
Shared motif: 'Suspension.'

"An empty hammock" is an image of a woven fabric, used as a place of rest, suspended between two secure posts. A "hammock" is a hanging bed made of sturdy cloth or netting suspended between two securing supports at each end. "An empty hammock" is one available to lie in, an inviting prospect that may sway one to stop work and take a break. Since the hammock is empty, there is also a question of never taking a break. A hammock is suspended between two poles, trees, or secure points from which it hangs, suggesting a two-sided issue; being caught between two extremes, hung up on two possibilities: "Should I rest, or should I work?"

"Two men placed under arrest" is an image of two people being suspended from freely acting, or two issues that put one on hold. Consider these "arresting situations": an arresting beauty may catch your attention; proceedings may be stayed or arrested in order to assess new or unusual information; an arresting suggestion can give pause for further thought. Two men can be arrested, but they are innocent until proven guilty. The central issue is the suspension of normal activity. Two men walking home from a bar at night may attract the attention of the "law." Their journey home is suspended for the time being until matters are sorted out, or, if there are holes in their story, there might be something to hang charges upon.

A hammock is a place for a rest; the attractiveness of an inviting hammock may be arresting. One may have to choose between work and rest, or one may have no choice but to suspend activities. During a televised sporting match, a pause for a commercial is an empty break in the action of the game. The hammock may be empty because of a suspicion that the poles or standards may not be able to take the weight of someone lying in it. When two people lie in a hammock, the issue swings between a comfortable rest and landing on the ground with a thud, calling attention again to the reliability of the supports that hold up the matter.

Apply this degree-pair with a mind to issues of time-outs, taking five, stretching the rules, bending the pillars or standards of laws, values, mores. Think of operating outside the laws and rules in innovative, slightly defiant ways. Look for double standards, throwing a changeup into the routine; applying critical intelligence to the pillars of society; being suspicious of the rules. Consider a tightly woven story that hangs on two main points; a story with holes in it causing one to pause and fill in the gaps; opposing versions of the same story; pressing decisions that bring all forward progress to a halt; clues or clews: a combination of threads or lines upon which to hang a story, or a hammock. One might be so attractive as to bring all activity to a standstill: an arresting beauty.

"The magic carpet" (19 Aries) and "A gang of robbers in hiding" (19 Libra)

Aspect: Square.
Quality: Challenge.
Shared motifs: 'Outside and above it all,' 'freedom from attachments,' 'wearing one's true robes.'

"The magic carpet" is an image of the ability to hover above situations. A "carpet" is a sturdy woven fabric used for covering the floor. "Magic" is the power or art of influencing matters beyond the range of the laws of nature, or to effect a remarkable or enchanting quality. A "magic carpet" might be a flying carpet defying the laws of physics: transporting to any place desired. Suspending natural laws implies effecting the extraordinary or not appreciating the gravity of the situation. In human awareness, the ability to disengage from the predictable course of events has both positive and not-so-positive implications. "Sublimation" is the ability to divert energy from one state to another, such as elevating desires to thought. Suspending awareness may imply detachment from the outcome of events, or a floating consciousness such as retiring into a world of one's own.

"A gang of robbers in hiding" is an image of plunderers living outside the laws of society, undercover. A "gang" is a band of persons going about together, united for a common goal. In the case of a gang of thieves, fellowship and loyalty last only while a common purpose is shared: honor among thieves tends not to be stable. "Robbers" are those who take unlawfully from others. Deriving from "reave," to plunder, robbers might leave their victims bereft of valuables, or in bereavement. "Robbers" also hide behind a "robe" or long heavy garment while disrobing others of their belongings. To be branded "a gang of robbers" does not necessarily imply a lack of character, honesty, and integrity.

Robin Hood, who presumably would wear a robbing hood to cover his identity, was forced to hide outside the law. Certain political and social regimes identify those who go about the world with integrity by the names "dissidents," "subversives." Sometimes finding one's place within society calls for acts of civil disobedience or the wisdom to take cover beyond the edges of prevailing laws. One's safety may depend on the ability to magically disappear in a crowd since it is wise not to be fully exposed at all times. Magicians are often synonymous with escape artists who defy the laws of containment. The question: is it freedom from base attachments or flight from genuine responsibilities?

Apply this degree-pair with a mind to the challenge of maintaining integrity within a compromising social milieu; the right use of cover; creative alternatives to the paths of convention. Think of magic as the wisdom to know when to stand above the fray; to transcend situations that could lead to bereavement; to ascertain the right moment to touch down. Watch for helpers in hiding ready to emerge when help is needed; escapism; waiting on the sidelines until one's influence can be effective. Consider sublimation as taking something to a higher level or taking the passion out of life, hiding behind empty thoughts; rising above it all or the urge to retire; moving to the margins of society in order to be true to oneself.

"A young girl feeding birds in winter" (20 Aries) and "A Jewish rabbi" (20 Libra)

Aspect: Quintile.
Quality: Creative genius.
Shared motifs: 'A vehicle of compassion for others,'
'a man for all seasons.'

"A young girl feeding birds in winter" is an image of compassionate nurturing of those in need during a harsh season. "Birds" are divided into those who follow the sun in a migratory search for spring and summer, and those who winter in their yearlong homes. Enduring winter hardships can evoke a compassionate response in others more safe and secure from cold and barren seasons. "Feeding" is an action of providing nourishment, fostering life for those who have to forage for food. "Food" is akin to "pastor," originally a shepherd or one who watches over the flocks as they feed in the pasture. "Repast" has been adapted in English as a word for food, hence a meal.

"A Jewish rabbi" is an image of a spiritual head and teacher whose responsibilities lie in interpreting and disseminating matters of the laws of living. The rabbi becomes a vehicle for bringing ancient wisdom to bear upon the present times. He is out of season by virtue of his link with the past, yet he is the source of nourishment for his community. As a leader, a rabbi's task is to feed his community in order to help others find their right place and time regarding their heritage.

Consider the story "The Ugly Duckling." Through the winter, the outcast duckling has to swim constantly to keep the pond from freezing over completely or else become frozen fast into the ice. Without the help and kindness of others, the misfit duck cannot survive. Providing sustenance for those ruled to be outsiders, or those who are temporarily out of their element, is a natural display of compassion: winter warmed with kindness. To call a rabbi a pastor is perhaps like calling a swan a duck, yet the wise, nourishing counsel of the deeper laws for living oversees the welfare of others in the same shepherding fashion. The laws that govern fulfillment of life's potential require one to be a man for all seasons, tolerant, generous, helping all to find their element, to grow into the season of a recognizable true identity.

Apply this degree-pair with a mind to creative generosity to help situations along; to guide others to their own day in the sun; to a compassionate sensibility that transcends rigid rules. Think of teaching; nurturing; sustaining rather than suspending; stewarding future potentials. Watch for a felt appreciation of today's outsiders being tomorrow's leaders; providing food for thought; feeding the mind. Consider a man for all seasons; nourishing wisdom as opposed to smug intellectualism; generosity of the heart as opposed to giving free handouts.

"A pugilist entering the ring" (21 Aries) and "A crowd upon the beach" (21 Libra)

Aspect: Conjunction.
Quality: Focus.
Shared motifs: 'Finding one's place,' 'choosing one's arena.'

"A pugilist entering the ring" is an image of a sharp focus on challenging for one's place in the center. A "pugilist" is one who fights with his fists, two hands of five fingers each, punching with the hand closed tightly to make one's point. "Pugilist," "punch," "point," and "pugnacious" all belong to a family of words deriving from "pungent," a sharp, pricking sensation of taste or smell: something that strikes smartly, like an alcoholic beverage that carries a punch. "Fist" is related to "fusty," a sharp, musty smell from a wine cask, and "fustian," a cudgel-like disposition of coarse bombast. A "ring" is any circular object that, curiously in this case, is a four-cornered square: a circle squared in which a man stands, his limbs extended to their fullest range. The fight or contest begins with a ring of the bell, which sounds again at the end of each round.

"A crowd upon the beach" is an image of a throng of people pushing their way to the shoreline. A "crowd" suggests people gathered closely together in a cramped situation that may involve some pushing and shoving. A "beach" is a sandy shore that slopes to a body of water. On a fine Sunday afternoon, the beach may be so crowded that one cannot find a place to lay a beach blanket. Sometimes it is like making a beachhead in a military campaign. Everyone seeks to find an advantageous spot to claim as their own near to where the solid land meets with the water: like finding one's seat in a crowded boxing arena. In a sea of blankets and towels this is often a contest-like challenge.

Consider these arenas for entering the fray: crowds gathered around a ring to watch two fighters contest each other for center-ring glory; an individual fighting to find a place within a crowd. Each situation depicts a mandala of the human journey. One could become boxed into a corner or resort to shoving and using coarse language when the situation seems less than ideal. Securing a better place than others seems to be the prevailing social inclination. Winning one's place in the world seems empty without public recognition.

Apply this degree-pair with a mind to the focused contest between individuality and social organization; the natural inclination to define one's space; finding the range of one's power, the impact of one's punch. Think of the range of attitudes possible for joining the fray: pugnacity or agoraphobia; combativeness or fear of public spaces; feeling one has to fight for some room or confusion about being pushed around; seeing social dynamics as a three-ring circus. Consider taking a public bashing; sitting back on the lookout for knockout beauty; having one's ideals buffeted by crowd mentality; a feisty nature; being aroused at the sound of a bell or with pungent smelling salts to continue the fight; seeking the limits of what one can do by one's own hand.

"The gate to the garden of desire" (22 Aries) and "A child giving birds a drink at a fountain" (22 Libra)

Aspect: Opposition.
Quality: Awareness of.
Shared motifs: 'You can't always get what you want,'
'desires and beyond.'

"The gate to the garden of desire" is an image of a passageway into an enclosure containing that which has been absent, and therefore is sought after. "Desire" is an awareness of longing for something that has been missing: Latin, *de,* away from, and *sidus, sideris,* star. A "star" is a fixed point of light, often symbolically portrayed as a five-pointed figure, used for navigating or measuring time by the stars, echoing the sense of sidereal, concerning the constellations, and astrology, guidance gleaned from the motion of heavenly bodies. One is a star in the social arena when shining brightly through one's accomplishment or performance. A "garden" holds an abundance of riches such as sweet fruits, wholesome vegetables, fragrant flowers: it is a fenced-off concentration of fertile reward. A "gate" is an opening or passageway that functions as an access to something. "Gate" is echoic of "gait," a manner of walking, and the Sanskrit *gate,* meaning beyond: the way beyond.

"A child giving birds a drink at a fountain" is an image of innocence opening access to the source of satisfaction. "Water" is essential for life. A "fountain" is an ancient symbol of the source of life energy overflowing. While a fountain can be a natural spring of water, in this case it is likely a public drinking fountain, which the girl must turn on for the thirsty birds. "A child giving birds a drink" suggests an innocent generosity that, without hesitation or thought of reward, is made available to satisfy a thirst or craving for the water of life. "Drink" means to swallow, soak up, or absorb eagerly as through the senses or the mind. "Drinking a toast to someone" is to honor another by a symbolic raising of the glass.

Consider an awareness of an abundance of things sought after, things that suggest a promise of fulfillment: success, wealth, fame, comfort, pleasure. A noble desire may be a longing for the fundamentals in life. However, "desire" is often imbued with lust or envy: the grass is always greener on the far side of the garden fence. Contrast this with an innocent and natural impulse to give access to what is freely available, simply because that is all that is needed.

Apply this degree-pair with a mind to the difference between necessities and desires; being high on life as opposed to longing for peak experiences; generously giving rather than envying greener pastures. Think of temptations as opposed to satisfaction; wanting more as opposed to having enough. Watch for frustration regarding not finding the gate into the garden, or indulgence after having found the way into the garden. One's own bright star may not be far away: sometimes longing for something beyond is as simple as being where you are. Consider thirst as the motivation to go beyond mere desiring; lust as vibrant, abundant love for life as such; the capacity to toast one's enemies as worthy opponents; understanding that what one desires is an ever renewable resource.

"A woman in pastel colors carrying a heavy and valuable but veiled load" (23 Aries) and "Chanticleer" (23 Libra)

Aspect: Trine.
Quality: Maintaining.
Shared motif: 'Keeping a tight hold on pride and possession.'

"A woman in pastel colors carrying a heavy and valuable but veiled load" is an image of quietly protecting and bearing the weight of what you already have. "Pastel colors" suggest summer clothing of soft color tones or hues of gray. "Pastel" derives from "pasta," a waxy substance that tends to stick. A "heavy but valuable load" suggests something considered precious, like a newborn child, the responsibility for which one is naturally inclined to carry. Whatever she carries is covered, hidden, protected, from open view. The woman's appearance is soft and quiet like the early light of day. It is not clear whether the woman wants to show her "load." Perhaps there is reticence or shyness. Then again, sometimes the quietest of entrances announces presence most loudly. The woman may be showing off her new precious bundle in a quiet way appropriate to its value, or she may be attempting to go unnoticed, hiding her sense of worth.

A "chanticleer" is an image of a bright, proud announcement of the new day. A "chanticleer" is a proper name for a cock or rooster, meaning to sing or crow loudly and clearly. A cock crows at the light of day with an arousing fervor in stark contrast to the quiet early morning, announcing his presence, saluting the dawn, heralding the new day. There is a puffed-up pride that goes with the rooster's crow as he stands on a fence post. In each case, the woman and chanticleer are announcing something new, although the manner of announcing their entrance spans a wide range of possible styles: pride as opposed to self-effacing caution; brash, brassy, and loud as opposed to soft, quiet, and reticent.

Veiling a valuable bundle can be achieved in a variety of ways. Imagine carrying a heavy bar of gold. One might choose discretion as a means for not drawing attention to what one possesses. Sometimes the best protective cover is to be brash and loud, deliberately calling attention to oneself and thereby deflecting suspicious or covetous eyes. When the golden sun lifts into the morning sky, the chanticleer begins to crow. He might even assume that, were it not for him, the sun might never rise.

Apply this degree-pair with a mind to the self-aware expressions of possessions and positions; maintaining a firm grip on what is felt to be owned; a sustaining pride that motivates one to carry a great weight. Listen for a range of entrance styles: soft and discreet or loud and brassy. Watch for how accomplishments and possessions are carried: all wrapped up with pride; boastful or cocksure; with trepidation, fearing loss; as if one rules the roost. Consider a hodgepodge of possessions that weigh one down; sticky matters over belongings; sticking with one's post; clear voices; soft voices; veiling shyness with bravado; toning down the show of inner conceit; gray moods and bright dispositions.

"An open window and a net curtain blowing into a cornucopia" (24 Aries) and "A third wing on the left side of a butterfly " (24 Libra)

Aspect: Square.
Quality: Challenge.
Shared motifs: 'The unbearable lightness of plenty,'
'issues of surplus.'

"An open window and a net curtain blowing into a cornucopia" is an image of receptivity to catch the fruits of life. A "cornucopia," the horn of plenty, is a symbol of abundance, power, possessions, and wealth. A "window" is an opening in a wall to allow light and air into a dwelling. Eyes are said to be the windows of the soul, which, when open, allow for receiving from the external world. Windows are dressed with curtains, which can open to, shut off, or conceal light and curtail air. "Curtain," deriving from the Latin *cort,* court, is akin to "cortex," the gray matter of the brain. "Net" is a woven or knotted meshwork fabric used to catch fish, birds, or butterflies. A "net profit" is the clear profit after expenses and deductions. The struggle to profit from life situations is a gray area constantly open to assessment.

"A third wing on the left side of a butterfly" is an image of an extraspecial manifestation in life that can be gone in the blink of an eye and give cause for thought. A "third wing" is an extra factor in what is normally understood to be a two-sided matter. A third eyelid, for example, is a nictitating membrane found in birds and reptiles at the corner of the eye. In humans, this refers to the ability to wink or blink the eyelids, but is intriguingly also called a "haw." "Haw" can mean to hesitate in speech or thought, as in hemming and hawing, and is also a call to attention when driving horses to turn to the left. "Left-sided" issues are those pertaining to feminine nurturing capacities; to the analytical hemisphere of the brain; to left-wing concerns of social welfare. Something may occur, causing one to pause for thought, or to take a left turn, on what was originally considered to be an "either/or" situation.

Consider a rigid or brittle window on life that sees issues of profit and loss, power and possession, wealth and poverty as clear-cut, "either/or" matters. Imagine a third element coming into play that causes one to pull on the reins of the drive for profit and power: the unbearable poverty of third world countries, for example. One might begin to think there is a hole in one's philosophy of personal gain. Consider opportunities of abundant rewards in life as like trying to ensnare an extraspecial and delicate butterfly in one's net. In the blink of an eye, the opportunity may flutter by.

Apply this degree-pair with a mind to the challenge of assessing transparent gains against the fragility of overall balance; the weight of responsibility of wealth against the unbearable poverty and suffering of others; reconciling rewards with responsibility. Watch for imbalances such that things won't fly; being at the mercy of the winds of fortune; feeling the need to compensate for powerlessness. Consider winking; blinking eyes, fluttering eyes; twitching eyelids; third world issues; third eye awareness; an interval between tones; shifting into a third gear; being third class; hesitation; a pause for thought; the gray areas of profit and power.

"A double promise" (25 Aries)
and "Information in the symbol of an autumn leaf" (25 Libra)

Aspect: Quintile.
Quality: Creative genius.
Shared motifs: 'Having your cake and eating it too,'
'times of plenty; times of famine.'

"A double promise" is an image of going beyond personal concerns to fulfill the hopes and needs of others. "Promise" is that which sends forth, Latin *pro-mittere.* One might assess a situation as promising when there are grounds for fulfilling hopes and expectations of future excellence or satisfaction: gray clouds promising rain; a promising talent. Sending someone or something forth with a particular purpose is a "mission." "A double promise" suggests going beyond concerns for one's own well-being and prosperity to include the well-being and prosperity of others. There is no contradiction involved unless one submits to double talk: promising to be in two places at the same time; attempting to appear generous while remaining greedy.

"Information in the symbol of an autumn leaf" is an image of meaning unexpectedly conveyed by a specific signal of decay that pulls everything together. "Information" is timely or specific knowledge derived from facts or data. Communicating information is usually thought of as unforeseeable and meaningful knowledge conveyed in bits: someone dropping surprising bits of information about themselves; an open-and-shut court case taking an unpredictable turn when a witness drops a surprising bit of information during testimony. The term "symbol" derives from the Greek *symballein,* to throw together: a mark or token that throws disparate things together, yielding greater sense. "An autumn leaf" signals a turn of season, the end of a time of abundance and plenty. "Leaves" inevitably, yet unpredictably, fall from trees in autumn after having turned colors: green to yellow and red, red to brown and gray.

Consider the practice of "tithing": a tax, voluntary in religious practice, measuring a tenth part, five doubled, of one's yearly income to aid those less fortunate. Tithing is based on the belief, the trust, that one can afford to give a portion of one's wealth and abundance away without inflicting harm to one's own welfare. In fact, some would say that giving charitably to those more needful brings greater rewards, tenfold rewards, to the generous of heart. Falling autumn leaves are clearly a sign of decline, death, and decay, which might awaken an awareness that no one can hold on to power, wealth, and possessions forever. Cycles of feast or famine are inevitable. The genius of generosity sends forth a promising balance for all.

Apply this degree-pair with a mind to the genius of finding one's place in the world in harmony with the welfare of others; balancing personal desires with compassion for others; balancing self-interest with social welfare. Think of being so comfortable about your gold that you can give some away; the natural generosity of heart as opposed to poverty mentality. Listen for surprising bits of information that change the course of everything; dropping hints; overly sincere double talk; unexpected revelations; the golden rule. Consider creating wealth through generosity; carrying part of the social load; golden moments emblematic of promising rewards.

"A man possessed of more gifts than he can hold" (26 Aries) and "An eagle and a large white dove turning one into the other" (26 Libra)

Aspect: Conjunction.

Quality: Focus.

Shared motifs: 'Getting a grip on personal potentials,' 'the changeable nature of possession.'

"A man possessed of more gifts than he can hold" is an image of overflowing talents that, not being mastered, run away. "Possess" derives from the Latin *possidere,* to sit as master of, hence to own, to have power over something: a talent; something owned as one's property; oneself. "To hold" means to grasp as with the hand, to keep, restrain, occupy, or possess. "Gift" turns on giving and receiving, gifting and taking. Imagine the action of a hand when it opens to give something to another, releasing one's hold in order to gift another. When one receives a gift, the hand closes to grasp, to take hold of, what is given. To have a talent suggests the possible mastery of something that comes to one easily, a fulfillment of the potentials promised within the talent. "To be possessed of more gifts than one can hold" suggests an overflow of wonderful potentials that beckon to be fulfilled but that disperse one's energy in too many directions, resulting in mastering none.

"An eagle and a large white dove turning one into the other" is an image of changeableness of nature. The eagle and the dove are birds with diametrically opposed characteristics: a fierce bird of prey and a bird symbolizing peace, kindness, and gentleness. The high-soaring eagle with farsighted vision and patience grasps its prey in sharp talons. The large white dove, with tender regard to the security of home, carries an olive branch as an offering of peace and hope. Blending both capacities within human character is an admirable achievement. Knowing when to strike or defend; knowing when to offer peace: human greatness masters these potent powers with grace and ease. Indecisively changing back and forth, hawk to dove, shows a lack of mastery, change-ableness of character, wherein potential talons and talents run away with the man.

When a tea cup is overfilled, the tea spills and runs away according to its own na-ture. When a man carries too many parcels, attempting to keep everything in hand at once, some or all of the gifts fall to the ground. Possessing a talent suggests having a potential that can be fulfilled, mastered, or brought into hand. One can also be pos-sessed by a talent, obsessively pursuing the perfection and expression of a gift. Con-sider the temperamental genius turning from eagle to dove in changeable moodiness. Perhaps one is shy like a dove, aloof like an eagle, never fulfilling the promise of gift-edness in the world.

Apply this degree-pair with a mind to the focus on mastering one's gifts, talents, and capacities; integrating powers such that they harmoniously manifest in the world; being in possession of oneself. Think of an overabundance of gifts as a human condition; a bewildering array of potentials; not knowing which way to turn. Watch for erratic switching between moods and pursuits; antisocial traits; hiding talents away; letting a talent drop. Consider running obsessively after a talent; a talent run-ning away with you; the talent for cultivating talents; running hot and cold regarding one's own gifts.

"Lost opportunity regained in the imagination" (27 Aries) and "An airplane hovering overhead" (27 Libra)

Aspect: Opposition.
Quality: Awareness of.
Shared motifs: 'Reappropriation,' 'inward focus transcending present reality.'

A "lost opportunity regained in the imagination" is an image of an inward retrieval of creative possibilities. To be "lost" suggests a bewilderment or confusion, perhaps about something no longer possessed, something gone astray or wasted. An "oppor-tunity regained" is a favorable time or circumstance that is retrieved, a promising advantage that has returned to a fitting place. "Imagination" is the creative awareness of possibilities, a panoramic awareness ranging like an open sky of possibilities. One might scan the sky of possibilities for those promising a potential to be fulfilled or realized. The image speaks to talents or gifts left undeveloped, such as a talent or gift for singing that might be imaginatively reclaimed after leaving it on the shelf for many years. The emphasis is on something from the past being brought forward.

"An airplane hovering overhead" is an image of a powerful vehicle that seems to linger in the sky. Remembering that this symbol was conceived in 1925 when airplanes were in their infancy as a mode of transport, an "airplane" would have been an amazing achievement of a powerful machine of flight. "To hover" is to be suspended or to linger near one point in the air. "Hovering" suggests an unresolved state or condition such as being suspended in a potential state, not yet fully realized or made actual. "Overhead" is beyond the head, higher than the reach of the head of a standing man, suggesting something that might be reached for with the hand or through imagination. An airplane that appears to hover overhead suggests attention to something powerful above one's present position in the world.

Imagine being headed to an appointment amidst a myriad of everyday concerns, noises, thoughts, and plans, when up in the sky, a blinding glint of light catches one's attention. "It's a bird! It's a plane! It's . . . it's Superman!" Perhaps what is really seen is a plane reflecting sunlight, focusing attention on something pointed and brilliant. In that moment, everything in the bustling world—sounds, sights, thoughts, and intentions—drops away. The point of focus is flying, floating, in a calm, easy motion, yet it calls consciousness to orient to a single transcendent focus above everyday matters; not quite a polestar, but still a navigation point for consciousness.

Apply this degree-pair with a mind to the awareness of powerful possibilities that capture one's attention; promising potentials that stir excitement; thoughts of superhuman achievements. Watch for being lost in a world of imagination; hubris: human pride so excessive as to offend the gods; renewal of wonder and inspired personal projection. Think of fantasies of extraordinary accomplishments, talents, and dreams; brainstorming; feelings of having found oneself again. Consider reclamation; retrieval; feeling half-asleep, half-awake; ideas that really take off and fly.

"A large disappointed audience" (28 Aries)
and "A man in the midst of brightening influences" (28 Libra)

Aspect: Trine.
Quality: Maintaining.
Shared motif: 'Expectation and unexpected moments
of aid and grace.'

"A large disappointed audience" is an image of a large assembly for a hearing that fails to meet expectations. An "audience" is a hearing, like having an opportunity to meet with the king, where your words are heard and recognized. "Disappointment" is the frustration that arises when hopes and expectations are left unfulfilled. Parents, for example, can be disappointed when their children choose to follow their own dreams and talents rather than those projected for them: turning away from the family business to pursue one's own path. One may, after reclaiming an abandoned talent and having superhuman expectations for oneself, be temporarily disappointed at a lack of mastery, about the transitional period of getting one's chops up to par.

"A man in the midst of brightening influences" is an image of a situation, free from expectations, rewarded with a gift out of the blue. To be in the "midst" of something is to be within the center of a situation or activity. "Brightening influences" are those that bestow a positive, uplifting effect, emitting cheerful powers that can renew hope. Imagine singing a song for a gathering of friends and receiving unexpected praise and encouragement, or finding encouragement from an unexpected source. Maintaining one's path of realizing personal gifts and talents calls for a balance between feasible greatness and realistically apportioned encouragement.

Imagine projecting hopeful expectations regarding an Elvis concert only to find that hopes that have been cast ahead fail to be fulfilled: the tickets are sold out; Elvis doesn't show up; he doesn't sing a favorite song. Imagine the brightening influence when Elvis unexpectedly enters the coffeehouse one is in and sings that favorite song! When one is true to one's natural gifts, in calm, centered possession of oneself, an open awareness grows that allows for unexpected bestowal of divine grace, a kind of clairaudience. The difference is subtle, but one can almost hear it: going to a performance expecting to hear a concert only to find that Elvis has left the building; free from expectation, one is gifted as if by a song from Graceland.

Apply this degree-pair with a mind to balancing expectations and disappointments; tempering excitement with feasibility; rewarding an uncompromising sense of self. Listen for extraordinary capacities for hearing, listening; clairaudience; inaudible influences. Watch for realistic optimism; resiliency regarding the ups and downs of hope and disappointment; unpredictable moments of grace; not hitting the top of the charts but feeling encouraged anyway. Consider freedom from the expectations of others; temporarily feeling alone; moodiness that does not last long; coming down to earth regarding personal expectations for oneself.

"A celestial choir singing" (29 Aries)
and "Humanity seeking to span the bridge of knowledge" (29 Libra)

Aspect: Square.
Quality: Challenge.
Shared motifs: 'Being called to transcend,' 'seeking the extent
of one's grasp of heaven and earth.'

"A celestial choir singing" is an image of an inward listening that evokes awareness of heavenly influences. "Celestial" pertains to the sky, the overarching vault of heaven that beckons human sensibilities to a higher awareness. A "choir" is an organized group of singers, often singing songs of divinity. A choir of angels, for example, in the Christian tradition, is composed of the nine orders of angels who collectively sing the messages of divine influence while circling the heavenly throne: the music of the spheres. An "ennead" is a group of nine often associated with gods and divinity. In the Chinese tradition, celestial influence was understood to effect a divine right of rulership by way of the Mandate of Heaven, hence the "Celestial Dynasty."

"Humanity seeking to span the bridge of knowledge" is an image of the collective urge to pursue the fulfillment of the full reach of human knowledge. A "span" is the distance between two extremes, such as the distance between two supports of a bridge. "Spanning" is derived from the image of a fully outstretched hand considered to be about nine inches long. A second sense of "span" is to bind or draw together, as in a well-matched pair of horses or oxen. "Knowledge" is an understanding that reaches beyond where one stands, for example, understanding the ways of heaven and earth. Knowledge, in this sense, is the span that bridges heaven and earth, drawing heaven and earth together in the reach and grasp of human understanding.

Uplifting influences that follow disappointments effect a raising of sensibilities toward a higher order of influence, such as the divine music of the spheres. It is tempting, during such times, to seek divine justification for fulfilling expectations, to look away from the earth for the reason why. "Seeking knowledge" is a human endeavor in which man seeks to surpass himself through understanding: man is a bridge. The challenge lies in remaining open for further understanding while not exceeding one's grasp. Forsaking earthly existence in favor of divine justification is as troublesome as forsaking heavenly influence in favor of earthbound knowledge. According to Pythagoras, man is a full chord of eight notes, the ninth being the singing of the divine.

Apply this degree-pair with a mind to the struggle to reach beyond oneself for understanding; to pull together an understanding of trinities, or a trinity of trinities: nine. Think of the awareness that harkens to the divine principle beyond the sensible laws of harmony; harmonic overtones; a nine-day wonder or a great sensation lasting only a few days. Consider exceeding one's reach to justify a matter; a quiet inner sense that listens for something more; an exacting sense of harmony; impressions of otherworldliness; appreciation for a call from beyond; getting a handle on one's own power, which, like the height of horses, is measured in extended hands.

"A duck pond and its brood" (30 Aries)
and "Three mounds of knowledge on a philosopher's head" (30 Libra)

Aspect: Quintile.
Quality: Creative genius.
Shared motifs: 'Build it and they will come,' 'the gifts of
heaven and earth come to fruition in the realized man.'

"A duck pond and its brood" is an image of habitation appropriate for the gestation, hatching, and raising of weighty issues. "A duck pond" is a place of habitation highly suited for ducks to live in and raise their young. "Ducks" are birds able to swim and dive in water, walk on land, and fly through the air. While in water, ducks appear to float effortlessly; when taking off in flight, they skip along the water's surface: ducks and drakes. "Drake" is the name for a male duck derived from the term dragon. A "brood" is the young of a species or the incubation of eggs, which leads to pondering over something deeply.

"Three mounds of knowledge on a philosopher's head" is an image of the realization and preservation of a well-balanced understanding of life. "Three" is, according to Pythagoras, the perfect number, expressing beginning, middle, and end: divine perfection. "Trinities" abound in all world traditions: body, mind, and spirit; earth, sea, and air; heaven, earth, and man. "Mounds" are heaps of earth or rough material. "Mound" derives from both the Latin *mundus,* world, and the Dutch term *munt,* meaning protection. On a head, mounds refer to bumps, recalling the popular image of a Taoist sage with three prominent mounds on his head, signifying a harmony of a realized human with heaven and earth. A "philosopher" is a lover of wisdom. Pythagoras is said to have coined the term to distinguish divine wisdom from the human love of wisdom.

Imagine a philosopher brooding over ponderous, deep, weighty questions, in such a way as to pull it all together harmoniously. It would be like having one's ducks all in a row: down-to-earth; emotionally balanced and able to dive deep; soaring heavenly like the Chinese dragon, a symbol of divine power and creativity. One might float some ideas, ponder them deeply, tend them like a well-banked fire, so as to transmit wisdom through the young in order to have traditional wisdom in the bank for future generations. Some ideas will neither float nor fly, sinking like stones in emotional waters. Some ideas come up empty, like laying an egg; some take a long time to sit on before they hatch. There is a sense of naturalness about the whole process: pondering, nurturing, preserving, and flying like the Dragon of Heaven.

Apply this degree-pair with a mind to the genius of being at home with all elements of wisdom and understanding; in accordance with all things; the genius for tending to domestic issues as if they were sacred matters; the humor and ordinariness of consummate human realization. Watch for brooding natures; happy being sad; ponderous walks; ponderous foreheads. Listen for calls to follow in the family footsteps; following traditions swimmingly; the call to return to the nest. Consider taking to things like ducks to water; a happy sense of resourcefulness; quaking or quacking voices; easy targets; resilient natures; paradox; opining.

---

1. In his book *The Sabian Symbols in Astrology,* Marc Edmund Jones replaced the original word on the notecard, "white," with "wild," cf. Diana E. Roche, *The Sabian Symbols: A Screen of Prophecy* (Victoria, B.C.: Trafford, 1998) p. 43.

CHAPTER TWO

TAURUS-SCORPIO

"A clear mountain stream" (1 Taurus)
and "A sight-seeing bus" (1 Scorpio)

Aspect: Conjunction.
Quality: Focus.
Shared motifs: 'Going with the flow' or
'With which flow do you go?'

"A clear mountain stream" is an image of the nature of water to always find the easiest way down the mountainside. A mountain stream, because it descends from the heights, runs swiftly, yet is clear. The qualities of a mountain stream are freshness, purity, and clarity, suggesting an innocent, natural, and unsullied sense of being in the flow of things. This is in contrast to muddy water, which, in order to become clear, must remain still for a while. "The great rivers and seas are kings of all mountain streams because they skillfully stay below them" (*Tao Teh Ching,* # 66). This suggests that there is a greater destination for the many mountain streams. The resourcefulness of water lies in its nature to always find its way to the lowest point.

"A sight-seeing bus" is an image of many people carried to the highlights along a tour route. "Bus" derives from "omnibus," a vehicle that transports all. If one is on the bus, one is going along for the ride. There is an element of submission, receptivity, or letting it happen required: you buy your ticket and take your ride. The innocent quality of participation is passive, seeing new sights along with many others. You are either on or off the bus. Some people abhor tour buses, preferring to run on their own to the unseen nooks and crannies off the beaten track. On a sight-seeing bus, the destination is, at once, the points of interest along the way and the return to the point of departure.

Think of the qualities of character required for going along on a sight-seeing tour: natural openness and receptivity. There is a natural sense of beginning, middle, and end; starting point, destination points, and return. The mountain stream begins a journey that eventually returns to the sea. The sea is the source of moisture that is carried through the air and returned to the mountains as snow or rain. In the great cycle of all things, one must choose one's own way: a singular, unique mountain stream, or one of a group that watches the world go by.

Apply this degree-pair with a mind to a natural sense of purity and openness in starting out; going with the flow; an ease regarding the return. Think of the difference between a singular, individualized way of being as opposed to going along with the crowd. Sometimes it's better to watch through a tour bus window with a group of like-minded others; other times it's better to flow freely on your own. Watch for a sense of delight for new things; the ability to get around obstacles; to patiently wear down hard cases; bubbling personalities; seeking the easiest way; submitting to the group in order to avoid conflict. Consider overexpending energy to go everywhere; a happy sense of trust regarding one's destination; preferring to be a watcher; issues about who is behind the wheel; being in harmony or accord with one's natural way.

"An electrical storm" (2 Taurus)
and "A broken bottle and spilled perfume" (2 Scorpio)

Aspect: Opposition.
Quality: Awareness of.
Shared motifs: 'Discharge,' 'release and splitting off,' 'awakening.'

"An electrical storm" is an image of an arousing natural event that crackles with illumination while disturbing the atmosphere. "Electric" derives from the Latin *electrum,* amber. "Storm" derives from "stir," as in a disturbance in the atmosphere that stirs things up. It is like the "Aha!" experience: sudden, blinding; a discharge of energy that often brings about a change and release from a stagnant situation, perhaps a mini-satori. Imagine a dark night sky suddenly illumined by lightning or a long stretch of hot, muggy days broken by a good thunderstorm. It is as if the clear mountain stream has reached a place in the mountains where it plunges dramatically down as a waterfall, or the pent-up moisture held in dark, heavy clouds releases in a downpour of rain.

"A broken bottle and spilled perfume" is an image of the accidental or unexpected release of essence that permeates the air. "Perfume" derives from "fume," to smoke, and "per," meaning through, hence completely. A "perfume bottle" is an airtight container that, should it fall to the floor, breaks with a sharp, shattering sound. "Spill" originally meant "splinter," a slender piece of anything that splits off from the whole, like a spike of lightning splitting from the clouds. Too much perfume can be overpowering, surpassing its purpose to lightly enhance the atmosphere. Spilled perfume leaves an aroma that lingers, hangs around a long time. It permeates the air in a way that is not easy to dispel.

Imagine a situation that appears to flow along easily when, after a mounting of pressure, something disturbs the atmosphere. Sitting beside a woman on a bus who is wearing a powerful perfume might stir up uncomfortable feelings. Smell is related to memory and motivation: a pleasant fragrance may allure, recall fond memories, or have one turn in repulsion. Perhaps the woman accidentally drops her perfume bottle, releasing an overwhelming stench and causing friction to mount such that something has to give. One may have to suddenly get off the bus.

Apply this degree-pair with a mind to sudden awakenings; being suddenly plunged into disrupting situations; having a natural flow shocked in midstream like rain on a parade. Think of experiences that let the stink out; something old that breaks onto the scene; past events that continue to pervade the air long past their due; ideas that excite and motivate new awareness. Look for release and discharge in a wide array of situations: lancing a boil; drilling an impacted tooth; dramatic changes in the emotional weather; motivating factors for a new start. Consider the color amber; splinter factions, split-off urges or breakout awareness; tensions that sharpen the senses; sudden memories that can no longer be contained; smoking issues that bring about flashes of illumination.

**"Steps up to a lawn blooming with clover" (3 Taurus)
and "A house-raising" (3 Scorpio)**

Aspect: Trine.
Quality: Maintaining.
Shared motifs: 'The gradual uplifting path,' 'fragrances that divide; atmospheres that unite.'

"Steps up to a lawn blooming with clover" is an image of a gradual approach to the atmosphere of a situation. "Steps" are a gradual progression of movement, usually of a short distance. "Step down" is a gradual decrease, as in converting the current of voltage to a lower voltage, as opposed to stepping the current up. A "lawn blooming with clover" is a good pasture in luxuriant or prosperous condition. "Clover" is a flowering ground cover with a sweet smell and associated with luck: a four-leafed clover. "Clove" is an aromatic spice that, like cloves of garlic, can really punch up a meal. "To cleave" something is to split in two or penetrate like a pungent smell: reeking of garlic, or aromatically and pleasantly spiced. "Blooming" is blossoming, suggesting a thriving, flourishing unfolding of life. As a slang term, one might refer to a blooming fool or intensify a matter as in "Ask me no blooming questions; I'll tell you no blooming lies."

"A house-raising" is an image of building community. When building a house, one first lays a foundation and gathers the materials, and then as the final step, with the help of neighbors, one raises the house. Raising a house is a shared task that can still be experienced, for example, in Mennonite communities of North America. The communal aspect of a house-raising extends beyond the actual building of a house. Workers are fed with communally prepared, generous, and hearty meals. There is a shared celebration after the house is completed. There is a natural order, both in the building of the house and in the social process: step by step.

Imagine riding on a bus when a perfume bottle breaks, filling the air with an overpowering fragrance. One may want to flee, but there is no escaping the pervading smell. All one can do is rise above the repugnant situation and work to gradually improve matters: open windows, clean up the spill. Perhaps the communal meal after raising a barn is split in terms of those who love garlic and those who love honey and cloves. Accommodating everyone requires a series of patient steps. The general atmosphere might be soothed if everyone has something they like: stepping down the potentially disruptive voltage, so to speak. Working together to build community has an uplifting effect on everyone, perhaps calling for a celebratory drink or dessert stepped up with a little spice.

Apply this degree-pair with a mind to the efforts to maintain a gradual, uplifting harmony; to steady a situation through accommodation; rising up to, gradually realizing what has been seen. Watch for strong community ties; a patient flair for lifting a lawn into a garden of blooms; extending help to keep the peace. Look for a quiet, innate sense of natural order, natural hierarchy, in one's expression and work. Consider elevating relationship; bringing something to a higher level; a tolerance for working with others; a natural willingness to help despite lingering issues; a sense of natural development as opposed to engineering social realities; working like a busy bee.

"The rainbow's pot of gold" (4 Taurus) and "A youth holding a lighted candle" (4 Scorpio)

Aspect: Square.
Quality: Challenging.
Shared motif: 'Seeking.'

"The rainbow's pot of gold" is an image of dreams cast ahead toward the golden allure of a rewarding, rich destination. Chasing after a "pot of gold" is, in literal terms, futile, since the projected spot where a rainbow touches the earth is an illusion. One could go to pot waiting for the dream to come true. A "pot" is a vessel, round and deep, used for cooking. "Gold" is a precious yellow metal symbolic of value, wealth, and riches. One can have a pot of golden honey or win the pot in a rich poker game. Rainbows are unique in that they appear to arc to a place that should ordinarily be reachable. In human terms, this symbolizes the dreams of reward that enrich the spirit.

"A youth holding a lighted candle" is an image of an object of illumination held in the hand of vigor. "Youth" refers to early age or an attitude fresh and filled with vigor. A "candle" is a cylinder, often made of beeswax, which gives light when burning. "Holding a candle" echoes familiar sayings: "A bird in the hand is worth two in the bush," suggesting that possession is better than expectation, and "Can't hold a candle to . . . ," suggesting an unfavorable comparison. The latter expression derives from boys who held torches in the streets or candles in the theater during evening entertainment. "Candle" derives from the Latin *candere*, to glow or gleam as in incandescence, and is related to "incense," to set fire to, and in particular, sandalwood incense, a golden-colored, fragrant wood incense often used in ceremony.

Imagine, after finding a four-leafed clover, that one feels the luck of the Irish and therefore sets out to find the rainbow's pot of gold. Along the way, a nip or two of poteen, an illegally distilled pot whiskey, invigorates the spirits. A "gilded youth" might spend his gold on mere pleasures or foolishly attempt to "gild the lily," which really means to put a layer of gold over already refined gold, but has come to mean to touch up an already perfect thing with paint, or throw perfume on a flower. The expression "Tace is Latin for candle" means silence, *tace* is discretion: don't throw any light on a matter best left covered.

Apply this degree-pair with a mind to the challenge of the enthusiastic pursuit of reward; balancing dreams that enrich the spirit with appreciating what one already possesses. Think of illuminating spirit in a communal ceremony; carrying on spiritual heritage; institutionalized ceremony that can't hold a candle to one's own dreams; the wisdom to not reveal where one's gold lies. Be alert for fragrances of honey, beeswax, sandalwood, devil's candlestick, or devil's stinkpot; the tendency to paint over originals; spending money on pleasures. Consider keeping dreams to oneself; a love of candles; being incensed about poverty; awareness of the gold within; burning hopes; awakening a spiritual flame; an inner sense of destination.

"A widow at an open grave" (5 Taurus)
and "A massive rocky shore" (5 Scorpio)

Aspect: Quintile.
Quality: Creative genius.
Shared motifs: 'Impermanence and inflexibility,'
'separation realities.'

"A widow at an open grave" is an image of facing the open possibilities of separation realities. A "widow," a term ultimately derived from many linguistic roots meaning to separate, is a woman who has lost her husband. A "grave" is a place of burial that receives and holds the dead. Also meaning a weighty matter of great concern, "grave" has a nautical sense of scraping and separating barnacles from the bottom of a seagoing vessel. The sea is known as the "widowmaker" to the wives of sailors. In logging, a tree that splits vertically while being cut is also called a widowmaker due to the danger involved in bringing it down. An "open grave" is one not yet filled in, a situation of assessing mortality, or deciding what is to be buried.

"A massive rocky shore" is an image of a monumental point defining the juncture of separation between sea and land. A "shore" is derived from "share," originally a plowshare, the blade of a plow that separates the earth, and "shear," to cut. Ancients might shear sheep with a sharp shard to cut the wool away. The sailing sense of "to sheer" is to deviate off course. A "massive rocky shore" will, in a tick of geological time, become scored and worn into gravel (French *gravel*, *greve*: a sandy shore). Taoist wisdom notes that water is stronger than stone. Mountains and rocky shores are, throughout time, engraved by water, eventually, inevitably, to be worn down to dust.

Imagine the surf pounding a massive rocky shore while sailors' wives watch for their husbands and sons. The sheer force of the sea is awe inspiring as the waves repeatedly crash against the rocks, evoking penetrating thoughts as if one were standing over an open grave. At such times, one might wonder about less significant matters that have dominated one's life; for example, emotional disturbances that continue to linger like long-held grudges, pursuits of superficial pleasures and wealth, shattered relationships that stick like splinters in one's hand: one might ask what issues are worth taking to the grave. Human life comes to an end just as the sea ends at the shore. An intensified awareness of this human condition can cut through much of unimportance, opening possibilities for creative, authentic being.

Apply this degree-pair with a mind to the creative awareness that penetrates grave matters of life; awareness of forces that separate worth from the superficial, wheat from the chaff. Think of opening awareness; dignity, and insight; monumental reminders; burying the hatchet; sober realizations. Listen for gravelly voices, low tones, a mouth full of marbles, quiet speech. Be alert to attitudes: hard or soft, hard yet soft, dignified and grand, inflexible or adaptable. Consider letting matters free as opposed to letting them lie; champagne refinements to heavy issues; releasing pressure like popping a cork; serious faces; realizing how the ultimate separation unites all; a good wake.

"A bridge being built across a gorge" (6 Taurus) and "A gold rush" (6 Scorpio)

Aspect: Conjunction.
Quality: Focus.
Shared motifs: 'Taking life by the throat,' the 'Gordian knot.'

"A bridge being built across a gorge" is an image of a constructive approach to get to the other side. The bridge "being built," attempting to span an open distance, is still in a potential stage, not yet complete. Building a bridge is not an easy matter: reaching completion is a feat of engineering that calls for preparation and planning, and for everything to be in the right place. A "gorge" is a narrow opening between hills or a rocky ravine through which often flows rushing water. The word "gorge" relates to the throat, swallowing, gorging. Necktie fashion, the neckerchief or ruff, is ultimately tied to the word "gorgeous": luxurious, fashionable neck adornments of resplendent color. The kerchief is usually tied in a knot at the throat, suggesting a knotty issue regarding crossing the gorge or throat.

"A gold rush" is an image of quickening excitement that pushes ahead for potential rewards and riches. "A gold rush" recalls historical moments like the California and Klondike gold rushes. The luster and allure of gold and riches literally put development on fast-forward. One had to be quick to stake one's claim. "Rush" implies being in a hurry, but also a heightened sense of excitement and surging emotion as in the German term *rausch,* intoxicating excitement. The rush plant grows near water and provides reeds for thatching furniture or reeds for wind instruments. A rush of air over a thin, vibrating reed gives voice to gorgeous sound.

A Chinese proverb about a little fox crossing over ice calls attention to warily taking cautious steps lest, in its haste, the young fox gets its tail wet. If what is on the other side is too alluring, one might attempt to cross over in a single stroke or, like Alexander the Great, cut the Gordian knot with one decisive stroke of his sword. One may have a passion for gold, wear gold necklaces, or have a passion for rich food to gorge upon. Then again, necktie fashions and rich, sumptuous foods may be hard to swallow. Bridge building is an enormous human accomplishment. It is like solving an intricate problem, cutting the Gordian knot with a radical solution, eliminating the conditions that caused the problem.

Apply this degree-pair with a mind to the focus of finding ways to the other side; bridging difficulties; attempting to tie caution and excitement together in constructive ways. Listen for clearing one's throat; a knot in the throat; finding one's voice; a tight voice that does not yet project; a gravelly voice; throat problems; deep, resonant voices; golden voices; singing that brings a rush of emotional excitement. Think of instant relief; an attitude regarding water under the bridge; the Bridge of Gold: a spirit of blessing for plentiful crops; a Bridge of Sighs over which prisoners walk to Tomb's prison. Consider cutting through problems; rushed impatience; going single file; cheating the devil; crossing a bridge when one comes to it.

"A woman of Samaria" (7 Taurus) and "Deep-sea divers" (7 Scorpio)

Aspect: Opposition.
Quality: Awareness of.
Shared motifs: 'Truthing,' 'getting into deep water.'

"A woman of Samaria" is an image of a moment of truth. When Jesus meets the woman at the well, he reveals himself to her as the Messiah: a well from which one drink refreshes ever after as opposed to a well to which one must return daily to be refreshed. Then, when the woman says she has no husband, Jesus tells her she in fact has five and the man she is with now is not even her husband. We can assume, at this point in the story, that he has the attention of the woman of Samaria. The "well" is a powerful symbol of the source of life: that around which all human civilization is organized. "The city can be moved but the well cannot be moved" (I Ching, hexagram 48).

"Deep-sea divers" is an image of plunging in deep over one's head. "Deep-sea diving" is a compromising situation requiring a special breathing apparatus in order to survive in deep water. Since humans are not natural inhabitants of the sea, they need a heavy-metal, pressurized globe with a safety rope, an air tube, and heavy boots. One must be prepared to go deep, trusting and relying on equipment and one's crew. It's serious business bearing the weight and pressure of deep water. Hence, under certain conditions, the right equipment, safety, and air lines, one will take the plunge.

This degree-pair turns on the difference between unconditional and conditional honesty. The truth can lead to deep water just as half-truths can get you in deep. One may need a spiritual lifeline in order to survive, or one may be too hard-headed to see, hear, or speak the truth of the matter. A "gold digger" is one who has a mercenary attitude toward personal profit and the easy road to fortune, which involves personal compromise. "Displacement" can mean finding oneself where one does not belong: a diver displaces water; a Samarian woman is socially displaced by virtue of being a Samarian rather than a Hebrew, and by her role as a kind of moral outcast. A deep-sea diver has left society in every sense except for a single lifeline vouched safe by his trusted crew. Exploring unnatural, unfamiliar territory brings up issues of trust and reliability.

Apply this degree-pair with a mind to an awareness of moments that test compromising situations; exploring the deeper motives for actions; assessing what is truly reliable; having to consider matters more deeply before proceeding. Think of situations that expose the flaws within a "whatever it takes to get by" attitude to life; revelations about doing it right; if one is surrounded with gold diggers, who does one trust? Watch for tests determining the genuine article; assaying gold; knowing how to determine fool's gold from real gold; authenticity. Consider a knack for maintaining fine equipment; feeling like a duck out of water; exchanging social acceptability for personal integrity; feeling displaced from mainstream society; looking before walking.

"A sleigh without snow" (8 Taurus) and "The moon shining across a lake" (8 Scorpio)

Aspect: Trine.
Quality: Maintaining.
Shared motifs: 'Reflecting on how to slide easily,' 'the guile to buy time.'

"A sleigh without snow" is an image of a vehicle out of season, unable to slide. A "sleigh" is a vehicle designed to slide while being pulled over snow or ice. Deriving from words that mean to slide and slippery, "sleighing" and "sledding" depend on seasonal conditions to operate smoothly. The sleigh's runners are nonfunctional "without snow" on the ground. Perhaps the sight of a sleigh evokes memories of times past, or thought for when the snows will come. In its own element, a sleigh moves very smoothly over the snowy roads and fields. "Without snow," there is too much friction to make headway. It might even be a snowy winter, but the sleigh is in a museum or set up as a curio display for the season. In any case, something about it is displaced.

"The moon shining across a lake" is an image of guile regarding forgotten or wasted treasure. When the moon shines across a lake, it creates an appearance, a reflection of a reflection, that seems to beckon like an insubstantial bridge across the water. Legend has it that all things lost are treasured in the moon: wasted time, money and pursuits, broken promises, unfulfilled longings and desires, fruitless tears. A "moonraker" is a name for a wily simpleton originating with Wiltshire folk who, when caught raking a pond for smuggled brandy, told the customs officer they were trying to rake out the moon: a slippery story to excuse a slippery task, or to slide around a sticky situation.

If one is fooled by a mere reflection, then a deeper issue may be overlooked. There is a children's tale about a little goose who tricks a fox into diving after a "moon-cheese," which is, of course, a mere reflection of moonlight on a lake. The fox falls for the tempting round of cheese, only to let the little goose slip away. Like the sleigh without snow, the "moon-cheese" is out of place. One may have difficulty distinguishing what is real from what is potential, especially emotionally potential. Visualize sitting in a sleigh, waiting until snow comes. Think of reflecting on emotionally charged memories. Sometimes to be out of touch, out of season, with the times is a good thing; sometimes it is a mere defensive strategy to keep things the same.

Apply this degree-pair with a mind to the clever guile to slip around an issue; to retrieve a lost matter; to maintain a sense of stability until the season favorably turns. Think of wasted resources: money, effort, emotions; treasured reminiscences; reflecting on the past; longing that bridges to the other side. Consider slippery stories; slippery slopes that can get one into deep water; mere reflections of the truth; being ahead of one's time; ahead of the law; clever delays and diversions; quick wits; finding forgotten treasure; smoothing over frictions; a moonshine state of mind.

"A Christmas tree decorated" (9 Taurus)
and "Dental work" (9 Scorpio)

Aspect: Square.
Quality: Challenge.
Shared motif: 'Challenging discomforts about giving and
receiving one's power and riches.'

"A Christmas tree decorated" is an image of a brightly decorated symbol of gifts. "Christmas" refers to a time when there is usually snow on the ground. Strangely enough, the tree has been brought in from its natural setting to serve another symbolic purpose. Outdoors the tree would be naturally bathed in snow. Indoors it is bathed in lights and decorative ornaments. Once again there is a displacement. One may be upset about the cutting of trees for a brief holiday celebration, or one may appreciate the symbolic richness of sacrificing the tree for a sacred event.

"Dental work" is an image of the maintenance and care of teeth. Dental work is performed by "dentists," who were originally called "tooth drawers," a name that echoes an expression meaning to take away the power to do mischief, or to render one's bite harmless like that of a toothless lion. Unhealthy teeth impair the ability to chew the foodstuffs one needs in order to stay alive. Historically, the condition of the teeth was the leading factor in choosing a suitable marriage partner. Poor dental health almost always goes hand in hand with bad breath, consequently, working on the health and appearance of the pearly whites takes on major importance. Without good teeth, one can hardly take a good bite out of life.

One cuts teeth to gain experience; cuts wisdom teeth to gain discretion; cuts eye-teeth in order to gain worldly knowing, to see with sophisticated wakefulness. A child's first set of teeth are cut at an age when Christmas holds much magic and wonder; the second set when the child has grown old enough to see and understand more of the matter. The Christmas tree decorated indoors highlights a time associated with giving, and also a time of ingesting rich, festive foods and drink. Often there is an emotional intensity at family gatherings: one wrong word can have everyone baring their teeth. The need for dental work arises when what one has put into the mouth, sweets for example, leads to decay. The "toothache tree" is the name from American pioneers for the prickly ash that possessed fruit with properties for treating toothaches. At Christmas, as at the dentist's office and everywhere else, one must be careful regarding what goes in and out of one's mouth.

Apply this degree-pair with a mind to the prudent regulation of what goes in and out of the mouth; coming into age, into season; attempting to take a bite out of life. Watch for dental problems or a penchant for doing dental work. Perhaps celebrations like Christmas are hard to chew. Perhaps one cannot take even a bite, or finds conversation a toothless affair. Attempting to be comfortable in shared celebrations may be like pulling teeth. Consider stories that have no teeth; a toothy smile in an attempt to fit in; managing decoration and decay; balancing power and peace; stirring up strife when intending to end all strife: sowing dragon's teeth.

"A Red Cross nurse" (10 Taurus) and "A fellowship supper" (10 Scorpio)

Aspect: Quintile.
Quality: Creative genius.
Shared motifs: 'A feast born of compassion,'
'cutting through differences.'

"A Red Cross nurse" is an image of the compassionate self-sacrifice of someone willing to go to the front lines to help the wounded. The symbol of the "Red Cross" is universally recognized. In the midst of the harshest, most dangerous conflict zones, it signals safety and care without discrimination, to help out in whatever way possible. A red cross on a pure white background (in Muslim countries, a red crescent on a white background) signifies the fusion of courage, compassion, and humanitarian integrity. Often this is realized through providing blood for those who have had their own blood spilled in battle. The red cross is also the emblem for Saint George, patron saint of England who, legend has it, slew the dragon in order to rescue a maiden.

"A fellowship supper" is an image of a gathering born out of shared experience accumulated through time, which cuts through whatever differences separated individuals in the past. "Fellowship" derives from the Old English *feolaga,* meaning those who put their money together in a business partnership, or those who come together through a shared sense of worth or commom purpose. At its highest, "fellowship" transcends individual interests in favor of humanitarian goals. Whenever factions arise through secret agreements or motives, fellowship becomes divided in mistrust and quarrel. When people are united in true fellowship through their hearts, nothing can break their bonds.

Imagine veterans from opposing factions sitting down to dine together. It is a form of hospitality, as is a field hospital. Perhaps those who gather would not be there save for the efforts of the "Red Cross nurse." A host of possibilities arises: exchanging welcome for hostility; hosting even the hostile; even in the midst of hostilities, hospitable people and places can and will emerge. Often the rich rewards of true fellowship are won only after long and painful struggles of separation. Afterward, tears and laughter are shared in joy, good drink, and good food.

Apply this degree-pair with a mind to the humanitarian thrust that courageously cuts across battle lines; natural empathy for passionate causes that unite for a higher purpose. Think of gatherings that collectively reflect on a shared past; the genius to see beyond that which feeds petty hostility. Consider an ambling walk; peace won through breaking bread together; a knack for going anywhere; crossing borders easily; a blood-is-thicker-than-water outlook; putting teeth into compassionate work; an affinity with those who have suffered through the same struggles; patching up differences; a genuine heartfelt smile; sharing from the heart.

"A woman sprinkling flowers" (11 Taurus) and "A drowning man rescued" (11 Scorpio)

Aspect: Conjunction.
Quality: Initiating.
Shared motifs: 'Emotions that cultivate; emotions that overwhelm,' 'save or rescue.'

"A woman sprinkling flowers" is an image of a sparse watering of flowers in care and cultivation. "Sprinkling" is a sparse scattering of drops or small particles of water. Without adequate water, the flowers will not bloom. Too much water is as bad as not enough. Like a recipe, it is a matter of water in the right measure. Because the woman brings the water to the flowers, the resplendent possibilities of nature are, to a large extent, in her hands.

"A drowning man rescued" is an image of being at the mercy of the vast, overwhelming forces of nature and having to be brought back. "Rescue" derives from the Latin *excutere,* to shake out, to shake back, in the sense of taking something back from captivity, hence "to save," "to free," "to deliver from." "Drowning" derives from "drink," a name for the sea or the action of drinking a liquid. A "drowning man" suggests helplessness, requiring help from an outside source. He may be in a large body of water or drenched in drink: in either case, the situation has gotten out of hand. In desperate situations a man will cling to any shred of hope, such as a floating log, a passing boat, a dolphin: drowning men clutch at straws. Sometimes the overwhelming powers of life, like a great wave from the sea, lift a man and carry him to safety.

Imagine a fellowship supper where old comrades gather to drink and reminisce. Perhaps someone becomes overwhelmed with emotions, salt tears flooding from his eyes, such that he must be consoled by others. Perhaps others are drunk and need to be nursed back to sobriety, or helped home since they can no longer stand on their own. When a woman sprinkles flowers, she is venturing out to care for something in need of cultivation. "Sprinkling" water from a watering can seems to be a sparse achievement compared to being overwhelmed at sea. Imagine scattering tiny drops of water on a drought-parched field of flowers: scarcely enough. In an extreme sense, one could persecute another by withholding adequate water. Think of the roles played in the triangulation pattern of victim, persecutor, rescuer.

Apply this degree-pair with a mind to the following issues: sometimes a little bit of water makes all the difference; sometimes only a ship-swallowing wave will do. Sometimes it takes being plunged into a sea of emotion before one takes life seriously; sometimes a little bit of attentive kindness is all it takes to make the garden bloom. Watch for assumptions about who is thirsty and who doesn't need a drink. Consider making a career out of being lost at sea; feeling insignificant like a drop in the ocean; patiently nurturing something or someone back to life; being swallowed up by a force beyond your control; being in over your head; drinking to excess; grasping for anything; panic; being stingy; playing a role in an emotional drama; being on hand to help.

"Window-shoppers" (12 Taurus)
and "An embassy ball" (12 Scorpio)

Aspect: Opposition.
Quality: Awareness of.
Shared motifs: 'A glass ceiling,' 'display and invisible barriers.'

"Window-shoppers" is an image of taking time to consider what might be. "Window-shopping" is a pastime of looking at wares displayed in shop windows without actually purchasing anything. The "windows" of shops are "dressed," made to look attractive and appealing for customers, usually in ways that highlight items in a favorable light. A glass "window" separates the display from the shoppers, requiring them to enter the shop to buy an item before they can get their hands on it. Perhaps one is looking at gowns that might be worn to an embassy ball; looking at possibilities for social adornment, symbols of position and achievement. Whatever it is that is being displayed, it is, for the time being, out of reach.

"An embassy ball" is an image of a select gathering of the social and political elite. An "embassy" is the house and grounds of a foreign government. Territorially, it is sovereign land belonging to a foreign country, subject to that country's laws and overseen by a representative of the foreign country of the highest rank: the ambassador. A "ball" is a formal assembly for social dancing. We think right away about what everyone is wearing and sense the importance of display. Important contacts are doubtless being made, but it is the gathering of the pinnacle of social, cultural, and multinational elite and how they show themselves to the world through showing themselves to each other that counts. Therefore, the "embassy ball" is a window on the world as represented by the elite, the leaders, the privileged.

Window-shoppers may be conditioned for the lowest and most frivolous forms of social adornment and demeanor; or, perhaps worse, perhaps better, conditioned to be on the outside of the window, never to actually buy into what is being sold. The "embassy ball" is an exclusive gathering of the elite, gathered mostly for their mutual benefit. When positive, integrity and excellence shine. When not so positive, elitism, disdain, and specious superiority show forth. The window may be a glass ceiling separating degrees of social status.

Apply this degree-pair with a mind to the awareness of the invisible barriers that separate life possibilities from one's grasp; the mystery of being held to one's social circle; the appeal of higher forms of social and cultural expression. Think of glass barriers; glass ceilings; transparent manipulation; flattering displays. Consider having a ball regardless of social barriers; making the social rounds; feeling obligated by one's position; feeling free and on the street; feeling inspired by displays of elegance and dignity; being happy with the simple life; wondering about a foreign world.

"A man handling baggage" (13 Taurus) and "An inventor experimenting" (13 Scorpio)

Aspect: Trine.
Quality: Maintaining.
Shared motifs: 'Getting a handle on one's load,' 'tinkering,' 'carrying and collecting.'

"A man handling baggage" is an image of getting one's hands on what must be carried. "Handling" derives from "hand," implying getting one's hands on something to control, manipulate, or manage it according to one's own power. "Baggage" is chiefly a name for the luggage of a traveler, packages and trunks that hold items of possession. A porter may carry someone else's baggage as a service; a traveler may carry his own. "Baggage" also has a sense of weight or responsibility, as in "left holding the bag," carrying responsibilities, loads, or blame for the faults of others. In a derogatory sense, "baggage" refers to an immoral or flirtatious woman, deriving from foreign military service where soldiers' wives traveled with regimental stores and baggage.

"An inventor experimenting" is an image of tinkering with possible better ways. "Invention" is an ingenious creation or devising something new, something discovered or innovative. "Experimenting" means to try out. Experiments try and test new inventions for their usefulness or effectiveness. One might tinker with an array of apparatus, attempting to make something invented work, working with whatever one can get one's hands on. Imagine an eccentric inventor in a garage cluttered with all manner of saved gadgets, parts of discarded items, and supplies, many of which are pieced together in some new, inventive way. Tinkering with "stuff" depends largely on what is at hand to work with: an improved mousetrap; a better flush apparatus for the toilet. Sometimes inventions aren't worth a "tinker's dam": the disposable plug used to stop up a hole in a pot while the tinker repairs it.

Imagine window-shoppers who, having been lured into a shop to buy many things, now have to handle it all, carry the load purchased. Every purchase made, everything bought into, is baggage that comes with the weight of responsibility. The use and care of bought items lies in one's own hands. Even the disposal of unwanted items, the packaging and bags in which new things are wrapped, is a responsibility. Perhaps the weight of fancy garb lies in the cast-off pile of refuse: garbage. An inventive re-sourcefulness in this case would be exemplified by an inventor going through other people's garbage to recycle, reuse, and recreate something new and of use.

Apply this degree-pair with a mind to the baggage that comes with getting your hands on things; handling what one has in new ways; being sold on a new version of responsibility. Watch for an ingenuity for working with "stuff"; finding treasures in other people's garbage; recycling sensibilities; never throwing anything away; big box mentality: everything is to be had, then thrown away in order to buy more. Consider carrying emotional baggage; being stuck with leftovers and hand-me-downs; making due with little or nothing; approaching life as a happy load; buying into a life that is just a load; wearing the same thing over and over again, or never wearing the same thing twice.

"Shellfish groping and children playing" (14 Taurus) and "Telephone linemen at work" (14 Scorpio)

Aspect: Square.
Quality: Challenge.
Shared motifs: 'Making creative connections; new lines of discovery; attachment; detachment.'

"Shellfish groping and children playing" is an image of playfully attempting to get one's hands on something that might pinch back. "Groping" derives from "grip," meaning to feel about with the hands as when feeling in the dark for a light switch. "Groping around" is to search bewilderedly with an element of excitement and un-certainty about what one might get one's hands on, or what might get its hands on

you. As low tide exposes an extended shore, shellfish may be scurrying around, groping for sanctuary. More likely, however, people are out digging for shrimp and children are laughing, reaching into tidal pools and groping for small crabs. All this is
possible because the shoreline has been stretched by the rhythms of tidal interplay.

"Telephone linemen at work" is an image of men at work stretching lines of communication from pole to pole. The "telephone" is a modern invention for communication that relies on low-voltage transmissions carried through wires. A "lineman" is
one who works connecting the telephone lines, who repairs faulty or fallen lines. As
each pole is connected, the possibilities for communication are extended. If the lines
are down, linemen work to repair, to reconnect and reestablish the links. The linemen
work to set up the physical possibility for long-distance communication. It is an action providing service, of setting it up for others, for everyone.

Shellfish blindly attach to the first rock they find. Detaching shellfish from rocks
can be difficult: sometimes what is detached fastens firmly on one's hand like a crab's
pinching claw. A "tache" is a fastening, like those that close a belt, for example. Attached firmly, securely, telephone lines open lines of communication. As the tides
come and go, the possibilities for exploring, playing, gathering, groping through a
marine world, open up. When the tides go out, the opportunity arises for getting
your hands on some shellfish hiding under sand and stone in the newly exposed
shoreline. When telephone linemen complete their work, the lines of communication,
over long distances, are open.

Apply this degree-pair with a mind to the challenge of reaching into new territory; stretching out into new frontiers; feeling one's way in the dark. Think of safety
and exploration; excitement about the unknown; blindly finding one's place; blindly
making a connection. Be alert for attitudes of detachment; attitudes of attachment;
probing intelligence; being motivated by the unknown, the uncertain, and hidden
matters. Consider feeling pinched; squealing with delight about discovery, about
hearing the news; pushing the envelope; connecting things that are poles apart; alluring frontiers, foreign territories; being caught by the current tides of communication,
the latest take on information, knowledge; losing one's grip in the dark; misplacing
items; having a good touch for repairing the lines of communication.

"A man muffled up, with a rakish silk hat" (15 Taurus) and "Children playing around five mounds of sand" (15 Scorpio)

Aspect: Quintile.
Quality: Creative genius.
Shared motif: 'Inclinations against prevailing winds
and toward strange influences.'

"A man muffled up, with a rakish silk hat" is an image of a man whose inclinations and manner of speech are revealed through how he is dressed. To be "muffled" is to be wrapped up for warmth or concealment, perhaps in woolen mittens or a scarf made from the wool of the hairy wild sheep of Sardinia: mouflon. "Muffling" something is to deaden the sound, like speaking with wool in one's mouth. "Rakish" describes a jaunty, dashing appearance, often thought to be inclined toward a dissolute, wild character. A "rake" is a toothed implement used to scrape together mounds of matter such as leaves, soil, and sand. Using a rake causes one to lean. A "silk hat" is a tall, cylindrical hat covered with silk plush. Silk is a fine natural fiber used for luxurious clothes. "Silk," Latin *sericus*, literally means "pertaining to the *seres*," the Chinese. Hence a man might be muffled up, holding on to his hat while inclined toward an oriental wind.

"Children playing around five mounds of sand" is an image of creating entire worlds out of imagination and all of the senses. "Five mounds of sand" symbolizes the five sense capacities, but also the organizational principle of a mandala: four directions emanating from a central point. "Mounds of sand" are fashioned by raking together heaps of sand with a rake or the five fingers of the hand. One can also take a silk hat-shaped bucket, fill it with sand, and turn it upside down to make sand castles. Children creating a world playfully might arrange their mounds wildly, perhaps inclining this way or that, without constraint of any kind.

A play is "muffled" in baseball, for example, when a player muffs, mishandles the ball. This may turn out to be a happy mishap, however, since the runners may be caught while attempting to advance on the muff. Silk hats are a fashion statement of the upper class, high polish for highbrow events like an embassy ball. When someone not of that social rank wears a silk hat, suspicions may arise concerning the moral makeup or character: hence rakish. When one is trying to elevate one's position through apparel, it might be like braving a social storm of perceptions. When one is inclined to orient oneself toward strange, foreign influences, there is a chance of having to endure a stormy reception. Prevailing social orders may fear the incoming tide from a foreign land, which could wash their world away like sandcastles by the sea.

Apply this degree-pair with a mind for creatively making one's way in the world; creating one's world out of a foreign inclination; a creative touch that endures and renews despite the tides of change. Watch for suffering ill regard until the tides change; being temporarily muffled until one reaches the top of the mound; a stylish flare introducing a new fashion. Consider muffled voices, mumbled words; inclined postures; dropping the ball and getting away with it; a playful knack for apparel and appearance; openness to new ideas, new worlds; creating happy sensations; detachment from disintegrating worlds, from social perception, from transient social position.

"An old man attempting vainly to reveal the Mysteries" (16 Taurus) and "A girl's face breaking into a smile" (16 Scorpio)

Aspect: Conjunction.

Quality: Initiating.

Shared motifs: 'Having something to say, but not knowing how to say it'; 'chop water; carry wood . . . no, that's chop wood; carry water'; 'the seriousness of levity; the levity of seriousness.'

"An old man attempting vainly to reveal the Mysteries" is an image of an empty attempt at revealing that which cannot be fully known. "An old man" is a man of experience. "Attempting vainly" suggests a try at something that comes up empty, of no real worth, or attempting something with a manner of pompous self-conceit. "To reveal" is to disclose, uncover. "Mysteries" are secrets that cannot be known, are hidden, or that defy explication and human comprehension: that can only be known through divine revelation. Every attempt to reveal profound truths calls for a touch of humor since, as soon as you open your mouth, you've got it wrong.

"A girl's face breaking into a smile" is an image of a sudden shattering of a rigid expression. A "smile" is a facial expression that, depending upon the circumstance, can convey many things: amusement; cheerfulness; blessing; approval; smug conceit; sudden joy. "To break" is to separate something into parts or fragments, change the quality of something, suddenly freeing rigidity. "Breaking into a smile" suggests a change that lightens the mood, releases tension, like breaking a spell of seriousness.

Imagine a classroom where an old man is attempting to reveal, for example, the Mysteries of the Rosary: fifteen meditations divided into three groups of five, the Five Joyful Mysteries, the Five Sorrowful Mysteries, and the Five Glorious Mysteries. Try as he might, the students can only smile at the big words and weighty concepts of the old man. Consider when, in attempting to answer a child's question, words simply fail or even become a laughing matter. Mysteries are often to be revealed only to the initiated, those ready to hear. To the uninitiated, such revelations may bring a "sardonic smile," a smile that originates with the ingesting of the "sardone," *herba Sardinia*, a poisonous plant so bitter as to cause the face to convulse into a smile leading to death by laughter, hence humor of scornful derision. Think of the overly serious disciples of the Buddha asking overly serious questions only to receive silence or a smile in response. Think of a Zen master laughing while, with a bamboo stick, he smacks a student who has tried to answer a koan. Genuine communication is indeed a mystery. Sometimes a smile says more than a thousand words; sometimes Mysteries are delightful: how they are revealed is everything.

Apply this degree-pair with a mind to a focus on having something to say, but not knowing how to say it. Look for expressive faces that say everything; a giaconda smile: an anagram for "Is a cold enigma." Listen for the difference between heavy philosophies and lighthearted gestures that say a lot. Consider a good smile; stiff faces; an exaggerated sense of self-importance; mixing up important words; revelations through humor; breakthrough laughter.

"A battle between the swords and the torches" (17 Taurus) and "A woman the father of her own child" (17 Scorpio)

Aspect: Opposition.
Quality: Awareness of.
Shared motifs: 'Decisive independence or twisted matters,'
'birthing passionate campaigns.'

"A battle between the swords and the torches" is an image of struggle between that which cuts apart and that which twines together. "Battle" derives from the Latin *battuerre,* to beat, and the Old French *bataille,* a conflict or struggle. "Swords" are symbolic of the intellect, which cuts through with discriminating precision. "Torches" originally were twisted, flaming pine knots used for illumination or to passionately put to the torch something of the enemy's. A conflict between swords and torches symbolizes strife between powers of the mind and powers of spirit and passion. "Swords" cut; "torches" twist and twine together: decisiveness as opposed to twisting with torment.

"A woman the father of her own child" is an image of a spirited sense of self-fertilization and independence. "Fathering" means to beget, originate, or create. A single mother may function like both a mother and father to her child. More likely, however, this symbol speaks to bringing together masculine and feminine energies creatively for self-realization. Every human being must balance masculine and feminine energies within themselves. It is an inner process of individuation that gives birth to the child of creativity. The issue is one of spiritual fertility: an independent and immaculate conception. Those filled with their own spirit may well be suffering from immaculate self-perception.

Imagine battles sketched out over the pages of a Gothic romance novel or larger-than-life heroes and heroines of B movies. One may have romantic visions of the way things used to be or the way things ought to be. Damocles was made to sit under a sword suspended by a hair to teach him how precarious happiness is: a tortuous, tormenting position from which he was not to stir, literally not to twist. Imagine an individual glowing with heroic self-sufficiency: the aura of the spiritually uplifted fighting a noble cause. It might be a woman who, as a child, became disenchanted with the traditional ways of revealing Mysteries, and now seeks her own independent ways of revelation. Historically, great campaigns have been launched to champion a spiritual cause. There may be something romantically compelling about such struggles, or one may go one's independent way, waging an internal war for self-ignited pursuits.

Apply this degree-pair with a mind to an awareness of matters of spirit over ideas; the battleground of mind and spirit; passionate independence against archaic versions of the Mysteries. Watch for denial, such as teenage mothers who insist they have never had sex. Think of Gothic romances where passions collide with social and political realities; campaigns to supplant cold technology with agrarian simplicity. Consider artificial insemination, fertility issues; sterile ideas and outdated, romantic passions to be championed; a twisting unease about impending danger; tortured by good fortune; choosing between cutting away from or twisting together.

"A woman holding a bag out of a window" (18 Taurus)
and "A woods rich in autumn coloring" (18 Scorpio)

Aspect: Trine.
Quality: Maintaining.
Shared motifs: 'The refreshment of decay,'
'enhancements that just fall your way.'

"A woman holding a bag out of a window" is an image of reaching outside of one-self in order to freshen and receive whatever falls one's way. To "hold a bag out the window" suggests an open window: a barrier for viewing the outside world opened in order to reach out. A "bag" is a container, like a linen bag, which, since it is used to contain soiled linens, might need some freshening from time to time. Perhaps the woman is trying to let something fall inside, autumn leaves for instance. Psychologi-cally, an opened window suggests a mind to clear out the clutter to allow in regener-ative fresh air. Holding something out the window exposes it to the social world.

"A woods rich in autumn coloring" is an image of the splendid display of fall col-ors, a time of year when fully matured plant life begins to decay. The colors are rich, and there is a special air about the season. The season's beauty is in abundance, even while signaling the approaching winter. One can smell the season of decay while walking in autumn woods. The leaves crunch and rustle as the trees release their fo-liage, signaling a time of degeneration, out of which a new green phase of the life cycle will eventually emerge. Autumn leaves also announce an impending time when the trees will be stripped bare, fully exposed. The animals of the woods will have less protective cover, their movement betrayed by rustling fallen leaves.

Airing a linen bag enhances a situation such as a musty condition, but also ex-poses what has been hidden and what might cause a stink. The crowning glory of a woods adorned in autumn leaves actually brightens the world with its foliage. Before trees exfoliate, they enhance everything around by way of striking contrast, hence operating as a foil, that is, someone who, or something that, enhances the qualities of another. "To empty the bag" is a French expression meaning to tell everything: let-ting all the colorful secrets fall.

Apply this degree-pair with a mind to airing things: past secrets; old and moldy items or ideas; opening a window of consciousness to a wider experience; dusting off what has been collected and is just hanging around. Think of connections to paper: thin leaves of linen for paper making; folios, folded leaves of paper; books; printing. Watch for enhancement skills; a knack for showing something or someone up for who or what they really are. Consider a nose for a story; opening the book on some dirty secrets; feeling the need to catch something new; information that just falls your way; spring cleaning; stories thin on details; being left holding the bag; a bag of nerves; a tell-all nature; exposé; the bare facts; an attitude of "Que sera, sera."

"A newly formed continent" (19 Taurus) and "A parrot listening and then talking" (19 Scorpio)

Aspect: Square.
Quality: Challenge.
Shared motifs: 'Catching the drift,' 'the art of paraphrase.'

"A newly formed continent" is an image of a powerful force that creates a new land; a massive development of continuous land. The "continental drift" is the theory of the movements of continents across the earth's surface, separating from one supercontinent called Pangaea. For a new continent to form, it must break away from the whole, the Pangaea. When a story is serially relayed by others, little bits fall away and new versions are formed, sometimes with little resemblance to the original. Piecing together a story may take some time. Gathering bits here and there until the whole thing comes together is perhaps like gathering peoples together to form a new country.

"A parrot listening and then talking" is an image of picking up many little stones of information and passing them along: retelling. A "parrot" is a bird with the ability to imitate human speech and laughter. Deriving from the Latin *petra,* stone, and *peter,* originally a safe underworld rock or stone, "parroting" someone may be a means of honoring someone else's words, covering another's words, mocking or even plagiarizing, kidnapping, someone's words. A colorful bird, the parrot suggests colorful renditions repeated over and over.

The apostle Peter carried on the work and words of Jesus, saying, "Upon this rock I build this church, this faith," a declaration of an underground sort given the tortuous relations between Christians and Romans at the time. A continent may arise out of the ocean, or it may break away from a larger land mass. "Newly formed" suggests original stories of long and continuous presentation. Oral traditions relayed information, communications, stories of all sorts, sung in long, continuous, epic proportions, hence a repetition factor that is passed along. Sometimes parrots repeat embarrassing things that their owners would rather not have repeated. Sometimes the story becomes twisted, mocking the original in unsuitable ways or with derision. "Listening" implies conscious attention to understand what is heard. Attempting to relay what has been heard can sometimes create a whole new world unless one exercises self-restraint, continence, and decorum.

Apply this degree-pair with a mind for stories that reach far, are far-reaching; stretch reality; cover a large territory. Listen for continuous chatter; scraps of information; stories in wide circulation that have a massive influence; gossip; newspapers; groundless rumor; drifting bits of misinformation. Watch for stories built on solid rock; emerging nations; reworking originals; covering a song, a belief, a refashioned tradition. Consider mimicry; learning by rote; underground revivals; an inclination to gossip or be the subject of gossip; the Peter Pan syndrome; repeating words of others for protection; disdain for old ways of saying things; throwing stones.

"Wind, clouds and haste" (20 Taurus) and "A woman drawing two dark curtains aside" (20 Scorpio)

Aspect: Quintile.
Quality: Creative genius.
Shared motifs: 'Phenomenal change,' 'fleeting and uncovered,' 'revealing passageways to mysteries,' 'quickening.'

"Wind, clouds and haste" is an image of accelerated ideas that create a stir, excitement, or massive confusion. "Wind" is fast-moving air, but also a secondary sense of "to wrap around," like coiling twine. "Clouds" are masses of visible vapor that can cover, darken, or obscure. "Cloud" derives from the Middle English *clud*, meaning rock, having the basic idea of mass. "Haste" is swiftness of action, speediness, reckless hurry or urgency. The image suggests clouds quickly flying by, driven on hastily by strong winds, high flying, feathered wisps, or mists blown by morning winds. Traveling at high speeds, in a car for example, may create a wind, leave a cloud of dust or a vapor trail. Imagine a cartoon character like the Roadrunner speeding off with a cloud of dust left behind, or a high-flying jet leaving a vapor trail in the sky, feeling the afterwind of a large, fast-moving truck.

"A woman drawing two dark curtains aside" is an image of opening, revealing that which has been hidden. If the curtains were on windows, opening them would allow a flood of light into the room. If the curtains were over a passageway, opening them would reveal a threshold to a hidden passageway. There can be mysteries involved behind the curtains, esoteric secrets, or open secrets, that is, those that are silently and collectively agreed upon. Opening the curtains reveals or exposes what lies within. This Symbol seems to invite imagination to reach for what lies beyond the curtains.

Being in haste can sometimes lead to trouble: a ticket for speeding; a tendency to knock things out of the way; all the dangers of high speed. Haste suggests impatience or an attitude of being above others, of leaving others in the dust. When realms of mystery and power are revealed, the pulse may quicken. There are issues of readiness: whether one is ready to jump in or whether it is not wiser to bear a seasoned respect for power shadows. The clouds may have silver linings; they may just be dark clouds. The creative genius of rarified thoughts may be beyond everyone, or simply out of this world.

Apply this degree-pair with a mind for quickening experiences, adrenaline rushes, gusts of rarified intelligence. Watch for tendencies to probe the unknown, special powers, flirting with shadow dynamics. Look for extremes of revelation and being heavily covered; shedding light on something previously hidden; receding into the shadows; opening new realms that supersede the limits of the known world; speeding over the mundane. Consider many thoughts rapidly twisted together; twisting ideas to the point of revealing mysteries; exerting control through heavy mysteries, by manipulating the entrance to hidden passageways; a head in the clouds; knowing something about the world beyond; pushing new ideas, new powers, to the limit.

"A finger pointing in an open book" (21 Taurus)
and "A soldier derelict in duty" (21 Scorpio)

Aspect: Conjunction.
Quality: Focus.
Shared motifs: 'To toe or not to toe the line,' 'the appeal of authenticity or the appeal to authority.'

"A finger pointing in an open book" is an image of citing that which is transparently clear and authoritative. The "finger pointing" is the index finger, which in Middle English was called *scite-finger,* shooting finger, perhaps because pointing a finger at someone is accusing the person of blame, or mimicking the shooting of a pistol. An "open book" suggests that which is freely available as a source or reference. When a person is an open book, they are easy to read or, if inauthentic, easy to see through. "A finger pointing" can be either drawing attention to an open source of wisdom, or sharpening focus on a particular line citing authority. A "point" is that which has no parts; position but no magnitude, or that which is a limit terminating a line, hence it can never exist without a line nor without the presumption of knowledge of a line.

"A soldier derelict in duty" is an image of failing to fulfill one's obligations, not living up to one's duties. "Derelict" means to be abandoned or left behind. "Duty" derives from "owing," as in endeavoring to fulfill service owed to the ruler or state. "Soldier" derives from the Latin *solidare,* to make solid, and *soldus,* pay, hence a soldier's pay. Abandoning one's duties can cause trouble with the authorities, but then choosing not to perform duties may be a matter of conscience: a personal realization that the orders given are humanly, personally unacceptable. Refusing to shoot innocent, defenseless people is a failure to obey orders, but also a show of higher moral sensibilities: refusing pay out of conscience and a higher sense of worth and reward.

Before the "Queensbury" rules were implemented, fistfighting was based on one rule only: the fighters were to step up to a line in the middle of the ring and place their toe on it. Then basically standing still, the fighters slugged it out with no attempt to evade the blows. If a fighter was unable to toe the line at the call of the next round, he lost. This rule of contest points a finger to the line at issue. Crossing the line tends to mean breaking the law or rules, but often one comes to point where the lines drawn can only be left behind.

Apply this degree-pair with a mind for the difference between a book as a source of knowledge and wisdom, and a book that represents an absolute authority as in "It is written." Think of situations like being off-track in one's life; self-assertive defiance as a means to get on track, to be true to oneself. Watch for innovations that read or play between the lines; civil disobedience; disobedience out of civility, decency; actions and expressions that point to a greater book. Consider toeing the line; exposing authority; transparent wrongs; leaving one's gold and possessions behind; daring to overrule authority or live by the book; rules one clearly cannot live by; bending the rules.

"White dove over troubled waters" (22 Taurus) and "Hunters starting out for ducks" (22 Scorpio)

Aspect: Opposition.
Quality: Awareness of.
Shared motifs: 'Getting above it all or looking for trouble,'
'doves and hawks.'

A "white dove over troubled waters" is an image of the coming of peace and hope. As the universal symbol for peace and the Holy Spirit, the "dove" is a welcome sight in troubled times. A "dove," as an attitude, is a peaceful way to approach life, to deal with military issues. Being "over troubled waters" suggests rising above difficulties, transcending the apparent turmoil of a situation. Strong winds cause troubled waters. Perhaps new ideas cause trouble with the prevailing authorities, leading to a disturbing situation. "Finger trouble" is an expression for tending to push the wrong control, such as the "delete" key on a computer.

"Hunters starting out for ducks" is an image of expeditionary ventures. "Hunter" derives from the Old English *hentan,* to try to capture or catch, from *henten,* to catch or pursue, and "hit," to strike upon. Hunters "set out" armed and clothed for the mission. When the hunters arrive at where their quarry dwells, they bring trouble to the water. The hunter mentality is one of tracking down, alert and aware of hints of the prey. Duck hunters use shotguns, which spray pellets, which scatter shots in a circle pattern to increase the chance of a hit. Camouflaged by their apparel, hunters hide or disguise their intent.

"Troubled waters" often manifest as a mind disturbed, troubled by difficult circumstances. The awareness of troubles in the world may evoke a dovelike response of compassion, or it may trigger a need to escape. Hunting is, on one level, a skill to be admired: having the know-how and aim to bag one's quarry. There is an element of the predator present as well: cunning, focused, carrying firepower and therefore dangerous. Hunters set out with expectations of catching their prey: to bag a few ducks is reward enough. A bounty hunter expects pay for finding his prey: a mercenary occupation motivated by financial reward. A dove is a winged creature that can fly above the game of rewards, freely bringing relief to those in need.

Apply this degree-pair with a mind to extremes of bringing succor and finding oneself troubled; performing actions for pay or reward or rising above service for gain; awareness of the higher and lower dimensions of pursuing a reward. Watch for professions that aid: medicine, nursing; that hunt for new ways to deal with situations; that call for help; that push into unknown territory with a broad shot, yet with a focused goal. Consider policies that paint everyone with the same brush; shotgun diplomacy; having a sense of trouble brewing; willingness to get in the line of fire to assist the helpless; troubleshooters who know how to find where the trouble lies and fix it; knowing when to duck; an inner sense of nearness to God.

"A jewelry shop" (23 Taurus)
and "A bunny metamorphosed into a fairy" (23 Scorpio)

Aspect: Trine.
Quality: Maintaining.
Shared motifs: 'The ethereal glow that evokes other realms,'
'mirth and reality,' 'less is more, more or less.'

"A jewelry shop" is a contained space with an array of gems, precious stones, many of which are adorned with gold and silver settings in lavish, enhancing displays. "Jewelry" is akin to "joke," through the Latin *iocus,* meaning a verbal game of mirth, and the Old French *joel* or *juel,* a plaything, trinket, and also through a subsidiary root of the Old French *jeu,* play. One senses immediately a lack of seriousness about a shop filled with trinkets and trifles. The jewelry shop is a resource of sorts for shoppers of precious stones. It suggests a store of riches like a treasure chest or like the blessing motif in fairy tales: "I have gold and jewels in abundance and all these I give to you." Buying gold, diamonds, and precious gems requires some savvy as to authenticity: Is it real gold, or does it just glitter like gold?

"A bunny metamorphosed into a fairy" is an image expressing the passage from the realm of ordinary experience into a realm of extraordinary, rarified radiance. A "bunny" is a diminutive term for a rabbit, derived from *bun,* a Scottish word for rabbit's tail, the stump of the buttocks. A "fairy" is supposedly an imaginary being of enchantment, the name deriving from the Old French *fae* and *fata,* fate, and having a distinct resonance with *fati,* that which is spoken, a divine statement. "Metamorphosis" is to change form, transmute: therefore, an endearing name for a rabbit signifying its distinctive rump, changing into a supernatural being with powers of divine words.

Imagine sitting in a deep, quiet woods, silently contemplating, when out of the corner of the eye, one catches sight of a bunny. The young rabbit then seems to change into a fairy presence, a luminous energy hovering within the woodland hues. It is an experience of the action of metamorphosis from one realm to another, from one thing to another, or perhaps one is the butt of a joke. In Vedanta philosophy from India, a rope-snake analogy is used to teach the nature of reality. Walking at night, one may perceive a poisonous snake in the path. Frightened, one jumps away, but comes to realize it was just a rope on the ground. The experience is very real: fear, alarm, terror. It is a question of what is real: bunny or fairy; rope or snake; trinket or gold. Gemstones exude rarified, radiant light. Real diamonds are not just costume jewelry, just as real fairies are not bunnies dressed up.

Apply this degree-pair with a mind to the playful allure of words and enchanting realities; heightened sensitivities about reality issues; special awareness of other realms, entities, nature spirits, and energetic fields. Look for themes of radiance and sparkle in appearance and outlook. Listen for a world in a word; metaphysical jocularity; speaking one's fate; enchanting capacities of speech. Consider issues with one's rump; transmutable natures; the tendency to see reality in other realms; playful power with words; trading one's last cow for a handful of beans.

"A mounted Indian with scalp locks" (24 Taurus) and "Crowds coming down the mountain to listen to one man" (24 Scorpio)

Aspect: Square.
Quality: Challenge.
Shared motif: 'As the individual begins to rise in life, crowds
come down to challenge his ascent.'

"A mounted Indian with scalp locks" is an image of personal accomplishments and achievements of power. A horse is a symbol of power; "a mounted Indian" is an image of an individual in the seat of his power. "Many scalps" suggests visible tokens of accomplishments, like credentials hanging on a wall. "Scalp locks" are long locks of hair worn by some North American Indians as a challenge to their rivals. "Locks" are strands of hair forming a curl or cluster. "Locks" is derived from the flexible twigs that were first used to fashion a lock, implying both an ability to fasten and to bend.

"Crowds coming down a mountain to listen to one man" is an image of the masses descending from on high to assess a man's words, a counterintuitive image, since normally one would think of crowds going up a mountain to hear the words of one man coming down from on high. To come down to someone is really condescension; being gracious enough to attend a meeting, for example, led by someone who is not yet regarded as a star speaker. Behaving as if on equal terms with others, while maintaining an attitude of superiority: patronizing.

The "mountain" is a symbol of that which one must climb in order to individuate, climb socially, gain public recognition. Crowds are not associated with the peak of a mountain. They are usually dwellers of the valley, of the lowest common denominator: the word on low. Part of the journey of anyone's rise in the world is through the crowd. To be someone, one must distinguish oneself from the anonymous masses, fight through public opinion. If a crowd comes to listen to someone who has his or her credentials out for public display, they may approach with a skeptical, patronizing attitude. The task of the individual is to win them over, to demonstrate that the tokens of accomplishment are not mere trinkets but rather achievements well integrated, brought down to earth.

Apply this degree-pair with a mind to having to fight uphill against public perception; having to prove oneself; a condescending attitude regarding meeting one's public, winning one's place in the social world. Watch for badges of honor; wearing decorations, succeeding without credentials as opposed to resting on one's laurels, making a name for oneself. Look for long locks of hair; a proud posture; waiting for others to come to you. Consider a warrior of words; proving oneself to oneself; not needing to rise above others, flexible words and ideas that have a binding power; bending the crowd to one's way of thinking; resistance to public opinion; Coma Berenices: the lock of amber hair that became a constellation; comets; varnish; a defiant struggle against gossip and slander.

"A large well-kept public park" (25 Taurus) and "An X-ray" (25 Scorpio)

Aspect: Quintile.
Quality: Creative genius.
Shared motif: 'The invisible side of constructive creativity.'

"A large well-kept public park" is an image of the collective efforts of society that create a space for enjoyment well beyond the scope of any individual's efforts. A "park" is a public space that can be shared, enjoyed, in common with all walks of life, all levels of society. A "well-kept" park suggests popularity in that a large attendance calls for consistent cultivation and care for the shared space.

"An X-ray" is an image of high-frequency electromagnetic waves that penetrate beneath the surface. "An X-ray" suggests a capacity to penetrate below the surface presentation of things, like an X-ray photograph of a skeletal structure. This is a capacity to make visible that which is not visible to the eye. As a medical tool, an X-ray allows the inner structures of the body to be examined without the use of surgical invasion. Still, there is an invasion of an invisible, imperceptible sort: radiation. The positive uses of energy sources that produce radiation are undeniable, as are the possible ill effects of too much radiation. Even invisible rays of light cast a shadow.

The park is large, therefore the range of possible issues is wide. Central Park in New York is a bustling, beautiful park, yet a penetrating observation reveals its darker side. The homeless, the criminally desperate, the addiction underground: there are many places in a vast park for darker things to hide. Invisibility can be a desired mode of public comportment for safety or security reasons: wary of being picked out of a crowd. Seeing through things can be revelatory in a positive sense. It can also be seeing darkness where none exists; projecting negative perceptions onto a beautiful landscape. Imagine a concert in the park. Behind the stage and the headliner star performers lies the work, often more arduous, of a much longer duration, involving many invisible personalities who pull together in order to make the event happen. The creative, invisible crews and volunteers build, organize, and maintain large undertakings for the benefit and enjoyment of the public at large. The hidden crowd of workers here differs from the "crowd descending": behind-the-scenes creativity as opposed to an anonymous challenge to the worth of an individual's gifts.

Apply this degree-pair with a mind to the creative vision and effort that lies behind a well-groomed public presentation. Think of creative satisfaction regarding being a part of something larger than any one person. Look for a manner of ease that sees through the fiction of having to prove oneself to others; seeing through the projections of the public, the projections of others; invisible energies that bind people collectively; public personas that hide a secret private life. Think of the difference between the limelight and the vast, behind-the-scenes energy and hard work that make the limelight possible. Consider mutual applause; pervasive paranoia; happy-to-have just-been-there attitudes.

"A Spaniard serenading his senorita" (26 Taurus) and "Indians making camp" (26 Scorpio)

Aspect: Conjunction.
Quality: Focus.
Shared motif: 'Finding one's new place out in the world.'

"A Spaniard serenading his senorita" is an image of being camped outside the window of one's beloved, singing sweetly in the night. "Serenades," which tend to be sung as evening songs, are dreamy pieces that gently call one to a lovely, calm, clear reverie. A "serene" song is one characterized by tranquility, peaceful repose. A "serene sky" is calm, elevated, and free of turbulence or cloud. "Serenading" is an action meant to calm and heighten a sense of dreamy peace. When a Spaniard serenades his senorita, he is attempting to win her favor through soft, alluring songs of love, to win a home in her heart.

"Indians making camp" is an image of the time to settle in and rest for the night. "Making camp" is a scenario of the end of a day's journey, which, as nightfall is near, is the time to settle, to make a peaceful place to rest. Imagine Plains Indians pitching a tipi as the sun goes down. They select an appropriate site, one that is safe and tranquil, providing all that is needed: water, food, fuel, for an undisturbed night. The "camp" is outdoors in a location worthy of being, insofar as it can be, home, even if only for the night. In a similar manner, a serenader is camped in the open, shamelessly singing to the honor of his beloved indoors.

Serenading someone can be a camp performance: a comical style, intentionally or unwittingly a parody of the serenader himself. It can be comical to see new campers attempting to erect their tents. Strikers can be camped outside a factory or workplace. Sometimes the songs strikers sing can be banal, patently artificial protests:

campy. Striking up a camp song, or striking up a campy song: in either case, the out-pouring of song is an unselfconscious thrust out into the world. Indians make camp after traveling through the day: perhaps an image of a hunting party that has ventured far from home camp; perhaps an image of wandering hunters and gatherers; perhaps having been pushed out of their native homelands.

Apply this degree-pair with a mind to focus on finding one's home; an itinerant sense of being in the world yet ever longing for home; traveling from place to place in search of somewhere to put down roots. Listen for striking voices; peaceful songs and voices; sentimental qualities; romantic voices; voices expressing emotional vulnerability. Think of parodies and striking up in song; issues regarding pitch, both as a musical quality and pitching a message, a camp, a position. Consider the importance of serenity and calm for the joys of an evening after a long day; home-is-where-the-heart-is sentiments; settling into new territory: land, ideas, expression; effecting uplifting influences either by intention or foolish good fortune; willingness to be a fool for love, for one's sense of being at home.

"A squaw selling beads" (27 Taurus)
and "A military band on the march" (27 Scorpio)

Aspect: Opposition.
Quality: Awareness of.
Shared motif: 'Marching to the beat of a different
(or the same) drummer.'

"A squaw selling beads" is an image of having to assume a position or work that may, or may not, accord naturally with one's sense of dignity. Imagine an American Indian woman at an Arizona flea market, selling beads to the passing public. The smile on her face might be a little forced, suggesting she really hates selling beads: it is just not in step with who she really is. She may be very happy to display and sell tokens of her cultural heritage to those genuinely interested and appreciative. The fine turquoise necklaces, the intricate beadwork and hammered silver: a whole world beckons of cultural and historical richness as the sun reflects off such items.

"A military band on the march" is an image of a collective effort to coordinate an action in precision and unison. It could be a source of social and cultural pride to see the band marching in parades, victory marches, celebrations, the half-time entertainment, that is, something that fills up an interval, a break in the main event. The ability to keep in step with everyone else is very important. It is helpful to be able to play one's instrument, walk, and keep in step all at the same time. It is even better if one can dress like the rest of the band so as not to stand out in an inappropriate way. Playing the same tune as the rest of the band is highly recommended for the best results. Then, there are those who march to the beat of a different drummer.

"Selling" implies getting the highest price for one's goods, attaining maximum worth, as in selling oneself, publishing the merits of oneself, or it may be selling one-self short, selling out. There can be an attitude of betrayal, of having been sold out (after all, Manhattan Island was purchased for little more than a handful of beads). "Beads" are often strung all in a line, like rows of marchers. However, one may draw a bead on one's objectives. One may be rising to the top, smiling, perhaps artificially, all the way. Perhaps one doesn't have a prayer to reach one's own goals within pre-vailing social/commercial/intellectual/military circumstances, unless one has her own band of beads, prayer beads, her beads all in a row, in her own hands.

Apply this degree-pair with a mind to an awareness of something more satisfying, more in line with being true to oneself. Watch for marching to someone else's tune; having to force a smile; to keep in step; to stay with the drill. Be alert for having to parade one's honor; to sell one's honor, one's home: circumstances sometimes force one to grin and bear it, to smile through clenched teeth. Consider jaw problems; teeth problems; grinding teeth, resulting from suppressing or repressing speaking one's truth; fallen insteps, and the beady eye of individuality shining within an im-personal milieu; "wampum": strung beads and shells used for jewelry, ceremony, or as currency.

"A woman pursued by mature romance" (28 Taurus) and "The king of the fairies approaching his domain" (28 Scorpio)

Aspect: Trine.
Quality: Maintaining.
Shared motifs: 'Coming into one's own,'
'approaching or being pursued.'

"A woman pursued by mature romance" is an image suggestive of romance late in life, a late bloomer. "Mature" is a state of being ripe, advanced to fullness, of full age. "Romance" is the stage of love that stirs a strong sense of ardor not yet fully consummated in marriage. "Romance" stirs adventure and longing for faraway places of strange and fascinating allure. One can be wooed by vows to fulfill a promise made by another. "Pursuing" is to go after, to follow, out of a sense of devotion, for example. As humans wander and roam this world, seeking love and a genuine sense of being home, any glimmer of love and appreciation can reawaken memories and deep longings.

"The king of the fairies approaching his domain" is an image of return to that which is one's own. A "fairy domain" is a realm charged with mystery and rarified energy: an unreal reality. "Approaching one's domain" evokes a sense of belonging, a sense of being drawn to what is naturally one's own, like returning home. A "king" is the master of his domain, the head, the leader. Psychologically, this is an image of coming into one's own: a well-integrated and balanced sense of self. "Approaching" is getting close to, just as lovers might snuggle up.

Like "romance," the fairy realm carries a sense of wonder and mystery. A romantic atmosphere is one charged with magnetic attraction: two people strangely drawn to approach one another. Imagine, after a time of putting on a smiling face while selling beads, a woman, much to her surprise, finds herself being pursued by a little bit of magic, attention, appreciation. The woman's smile becomes genuine, because, feeling appreciated, it is natural to feel at home, in one's own domain, to feel like oneself again. Approaching such a domain is an exciting time; it has an air all its own that tends to take you away from the ordinary world. Being pursued by romance may not be desired. Not everything that pursues you feels just right: the pursuit may have an intent to capture or do harm. To this extent, the king may be ambivalent about approaching his domain. Is he in exile? Is there danger lurking if he returns?

Apply this degree-pair with a mind for securing a personal domain that exudes a touch of mystery; attempting to maintain a mature center while being called to a deep longing; trying not to lose one's head in love and romance. Watch for attentions that seem to come out of another realm; attentions that place one out of touch with reality; stories of personal creativity blooming late in life. Consider May-December romances; staying with a rigid routine out of fear of mystery, romance, and adventure; tendencies to dream about romance; a strange sense of security in never quite returning home; enchantments that keep one in one's place, or that take one far away; keeping in step just in case it might fulfill one's heart's desire; a little love and appreciation that takes one a long way.

"Two cobblers working at a table" (29 Taurus)
and "An Indian squaw pleading to the chief for the lives of her children" (29 Scorpio)

Aspect: Square.
Quality: Challenge.
Shared motifs: 'Pleasing cooperation,' 'power struggles.'

"Two cobblers working at a table" is an image of two people repairing shoes on their worktable. The two of them must work in cooperation to get anything done. Their craft is one that they share, and therefore they share tools, materials, and the workspace. They may strive for excellence in their work, however "to cobble" can also mean to throw together hastily, roughly. A "cobble" is also a small round stone, as those used to make a cobblestone road. If the cobblers are not getting along, it is conceivable that they might cobble, stone, one another.

"An Indian squaw pleading to the chief for the lives of her children" is an image of a mother placed in an unbearable situation of having to plead for the lives of those she loves most. A "plea" is an earnest appeal or entreaty. The woman is being subjected to an extremely anguishing possibility. "Pleading to the chief" suggests entreating, imploring with great intensity, the leader, king, judge, the one at the top by whom the verdict has been decided, at the mere fall of a hammer. Perhaps one has been a victim of a hasty decision, or the ruthless use of power that subjugates, makes one subservient to another. An earnest entreaty places the matter on the table for discussion. If the two parties are working together harmoniously, the position may be swayed to a more pleasing outcome: "If it please the court."

The lives of children can be placed as if on an altar, a table symbolic of elevated status as an offering to the divine. Imagine an Incan princess pleading to the chief while her children are being led to a sacrificial altar. Parents sacrifice much to raise their children: work to provide; encourage their growth; pray for their well-being. Relations between parents sometimes need to be patched up. Difficulties can lead to throwing stones at one another. Sometimes it is all a bunch of cobble: nonsense. What is chief, in the matter, is working together for some higher goal, purpose, for the sake of . . . The challenge is to determine what is really important and of genuine worth.

Apply this degree-pair with a mind to trenchant issues of communication and co-operation; disputes of ownership over that which can never be owned; attempting not to compromise oneself within compromising situations. Watch someone lording it over someone else's head based on a harsh verdict; the paradox of fighting over a house while losing one's home; the sense to surrender possessions in order to save one's heart. Be aware of abductions, child visitation privileges, judges' decisions, parental sacrifice; making the children sacred; holding the children on high; children who rule their parents; mature of age yet acting immaturely over trifles; young of age yet acting maturely over what really matters.

"A peacock parading on an ancient lawn" (30 Taurus) and "A Halloween jester" (30 Scorpio)

Aspect: Quintile.
Quality: Creative genius.
Shared motifs: 'The human and the divine comedy,'
'dispelling the hard edges of reality.'

"A peacock parading on an ancient lawn" is an image of a proud display of possession and accomplishment. A "peacock" is, strictly speaking, the male of the peafowl, which is distinguished from the female by its large fanning tail of iridescent color. When a "peacock parades," he puts on a colorful show that can either be delightful or ostentatious. A peacock strutting his stuff can be a comical display, even vulgar. In terms of human character, the peacock can lean towards pride, aloofness, vanity, self-absorption: proud as a peacock. Strutting your stuff can also be a matter of confidence and pride in what one has accomplished, what one has to show the world. There is a thin line between ostentatious flaunting and exuding confident self-esteem. Often humor softens haughty conceit. One might say, smilingly, "If you got it honey, don't hide it!"

"A Halloween jester" is an image of creatively fusing two seemingly discrete elements: the hallowed and divine with humor and comedy. Imagine a dignified procession of your friends in the elaborate costumes of church leaders. "Honey! The Pope is here to see you again." A jester is a joker or fool. In medieval court, the fool was the near and constant companion of the king, often a valuable advisor, and the only one allowed to make fun of the monarch. The fool's function was to deflate royal grandiosity from time to time, bring the king down to earth, to prick the overinflated balloon of pompous regality, so to speak.

Contemporary Halloween is all about dressing in costumes, having fun at costume parties, trick-or-treating. Traditionally, "Hallowed evening" comes from Celtic, pre-Christian origins, marking the time of *Samhain*, or the end of the season of growth and harvest and the beginning of winter. It is said that the membrane or mask-like veil between the worlds opened at this time, allowing fairies and spirits to enter this world. Like an ancient lawn, such traditions take a long time to build. "Hallowed e'en" has been disguised as something else. Even so, once it arrives, it is time to show your stuff, celebrate. There is no blame in dressing it up a bit.

Apply this degree-pair with a mind to the genius to dispel the harsh edges that seek to rigidly define home and heart, reason and imagination, this world and that, reality from unreality, romance from pragmatics. Watch for rich, beautiful display, proud exhibition, with a wicked humor strutting nearby. "Fool" derives from the Latin *follis*, meaning bellows, therefore watch for windbags, overblown conceit, and over-the-top humor. Consider the genius to work beyond the struggles of power and cooperation; a balance of discriminating intelligence with intangible impressions; the ability to laugh at oneself, to see the divine humor at play in all things; to see the humor in human folly; a genuine smile; feeling at home; a consummate attitude of "there is much to admire and much to smile about."

CHAPTER THREE

GEMINI-SAGITTARIUS

"A glass-bottomed boat in still water" (1 Gemini)
and "A Grand Army of the Republic campfire" (1 Sagittarius)

Aspect: Conjunction.
Quality: Focus.
Shared motifs: 'A pause for deep reflection,'
'a call to remember,' 'a window on the old guard.'

"A glass-bottomed boat in still water" is an image of circumstances that call for seeing through one realm into another, from an intellect realm into an an emotion realm. A "glass-bottomed boat" is a water vessel with the capacity to allow passengers to see what lies in the water below. "Glass" is a transparent substance that is solidified from a molten state into a rigid, brittle form, used to separate two areas while permitting light and visual perception to pass through. Tour boats with glass bottoms take tourists out into bodies of water that contain shipwrecks or natural marine wonders. Looking down into the water, one can see aquatic memorials of sunken ships. It may be an emotional experience remembering those who have fallen, however the water is still, suggesting calm, centered reflection of what lies below and behind; like a group gathered around the window or television screen to view and monitor a shared experience of underlying emotions.

"The Grand Army of the Republic campfire" is an image of a gathering around a shared center of warmth. "The Grand Army of the Republic" was an organization born out of the Civil War. Veterans of the Union army and navy organized with a purpose to strengthen bonds of comradeship, establish pensions for veterans, and observe remembrance of fallen comrades. The United States' Memorial Day holiday, usually the last Monday in May, was established directly from the efforts of the G.A.R. "Campfires" are natural focal points for gatherings, evoking a sense of keeping a spirit alive, warming up to the experiences of comrades-in-arms.

While not confined to an army gathering, coming together becomes a focal point for subscribing to a sense of one's life as lived in common with others who have fought in the same vein. "Glass" allows objective clarity while acting as a barrier that protects or defends against getting in too deep. As a window to that which is normally out of view, glass separates two realms, suggesting an ability to operate on two levels at once: sublimation into an airy vantage point, or fiery passions fueled on memories.

Apply this degree-pair with a mind to energies that thrust forward within shared passions to affect the world; a focus to remember comrades and continue to carry the torch; a coolly detached sense of rightness about emotions. Look for gatherings and groups that tend to be organized around self-serving interests; open to public exposure; possible underhanded dealings and subterfuge. Listen for a Rah! Rah! spirit; affected appeals to gather around the campfire; songs, books, and movies evoking emotions and sentiment for a past sense of glory. Consider abilities for reading the subtext; reminiscence; social reunions; pathos: evoking sympathy, sadness, or pity in expression; capitalizing on sentiment in the wake of hardship; super-observance; the world-according-to-camp mentality.

"Santa Claus filling stockings furtively" (2 Gemini) and "The ocean covered with whitecaps" (2 Sagittarius)

Aspect: Opposition.
Quality: Awareness of.
Shared motifs: 'Spirit of giving,' 'stealing,'
'covering deep truths,' 'stirring up spirit.'

"Santa Claus filling stockings furtively" is an image of rewards and gains in the guise of the spirit of giving. "Santa Claus" is an Americanized name for *Sante Klaas,* the Dutch and German name for the patron saint of children, Saint Nicholas. A "saint" is a person of great virtue or holiness. "Santa Claus" has become associated with the spirit of giving at Christmas, especially gifts for children. The virtue of selfless giving is a practice exemplified by the filling of children's stockings hung on Christmas Eve: divine gifts that magically happen to fall in stockings hung with hopes of beneficence. Belief in Santa Claus is widely thought to be the domain of children, one that, with maturity, is outgrown. A child may discover that Santa is a man dressed in costume, hence the need to "fill stockings furtively." Discovering the disguise could easily dispel the joy and wonder of receiving gifts.

"The ocean covered with whitecaps" is an image of the froth stirred by wind over water. An "ocean" is a great body of saltwater. To be "covered" is to be concealed, hidden, or protected, as with covering something with a piece of cloth. "Whitecaps" are waves that rise in a peak of turbulent wind and water, creating bubbles, foam, and froth. To be "covered in froth" is to be coated with light, insubstantial foam, hence a frothy conversation is one that is foolish and trivial. "Whitecap" is the name of a former lawless, secret organization in America, so named for wearing white caps, who engaged in violent crimes against individuals deemed morally unacceptable. The appearance of whitecaps is only a surface manifestation hiding a much deeper, more powerful current: the tip of the iceberg.

Even a ferocious wind stirs only the water's surface. The image of inner truth is a vast, deep reservoir of riches. The effect of wind on water is to lift small parts of the whole to a higher peak: each wave is a highly individualized, heightened perspective of a wider horizon. "Filling stockings furtively" is to do so secretly, stealthily, stealing away while escaping notice. A thief might be stuffing his stocking with other people's valuables. A theft might stir up a lot of trouble or pique awareness of a deeper issue. It depends on which cap you are wearing: one for fun, joy, like Santa's cap, a symbol of generosity and kindness of spirit; or a hood shrouding one's true identity.

Apply this degree-pair with a mind to an awareness of deeper issues lying below the surface appearance; the motives for apparent generosity; suspicions about being fooled. Watch for costumes, disguises, and caps; coverings that lead one to wonder what lies beneath. Be alert for gifting anonymously; stealth under cover; organizations that wear the hat of charity, or wear a hat for self-interest and gain. Consider tucking valuables away for a rainy day; trivial conversation; social ideals of purely imaginary substance; a knack for detecting undercurrents; banking in secret; controlling the distribution of wealth.

"The garden of the Tuileries" (3 Gemini)
and "Two men playing chess" (3 Sagittarius)

Aspect: Trine.
Quality: Maintaining.
Shared motifs: 'Rules and revolution,'
'maintaining order or testing the rule.'

"The garden of the Tuileries" is an image of royal palatial remains open to the public. The "Tuileries" palace was burned down during the Commune of Paris in 1871. The "Commune of Paris" was an organization that seized control of the government during the French Revolution. Their communal, social, and revolutionary principles were in direct contrast to the law and order of the status quo. The gardens continue to be maintained as a peak moment of culture, carried forth as a symbol of an expression of creative stability, open to all. "Tuileries" is a name derived from the tile yards formerly on the site.

"Two men playing chess" is an image of two men playing the game of kings on a tiled board. "Chess" derives from the Old French name *esches,* the plural form of the interjection warning an opponent of impending danger: "Check." Chess is played on a checkered chessboard, a square with sides divided into eight square spaces, often composed of black and white tiles. "Tile" derives from the Latin *tegere,* to cover, referring to the thatching on a roof or interlocking tiles that cover a house. "Protect" and "detect," cover and uncover, derive from the same strategic and architectural know-how: the Latin *techne,* the technological skill to build, cover, and weave.

"Tile" is an old slang term for a hat, being to the head what roofing tiles are to a house. "Freemasonry" is a secret organization originating with the tradesmen of ancient times. "To tile a lodge" is to close and guard the doors, preventing the uninitiated from entering. "Chess" is a highly skilled game with definite rules defining the moves of the thirty-two chessmen. Played according to the rules, the chess game calls for intelligence, strategy, and creativity. A breakdown of the rule of order would be like the chessmen getting up and telling you where to go: a revolution. Playing the game is an allegiance to the rules of the status quo. Revolution is the refusal to follow the rules of the game: tearing down the king's palace but leaving the gardens open and available to all.

Apply this degree-pair with a mind to the need to maintain a stable order of rule; to keep in step with the defined movements of the social status quo; to test, overthrow, or uncover the the real rules of the game. Look for rules that maintain order;

vestiges of a cultural past that inspire new moves; personal strategies that aim for checkmate in political endgames. Be aware of sacrificing pawns for a kingdom; secret agendas; social ideals outside of the law; feeling hemmed in by imposed constraints; attempting revolutionary innovations within the rules of the game. Consider knowing when to keep a secret; keeping a lid on one's strategy; defensive moves to protect communal welfare; secret communities that blend in; a knack for detecting flaws in how things work.

"Holly and mistletoe" (4 Gemini) and "A little child learning to walk" (4 Sagittarius)

Aspect: Square.
Quality: Challenge.
Shared motifs: 'New steps, old steps,' 'embracing, spurning.'

"Holly and mistletoe" is an image of the turning of the the old to the new. "Holly" is a plant that is sacred in Celtic tradition. One of the chief uses of holly is that of a protective energy. The sharp spines of the male holly leaf serve as a defense against unwanted influences; the smoother leafs of the female holly tree bear bright red berries. "Holly" was used as decoration from as early on as the Roman festival of "Saturnalia," a period of freedom from all constraint, law, and order beginning on December nineteenth. "Mistletoe," also known as golden bough, was sacred to the ancient Druids. A parasitic plant that grows on other trees, mistletoe was thought to hold the soul of the host tree. The white berries of the mistletoe, which are poisonous, turn a golden color as they dry, hence "golden bough."

The connection between the two plants derives from Druidic times when the evergreen holly with its red berries was thought to bring beauty to the world while the sacred oak tree was barren during the winter months. Mistletoe was gathered, especially from the oak tree, in winter, while wearing sprigs of holly in the hair. The oak tree symbolizes the new year of the waxing sun. Taken together, the three plants symbolize the time of the transfer of power from the old king to the new, the old year to the new year.

"A little child learning to walk" is an image of learning to stand on one's own two feet: tentative first steps of evolution. "Walk" derives from the Middle English *walken,* the Old English *wealcan,* to roll, and ultimately from the Latin *volvere,* to roll or cause to roll, hence revolve, evolve. Standing and walking on two legs was a decisive evolutionary phase for mankind: *homo erectus*. Every period of development involves a revolution, like the turning of a wheel; an evolution that turns from the old to the new. The early steps of a "little child" stand in contrast with the sturdiness of a full-grown oak tree, which symbolically offers a steadying support. Early steps are tentative, drawing strength from older, steadier sources of support.

Apply this degree-pair with a mind to the transition from the old to the new; the challenges of new, revolutionary ways of doing things as opposed to old, established ways that have run their course. Think of resisting the urge to help, embracing new ideas, or resisting change with toxic regard for new challengers. Watch for awkward first steps that need something to lean on; a strolling style of walking; struggles to establish new regimes on solid ground; walking sticks; bouncing right back up after a momentary fall. Be alert for patterns of evolution, stepping into a new realm of development, or patterns of devolution, one step forward and two steps back. Consider tapping into old resources; issues with the feet; new ideals that merely shuffle the rules for social position; sinking roots into tradition; aggressive takeovers or slowly usurping power.

"A radical magazine" (5 Gemini) and "An owl up in a tree" (5 Sagittarius)

Aspect: Quintile.
Quality: Creative genius.
Shared motifs: 'So old it's radical,' 'the "now" vision.'

"A radical magazine" is an image of a periodical publication of extreme views demanding immediate and widespread social and political change. "Radical" means pertaining to the root, the foundation, or what is fundamentally essential. "Radical views" are extreme views that, in a social or political sense, are to be applied to their fullest extent. There is a creative irony in all things radical: the new is almost always a going back to the roots of the old ways. Clashes between the new, radical ways of thinking and the old guard of the establishment thus become matters of "what is new is old"; "what is old is new." A magazine can be a published periodical, circulated at regular time intervals, or a storehouse where anything, but especially ammunition or firepower, is kept on supply.

"An owl up in a tree" is an image of the perch of the eyes of wisdom. The "owl," an emblem of Athena, goddess of wisdom, settles high in a tree with great ease while others may find that perch precarious. The difference lies in being settled, established root and branch, as opposed to being out on a limb or without a proper foundation. Owls are known for their uncanny night vision and the ability to turn their heads with such agility as to be able to see all the way around. From such lofty heights, one can see the lay of the land. "Wisdom," therefore, would come from being well established, well rooted, with a panoramic vision that can take in all things. Inversely, wisdom may be seeing all things from a well-grounded perspective.

A radical perspective may wish to change things root and branch, utterly, completely. The issue is whether the change called for is rooted in solid ground or whether it is a passing whim about which one doesn't give a hoot. A hoot owl may be the voice of satire or scorn such as the Greek proverb "to send owls to Athens," meaning to do something superfluous like carry water to the river. "Athens" was named for Athena after a dispute with Poseidon over who would be the city's patron. The sea god offered a war horse; Athena produced an olive branch for peace.

Apply this degree-pair with a mind to creative endeavors of vision for personal and social ideals; a humorous touch regarding the radical ideas that arise periodically; the humor in "what is old is new again." Listen for stump speeches and soapbox oratory; hoots of laughter; returning to roots music. Watch for retro trends; being "blind as an owl," that is, cannot see what is under one's nose; going to old stores to load up on new ideas. Consider vision problems; farsightedness; night vision; difficulties getting one's head around new ideas; neck problems; a wise-owl ease with the responsibilities of liberty, the hierarchies of equality, the dissent of fraternity.

"Drilling for oil" (6 Gemini)
and "A game of cricket" (6 Sagittarius)

Aspect: Conjunction.

Quality: Focus.

Shared motifs: 'Industrious character,' 'the crux of the matter.'

"Drilling for oil" is an image of an enterprise tapping into a natural resource. "Oil" is a liquid substance formed over time through natural processes within the earth from animal, vegetable, or mineral origins. Deriving from the Greek *elaion*, olive oil, "oil" became petroleum from the compound in Middle Latin *petra*, rock, plus *oleum*, oil. "Drilling" means to pierce or bore, as in to bore through layers of earth and rock in an attempt to discover a pocket of oil. Beneath the surface lies a core of wealth with a huge potential impact on social, economic, and political arenas. "Drilling" does not guarantee striking oil: making a lucky or valuable discovery. There is ever an exploratory element involved: striking it rich or striking out. Sinking a well suggests penetrating industry, that is, an industrious character with a steely resolve to go deep.

"A game of cricket" is an image of an open-air game, the crux of which rests upon goal stakes at which one bowls. Consolidated in England, "cricket" has spread to territories formerly under British rule, hence a commonwealth theme born out of the imperial ambitions of the past. The game itself has its own rules that, when not followed, give rise to the expression "not cricket": not fair or sporting. Contending with difficult conditions, such as soggy, rain-soaked grounds, makes fielding a hit ball an awkward matter or a sticky wicket, a situation calling for delicate handling.

In order to drill for oil, one needs an oil rig to assemble a shaft of perpendicular pipe fitted with a drill bit. Rigging a game would not be cricket. Making a play for oil can tap into a naturally formed resource that fuels industry and commerce, but can also lead to sticky situations such as pollution and ulterior political and economic motives. The rules of the game are the underlying structures that uphold good sport, like a "crutch," an upright instrument of support, and "crux," a perpendicular post supporting a horizontal beam. Their constancy ensures regularity and routine, drills, that over time establish traditions and conventions: the riggings by which one's ship sails. Boring into the earth calls up images of parasites that live off organisms by boring through the outer protective layer. Oil is formed over millions of years from living organisms trapped in suitable geological conditions. The oil industry is, therefore, based on drilling into archaic pools for contemporary purposes.

Apply this degree-pair with a mind to going deeper, penetrating thought that relies on the old to fuel what is new; a focus to get to the crux of the matter; establishing reliable supports for industry. Watch for falling into routines that stay on the surface of matters with deep implications. Look also for historical ironies like imperialism giving rise to more level playing fields, archaic resources being burned up in smoke. Consider valuables that lead to sticky situations; assumptions about living off others' resources; money games; rigging matters in order to propel advancement; becoming stuck in one's ways.

"An old-fashioned well" (7 Gemini)
and "Cupid knocking at the door" (7 Sagittarius)

Aspect: Opposition.
Quality: Awareness of.
Shared motifs: 'A call to open to what is deeper,'
'desiring what is fashionable.'

"An old-fashioned well" is an image of a manmade object that is the source of water, the source of life. A "well" is that which organizes human civilization. The I Ching says of the well, "The town can be changed but the well cannot be changed." Without a source of water, no town or city can sustain itself and therefore, of necessity, is forced to relocate. This is clearly an old-fashioned idea, since modern cities, like Los Angeles, tap into a water supply from somewhere else, and pipe it in. This can be likened to a bucket that does not go all the way to the bottom of the well, to the foundations of life: a superficial and dissatisfying way of being. "Old-fashioned" refers to the ways of the past, to customary ways that are obsolete, in disuse. The well, as a symbol of the inexhaustible source of life, can never be out of fashion. Only the human relationship to the well can be one of neglect and superficial disregard.

"Cupid knocking at the door" is an image of awakened desire. A "door" is a barrier separating an interior from an exterior. It is the passageway that allows an entrance or a departure. Letting Cupid in, to become entranced, suggests an arousal of desire that stirs emotion deep within. "Cupid" is depicted as a small-winged boy-god who rather mischievously shoots his arrows at his hapless victims. In Greek mythology, the gods did not see being struck by one of Cupid's arrows as a desirable thing. It often led to trouble.

"To fashion" a well is to make a well, a manmade structure designed to access the source of life. Awareness of the deep resource of refreshing water, whether the well within, the well of knowledge, the well of cultural resource, or the well of the town, is not something to be knocked. One might be aroused to seek the water of a deeper well. One might leave the well in disrepair while pursuing more superficial objects of desire. "Cupid knocking at one's door" is a visit of divine energy. Divining where to dig for water is an arcane art that employs a rod and calls for a knack for discovery. Opening the door at Cupid's knock leads one to uncover a good well that, perhaps, has been there all along.

Apply this degree-pair with a mind to discovering archaic sources of nourishment; the allure of fashionable trends that whet one's thirst; an awareness of the responsibilities of one's source of wealth. Look for an alertness for issues of satisfaction and mere desire, that which quenches the thirst for love and life; superficiality, shallow satisfactions as opposed to awakening deep, inward sources of the divine. Consider golden dreams of lands of love; insatiable desires that keep one stuck in the same place; choosing out of insecurity or out of unshakable trust; being troubled by an inherited situation; "knock for six": in cricket to hit the ball off the field, scoring six runs; "knock over with a feather": overcome with surprise; astonishing developments; "knock off": to steal or to cease work; knock-knees.

"An industrial strike" (8 Gemini) and "Rocks and things forming therein" (8 Sagittarius)

Aspect: Trine.
Quality: Maintaining.
Shared motifs: 'Alchemy,' 'cooking,' 'stirring things up.'

"An industrial strike" is an image of a situation wherein the locus of industry is surrounded by the discontented workers. When the work stops, industry grinds to a halt. Energy is directed instead toward issues of inequities, of worth, of brewing social awareness being stirred up in the work force. Industry is a concentrated activity that manufactures useful, beneficial works. Grievances that lead to a strike are almost always ignited along the fault lines of social inequities, the horizon of different strata of social position: workers and management; workmen's pay and owners' profits. Such issues become inflamed as the pressure builds between two distinct strata, moving in different directions.

"Rocks and things forming therein" is an image of the deep internal creative forces of geological time. "Forming therein" suggests the inner space wherein rocks and things like oil, water, diamonds, and minerals are formed. Drilling into the earth for oil, or digging a well for water, leads naturally to an invisible realm beneath the surface where things are formed. Many crucial resources are formed within the cauldron of the earth, including plain old rocks. "Things" can be material or immaterial. There is a close relationship between thing and think (German: *ding* and *denk*): ideas forming within, or ideas that solidify like rocks.

"To strike" is "to deliver a blow" with suddenness. "Striking workers" are those who knock off work out of protest. "Striking a balance" is to find a mutually agreeable compromise. Within the earth, horizontal stratification of different layers can intensify pressure that leads to the formation of different materials, volcanic potentials, frictions that can shake the world. The captains of industry may find their ship on the rocks should the workers whose efforts propel production rock the boat. The divisions of labor may hold immovable positions or strike up a pose like the Rock of Gibraltar. If the shoe pinches, the foot is sure to protest. In a quarrel, the advantage may rock from side to side, tilt in one's favor, or just disturb the equilibrium. When resistance is mutual, something has got to give: one might have to strike out in another direction, branch out into a new activity.

Apply this degree-pair with a mind to energy expended to maintain solid foundations that stubbornly resist pressures to change. Think of pressure cookers, cauldrons, alchemy: all things that build in pressure that inevitably must release powerful energy for creative and destructive purposes. Look for pressures that build subjectively, things cooking within the human psyche, and social pressures regarding the division of labor; being between a rock and a hard place. Consider choices between shoring up old ways or opening up new ways; friction sores; being in a pinch; a knack for mediation, for saying the right thing; having sudden ideas; turning issues over in one's mind.

"A quiver filled with arrows" (9 Gemini) and "A mother with her children on the stairs" (9 Sagittarius)

Aspect: Square.
Quality: Challenge.
Shared motif: 'Many potentials unfolding a step at a time.'

"A quiver filled with arrows" is an image of a full array or arsenal of effective capacities to draw upon. A "quiver" is a container that holds shafts such as Cupid's arrows, or, from the German for quiver, *kochar,* a golf bag. One might quiver with excitement, or tremble with fear. One might have a quivering voice that rapidly shakes with a trill, a musical series of eighth notes. When a quiver is filled, it is full, satisfied, like a heart that is full of love or desire or a thirst that has been satiated. "To be filled" is also to be on the verge of spilling over, overfull, implying that something is at the point of giving way. Imagine cooking in a cauldron, stewing something that is ready to bubble over.

"A mother with her children on the stairs" is an image of maternal guidance for unsure, tremulous steps up or down the stairs, the graduated steps of learning. "Stairs" are a series of steps that change one's position of elevation: ascending or descending. A child's first steps can be shaky, perhaps quaking at the flight of stairs before them. The journey through school is one that rises through a series of grades until one graduates. A nurturing, helping hand, like that of a mother or a teacher, attempts to guide the way as surely as the flight of a straight arrow. The challenge is to take it one step at a time rather than all at once. A child's enthusiasm may bubble over with ambitious steps. Many children on stairs may be a handful, portending a stumble or a fall.

Arrows that can be drawn upon with one's own hand suggest pointed barbs that can be directed toward their mark. Drawing a single arrow at a time is a good idea, even if there are several challenging targets, like a flock of quacking ducks, that one might wish to hit all at once. Providing a helping, guiding hand for many children on the stairs necessitates picking the one or two most in need of steadying. Seeing young children on the stairs can have one quaking in one's boots with quick, trembling concern for their safety.

Apply this degree-pair with a mind for the challenge of knowing which potential, of many, one should draw upon; which direction, if any, to go; struggles with the fear of potential loss or failure. Watch for getting a handle on the right means or instrument for the most fitting target as opposed to shooting off in all directions at once. Listen for angry barbs; the clatter of footsteps and quacking voices; voices that shake or quake; songlike tremolo. Consider cooks; teachers; having many jobs at once; golfers; uncertain professional goals; retraining; feeling degraded through having to step down in order to retrain; feeling the need for a helping hand; the eternal student; the guidance counselor; taking a step back before moving forward two steps; feeling attacked with barbs such as "Those who can, do; those who cannot, teach."

"An aeroplane falling" (10 Gemini)
and "A golden-haired goddess of opportunity" (10 Sagittarius)

Aspect: Quintile.
Quality: Creative genius.
Shared motifs: 'Diving in; being uplifted,' 'the sky is the limit,'
'coming down to earth.'

"An aeroplane falling" is an image of a powered, heavier-than-air flying vehicle with fixed wings in free fall. "Aero," the Greek word for air, is currently used in compounds such as "aeroplane" or the more contemporary "airplane." "Plane" refers to a level surface, such as the surface of the earth, which is relatively flat from the perspective of human experience. "Plane" also means a flat surface producing lift, the result of the action of air or water moving over it. There is a question of level: strata of earth; layers of atmosphere. Being at the controls of a plane permits a graceful flight, smooth landings, and aerial acrobatics, including breathtaking, whirling nose-dives.

"A golden-haired goddess of opportunity" is an image of an inherent sense of good fortune, golden opportunity, uplifting confidence regarding a heavenly presence of rewarding possibility. "Gold" symbolizes riches, life, appreciation, beauty, and love. "Golden hair" is a symbol of power, the summer aspect of *Aphrodite Comaetho,* "Bright-haired Aphrodite." Aphrodite, or Venus, is said to have been born rising out of the foam of the sea. The mother of Eros, or the arrow-shooting Cupid, Aphrodite's name combines *aphro,* foam, and *dineo,* "I whirl," or *duo,* "I dive." As a goddess, the golden-haired one suggests a heavenly source of good things, opportunity, uplifting rewards, a wide expanse of golden possibilities.

Imagine shooting an arrow into the air. The force of gravity will eventually take effect, returning the arrow to earth. Airplanes are powerful vehicles capable of flight. Designed to create a lift effect with their wings, planes can be skillfully maneuvered through the air and brought back to earth with a smooth landing. The lift controls are such that a skilled pilot can perform hair-raising nosedives, whirling spirals headed straight toward the ground, and still pull out of the dive in time, amazing those who watch from below. Flying is not a natural physical capacity of human beings. Without the proper training and a reliable airplane, attempting to fly like the gods is a hare-brained idea. Training for something to which one has no inner attraction, choosing a practical discipline of study over what one really loves, is a plan that usually does not fly for long. Following one's inner desire and bliss is often smiled upon by the golden-haired goddess.

Apply this degree-pair with a mind to the creative flair for seizing a golden opportunity, lifting-off innovative ideas; a genius for capitalizing on lofty possibilities. Watch for the heightened importance of hair, hair-raising, the way hair falls, a shock of hair; golden hair; long, twirling hair. Be aware of subtle earth-goddess themes: Demeter, who ripens the fields into golden grain; Sif, the golden-haired wife of Thor, whose hair was lopped off by Loki, necessitating a hair replacement of finely spun gold. Consider navigating ups and downs with a confident flourish; successful first attempts or maiden voyages; "Venus hair" or "maiden hair": very delicate and graceful; "maiden over" in cricket is one from which no runs are made, implying that playing the "cricket" of societal expectations may not be one's true path.

"A new path of realism in experience" (11 Gemini) and "The lamp of physical enlightenment in the left temple" (11 Sagittarius)

Aspect: Conjunction.
Quality: Focus.
Shared motifs: 'The path less traveled,'
'realistic empathy; (em)pathetic realism.'

"A new path of realism in experience" is an image of an awakening to things as they actually are. One can be overinfluenced by otherworldly beliefs, by collective assumptions, unexamined views that anyone can blindly follow. "Realism," in a philosophic sense, is a view which holds that abstract ideas have an objective existence surpassing concrete objects in terms of their "reality." Symbolically, "realism" is like sobering up, or waking from a dream. For example, one may rely solely on one's own experience, dismissing secondhand information as gossip, in ascertaining what is real or worthy of consideration. In artistic expression, "realism" is the attempt to portray things in accordance with their perceptible nature. On the other hand, "realism" can be the view that the phenomenal world of experience is illusory; that the real world lies elsewhere, behind appearances, a higher reality above.

"The lamp of physical enlightenment in the left temple" is an image of being guided by an illumination, an ideal sense of physical reality. Imagine getting up in the night and walking into an object in the darkness. In that moment, a flash of enlightenment blazes through the experience of physical pain, turns on the "lamp" so to speak. One might be very sleepy, stumbling on a path that in the light of day would never be taken. A felt experience can evoke pathos, suffering, which motivates thought for a pragmatic and realistic course in the future.

One may have empathy for the plight of others. "Knights Templar" who protected pilgrims on their way to Jerusalem were given quarters on the site of Solomon's Temple. "The Temple" is a name for the seat of the Knights Templar in London. "Mount Temple" in Jerusalem is said to be the other of two main sacred sites. All that is left of the temple, said to hold the Arc of the Covenant, is the Wailing Wall: surely a symbol of great pathos. The left temple of the head may refer to the rational, analytical function of the brain, although the left side ever refers to the feminine, creative, receptive capacities of the mind and body. Intense emotional experiences may bewilder, or lead to an ability to separate emotional involvement from the cool head of assessment. "Physical enlightenment" can come from stubbing one's toe on a material object: kickability is a very pragmatic way to determine what is real. Shining a light on the matter literally makes one's steps easier to take.

Apply this degree-pair with a mind to physical manifestations that evoke empathy and insight. Watch for new ways to understand personal, emotional, spiritual, and physical reality. Taking the path to the left may literally illumine many things: walking the path less traveled; being brainy at the body's expense; physical well-being in accordance with one's philosophical leanings; the clumsy professor. Consider sudden shifts in one's path of life; poetic sensibilities born out of trust; pragmatic applications for effective purposes; belief in fact or belief in faith; idealizing the everyday.

"A topsy saucily asserting herself" (12 Gemini) and "A flag that turns into an eagle that crows" (12 Sagittarius)

Aspect: Opposition.
Quality: Awareness of.
Shared motifs: 'Piquing awareness,' 'animating brilliant points.'

"A topsy saucily asserting herself" is an image of boldness coming from an unexpected source, like a slave being boldly assertive to the master. "Topsy" is the name of a fictional character, a black slave child, in Harriet Beecher Stowe's *Uncle Tom's*

Cabin. The implication is that of speaking with apparent disrespect to one's superiors; adding a dash of excitement to a situation; adding piquancy to a dish. "Piquing awareness" can make things interesting, like adding spice to the pot: provocative spice arousing interest. It can also evoke resentment, a feeling of inappropriate, impudent behavior.

"A flag that turns into an eagle that crows" is an image of an inanimate symbol coming to life and triumphantly expressing itself. A flag attached to a pole is a standard designating a country, state, or organization. It may be a signal to stop, perhaps due to an urgent need or danger. When a standard or condition of a thing or state grows weak, it is said to be flagging. "An eagle" is a majestic bird of prey. The constellation "Aquila," the Eagle, contains the bright star "Altair." The American flag, the "Stars and Stripes," together with the bald or American eagle, are the two best-known symbols of America. "Crow" is the constellation "Corvus." "To crow" is to exult or boast.

When questioned about her origins, Topsy in *Uncle Tom's Cabin* replied, "I just growed." One can imagine a slave girl boldly asserting herself; how piqued her masters may be at such impudence. When certain standards are turned upside down, they are said to be topsy-turvy. Societal convention would like to have things on the straight and narrow, but they are sometimes thrown into confusion. The sauce for a dish may cause a stir, leading one to say, "That tops everything!" Carrying a flag signals the stripes one wears. Awareness of issues for debate can become very animated, especially if one goes directly to the point, as the crow flies, so to speak. To some, this may be unsavory; to others, just the bit of spice to pick things up.

Apply this degree-pair with a mind to an awareness of experiences that defy one's version of reality; startling revelations that bring everything to life; standing up for the flag, for the establishment, or for expressing unsavory aspects of the establishment. Watch for words, works, or writings that take on a life of their own; soaring, pompous pride; exultation in symbolic righteousness. Listen for spicy interjections, shrill opinionation, saucy controversy, stiff calls for allegiance, staunch defense of weak positions. Consider breaking through invisible barriers; defying prejudices; flying in the face of bias; the unlikely hero; being candid; being independent in word and deed; a knack for naively exposing prejudice; an affinity for spicy foods or anything that sharply enhances an experience.

"A great musician at his piano" (13 Gemini) and "A widow's past is brought to light" (13 Sagittarius)

Aspect: Trine.
Quality: Maintaining.
Shared motifs: 'Playing on the past,' 'a symphony of feelings,' 'musical dynamics.'

"A great musician at his piano" is an image of a person of accomplished talent sitting at a chosen instrument of expression. "Greatness" is that which is incomparable, that which surpasses the ordinary and suggests mastery. A "piano" is a musical instrument of the percussion family comprising a wooden box containing a metal soundboard, and metal strings which are struck with felt-covered hammers operated by pressing the black and white keys of the keyboard. "Piano" is also a musical dynamic designating quiet. "Great musicians" often play masterworks from the past. Some are known for technical mastery or an exacting precision devoid of personal flavor or spice; and some for a great command of highly expressive personal interpretation.

"A widow's past is brought to light" is an image of a revelation evoking sympathy, empathy, a dramatic tinge of pathos. A "widow" is a woman who has lost her husband through death. Imagine striking situations where a person's past sorrows are inadvertently brought to light. The entire atmosphere changes in tone, like a dramatic shift from major to minor key of a musical piece; a high pitch is dampened during a grave moment; a fast and lively discussion changes to a somber tempo: *vivace* turns *adagio*. Things brought back from the past into the present can stir admiration and appreciation, or awaken memories of sorrow and grief. Casting a spotlight on an issue can highlight a well-rehearsed accomplishment or draw attention to a tendency to dwell in the past, turning something over and over again in the mind.

Concert pianists dress in black, but can perform for an audience expressing rousing approval. A widow is dressed in black, but she might be smiling, enraptured in a warm memory.

Commanding center stage can be achieved through talent and hard work, or by dramatic emotional manipulation. The essence of the matter lies in whether the flavor of greatness is brought forward, or whether the spice has lost its piquancy, gone stale, become old news. A "great musician" may lord it over his pupils while they slavishly practice their scales. A moving piece of music may strike an overwhelming emotional chord for a widow, revealing a sad, lingering tone that slowly diminishes.

Apply this degree-pair with a mind to the effort to maintain command of the dynamic range of emotions and pathos; keeping one's past quiet behind a proud and brave face; attempting to remain composed when past sufferings are suddenly revealed. Watch for center-stage indulgences, emotional dwelling; emotional vibrations that continue to linger; putting a damper on a lively situation. Listen for grave undertones; voices that cannot hide emotion; imposing a formal posture on a full scale of emotional highs and lows. Consider one piece of music that brings back a trenchant memory; a penchant for an "Irish Wake"; playing past masters; comeback capacities; preferring only the white keys.

"A conversation by telepathy" (14 Gemini) and "The Pyramids and the Sphinx" (14 Sagittarius)

Aspect: Square.
Quality: Challenging.
Shared motifs: 'Monument, memory, and mystery,'
'intimacy beyond the senses.'

"A conversation by telepathy" is an image of communing without spoken words. "Telepathy" is comprised of *tele,* complete, and *pathy, pathos,* feeling or suffering, meaning a "felt intimacy with" someone or something. Humans communicate silently at all times, but silent conversation embraces a strange territory, characterized as extrasensory communication. To be beyond the senses is an inscrutable matter evoking a sense of mystery and enigma. Experiencing complete intimacy that communicates beyond the senses is like being in close touch with that which cannot be touched, such as a deeply felt memory of someone or something from the past with which one converses.

"The Pyramids and the Sphinx" is an image of mystery and monumental wonder. The "Sphinx," a mythological figure of an animal body such as a lion, with a human head, usually a woman's, is the quintessential symbol of mystery. The riddle of the Sphinx is a question about the three ages of man, which, if not answered correctly, would bring about one's demise. "Pyramids" are monuments to the dead, a funerary complex within which a narrow throatlike passageway leads to the inner sacred chamber or temple. Together, the Pyramids and the Sphinx pose an enigma, a hidden mystery that is inscrutable, defying close examination; a riddle, the answer to which cannot be spoken.

To be "sphinxlike" is to be inscrutable, evoking a sense of mystery, enigmatic. "Sphinx" is related to the Greek *sphingein,* to close, to strangle, hence things about which it is difficult to say anything, choking on your words, trouble spitting it out. "To scrutinize" is to examine bit by bit, like tearing a piece of fabric into shreds of cloth: rags. Anyone claiming to be "telepathic" may take a ragging from those un-sympathetic to such matters. On close examination, there may be nothing there, nothing of substance. Perhaps one struggles to speak, or words are caught in the throat. Getting inside the heart of the matter may take an inner sense, a kind of com-muning that defies speech, logic, and reason. Monumental questions are, in one sense, questions that reach far back in time, monuments to the dead, focal points for communing with a great mystery beyond. Stone monuments are impenetrable, phys-ical symbols of that which is buried deep within.

Apply this degree-pair with a mind to the challenge of understanding monumental and enduring memories; a felt sense of communing beyond words; the need to give weight to one's thoughts and impressions. Think of intimacy in thought and feeling; knowing because one feels; philosophies based on past sufferings. Listen for quiet tones; chanting; droning; suppressed expression, throat issues, unspeakable matters. Consider intimate affinities with the past; awareness of insubstantial presences; the use of enigma to control or manipulate; the use of mystery to make a deeper impression.

"Two Dutch children talking" (15 Gemini)
and "The groundhog looking for its shadow" (15 Sagittarius)

Aspect: Quintile.
Quality: Creative genius.
Shared motifs: 'Double identity; double meanings,'
'spectral brothers.'

"Two Dutch children talking" is an image of a conversation in a shared foreign, yet recognizable language. Dutch as a spoken language has a long and venerable history, yet to those who do not speak Dutch, it may sound incomprehensible. Children often make up a secret language of their own. The very young seem to communicate in sincere gibberish. "Dutch children" hail from the Netherlands, a country so named as to describe the areas below sea level that depend on dikes to defend arable land from the sea. The underworld as the realm of the dead recalls the "the Flying Dutchman," a spectral ship said to portend disaster.

"The groundhog looking for its shadow" is an image of a heightened sense of alertness or wary regard for what might lie behind. A shadow can only be cast on a sunlit day. "Groundhog Day" is a festival day based on whether a groundhog, upon waking from hibernation, can see its shadow or not. If the groundhog sees its shadow, it is said to portend six more weeks of cold winter weather. Seeing one's shadow is to see an insubstantial other, one that is not you, but is entirely dependent for its existence upon you. One who casts no shadow in the light of day is not among the living.

"Two children" is a double situation. "Going Dutch" is sharing the expense equally. A "Dutch door" is a door split in two horizontally, allowing top and bottom to swing open independently. "Double Dutch" can mean incomprehensible talk or refer to a children's game of skipping that uses two skipping ropes, held by two children, turned in opposite directions, like a double cross, if you will pardon the double-entendre. "Me and my double" refers to that which is ever with me, yet is not me. English-speaking people use "Dutch" in a bewildering array of humorous, if slightly derogatory, expressions: a "Dutchman's drink" is the last one in the bottle; one can be in "dutch": trouble; give or catch "dutch": heck or a scolding; or be "dutch lucky": benefit from undeserved luck.

Apply this degree-pair with a mind to communication that is a bit of a stretch, hard to understand, speaking of matters beyond the ordinary. Watch for themes of pairs, doubles, twinning. Look for being attached to one's shadow motif; being aware of a shadow; creating a private language shared with one other; a creative use of word doubles; a fascination with things like "Atlantis," an island overwhelmed by the sea; with netherlands, the shadowy realm of the dead. Listen for voice traits that are garbled, or a proclivity for double talk, or words playing on two meanings: the double-entendre. Consider finding ingenious ways to speak what is difficult to express; bringing humor to mystery; neologisms; clever approaches to difficult matters; making the impossible seem plausible.

"A woman suffragist orating" (16 Gemini) and "Seagulls watching a ship" (16 Sagittarius)

Aspect: Conjunction.
Quality: Focus.
Shared motif: 'On one's own day, one's words are believed.'

"A woman suffragist orating" is an image of an expressed opinion in favor of someone or something, historically associated with women's right to vote.[1] "Vocalizing" one's view in support of an issue suggests a public voicing of a social condition expressed passionately, with conviction. "Suffrage" refers to seeking the right to vote, to be counted, an entreaty for a decisive right, support, or sustenance through organized protest. "Oratory" is the art of formal speech, a focused application of the voice for specific public and social issues.

"Seagulls watching a ship" is an image of a vigilant attendance to a potential source of food and nourishment. "Seagulls" are well known for their shrill chorus that pierces the air whenever there is a scrap of food over which to fight. However, "seagulls watching" suggests waiting with silent intent, focused on a shipload of potentials. Seagulls watch for scraps of food discarded from ships or picnic tables in the park. Imagine a seaside park where many people are eating lunch. A woman may be standing on a soapbox in eloquent oration about rights when someone tosses a half-eaten sandwich away. Suddenly a dozen gulls are shrieking so loudly over the prize to be won and hastily swallowed that the woman's voice can no longer be heard.

Not everything tossed your way is easy to swallow. Even gulls reject some, albeit few, things. One may be gullible when it comes to matters of social justice, accepting a few scraps of oratorical platitude from authorities who bestow such pronouncements. One may be full of vigor at the call to speak out against obvious inequities, encouraged by the surrounding support of others who cry out in unison of voice and purpose. It helps to have a sharp eye for the right time to strike, as it were, the right time to speak in order to ensure the greatest effectiveness of one's words. Inhabitants living by the sea soon learn to tune out shrieking cries of hungry seagulls.

Apply this degree-pair with a mind for a sense of the right time to have one's words heard and believed. Watch for situations where the squeaky wheel gets the grease; where one just tunes out all the squawking. Turning a deaf ear on issues voiced may only lead to an uproar later on when some scrap of information is dropped. A vigilant, sharp eye watches for the moment when one is least likely to be duped. Consider characteristics of pride, brash airs of entitlement, shrill vocal qualities, farsightedness, and astute instincts for sizing up a situation; appetite dominating intellect; indignation ruining appetite; feeling one has to shout to have an equal say; a tendency to be led by the loudest social voice; refusal to be quiet when sensing that something is wrong.

"The head of health dissolved into the head of mentality" (17 Gemini) and "An Easter sunrise service" (17 Sagittarius)

Aspect: Opposition.
Quality: Awareness of.
Shared motif: 'Health, sacrifice, disintegration, and renewal.'

"The head of health dissolved into the head of mentality" is an image of an outgrowth from one situation into another; from well-being into a refined intellectual awareness of an issue that comes to a head. "A head of health dissolved" is not necessarily negative. "Dissolving" is a process of disintegration, a necessary phase of growth from one condition into another. For example, one may be happy with something when, through growing awareness, the idea or belief begins to fall apart. Health conditions lead, through a process of disintegration, to an awareness of higher ideas, to an awareness of higher manifestations.

"An Easter sunrise service" is an image of a communal gathering for a ritual ceremony concerning rebirth, renewal, and resurrection.[2] In its Christian context, "Easter" is a day of rejoicing and feasting after the fasting and penance of Lent. Both "Easter" and "sunrise" are associated with renewed life, as is the Easter egg tradition. "Service" implies an action that benefits or helps another or a community. There is an element of sacrifice involved in serving another: one gives up an independent, integrated sense of oneself in order to serve some other, higher purpose.

One might sacrifice one's health to serve an idea or ideal. One might fast for forty days in order to purify or renew oneself: enhance one's awareness of a higher reality or belief. It may seem counterintuitive that wasting away could be good for your health. Eggheads tend to be something less than the epitome of health. Sometimes, like Humpty Dumpty, mental and physical health is hard to put back together again:

the process of dissolving, of positive disintegration, presupposes growing beyond current conditions into something else, not piecing back together a previous situation.

Apply this degree-pair with a mind for positive disintegration: dissolving into a higher awareness that benefits both oneself and others; and not-so-positive disintegration: sacrificial deterioration of a healthy condition for the sake of an idea. Creative growth can have a decadent aspect: sacrificing one's own health, like an eccentric writer or artist, for the general well-being of the public. Watch for "Humpty Dumpty" motifs: ideals constructed like a high wall; falling from one's lofty conceptions; attempting to piece oneself together again; renewal that can't be constructed or engineered. Consider sublimation; food for thought; living off ideas alone; awareness of the higher meanings of food and sustenance; concern for feeding the hungry; convictions regarding not living by bread alone.

"Two Chinese men talk Chinese" (18 Gemini) and "Tiny children in sunbonnets" (18 Sagittarius)

Aspect: Trine.
Quality: Maintaining.
Shared motifs: 'Maintaining one's own world,'
'a protective veil.'

"Two Chinese men talk Chinese" is an image of a conversation in a foreign language. The Chinese language derives from a different language stream than Indo-European languages such as English. It has tones and rhythms foreign to the English ear. From the perspective of someone who speaks only English, the first experience of hearing Chinese spoken evokes a sense of strangeness, yet amazement and tacit recognition that something is indeed being communicated. From the point of view of the two Chinese men, talking in Chinese is like a return to a familiar, safe place: they are at home in the world of their shared language. "Two Chinese men talk Chinese" in order to protect and preserve their language and culture; they join together in a common language to deflect complete estrangement.

"Tiny children in sunbonnets" is an image of the vulnerable innocence of youth in the full light of the sun, protected by only bonnets. A "sunbonnet" for tiny children is usually made of soft cotton, provides a protective covering for the neck, has a brim framing the face, and ties under the chin. When the very young are talking, having a bonny chin wag, it hardly sounds different than listening to Chinese men talking Chinese: a foreign and bewildering world of jabbering and gesticulation, a mix of staccato and legato with singing tones. It matters little what the language is. Two Scotsmen, with their bonnets or tams, can leave outsiders bewildered by their bonny brogue.

Sunbonnets protect and shelter from the sun: the full light of reality that can burn "wee bairns." If we wear our language, whatever language that may be, like a sheltering and protective hat, we might become insulated from all the many ways of communicating under the sun. If, on the other hand, we remove the assumption of our primary means of communicating, of organizing our thoughts and our world, as we might remove a hat, the world of communication becomes vastly richer, more delightful, strange, and marvelous at the same time. Sometimes exposure can bring danger and prejudice; sometimes a protective veil arouses suspicion simply by looking and sounding different.

Apply this degree-pair with a mind to protecting and preserving identity through shared ideas and ideals; maintaining stability under a cover of safe protection; renewing a sense of belonging through ways of communicating held in common. Watch for strangeness; otherworld, foreign, gibberish as opposed to rational linear speech; a sense of being in a world of one's own. Be alert for framed faces; hats of all kinds: berets, tams, caps, headdresses. Consider shelter and protection; paranoia, suspicion, and ridicule; secret or private languages; a round face, a brimming smile, a framed face, youthful health, wagging chins.

"A large archaic volume" (19 Gemini) and "Pelicans moving their habitat" (19 Sagittarius)

Aspect: Square.
Quality: Challenging.
Shared motifs: 'Moves that bring traditions with them,'
'preservation and assimilation.'

"A large archaic volume" is an image of an antiquated work no longer in general use. Imagine large scrolls from an ancient culture that are protected for special purposes such as preserving a language, or as an example of how things used to be. In terms of contemporary usage, the volumes are obsolete. In terms of archival interests, the volumes are exquisite treasures to be maintained, studied, kept alive for purposes that transcend practical usage.

"Pelicans moving their habitat" is an image of a community of waterfowl moving en masse to a new home. Perhaps the intrusion of man and his attendant insistence on practical, profitable use of land has caused the pelicans to seek a new home. Imagine wetlands being drained; shorelines being fouled with pollutants; the loud roar of heavy equipment crowding out the natural inhabitants. Mass migration to find a new home can come about for many reasons, but usually comes down to a few archaic necessities: food, livelihood, finding a home, escape from peril.

"Pelicans" are noted for their large bills, the lower portion being a hanging pouch for holding fish, food. This allows them to carry their food long distances and, in a manner of speaking, stretches their gastronomic possibilities. Immigrants may bring their own food, their own cuisine, to a new country. Preserving archaic or traditional foods can enrich contemporary tastes, such as having dinner out in Chinatown where one is never sure what it is you have just ordered. Sometimes one wonders what all the noise is about or finds ancient fare unappetizing: "Help yoursel' to a wee bit o' ma haggis laddy!"

All manner of things can be stretched to large and loud proportions, such as a written tome entitled *On Haggis: A Short History of Its Origins and Preparation in Six Volumes: The Early Years: Part I*. Perhaps the mouth is big or what is said is overly loud, overly long, or just plain obsolete. Perhaps an old recipe becomes the new thing in a new land, such as Essene bread based on a biblical recipe. The challenge lies in the mixing of new lands and new foods, old foods and new lands, old ideas about eating, new ideas about food in ethnic enclaves of foreign communities.

Apply this degree-pair with a mind to the melting pot of language, food, and culture; the struggle to fit in with a world of diversity. Watch for gregarious manifestations of culture, tradition, habitat. Obsolescence for one may be a call for preservation to another. Think of Latin or Sanskrit, dead languages kept alive by scholars, lengthy works or works of longevity; a preference for the old ways in a new world, such as hearing Mass in Latin. Listen for loud voices; a knack for mimicking accents; voluminous stories. Consider the challenges of eating new foods, living in new lands, mixing disparate ways of life; isolationist tendencies; seeking sustenance with which one can live.

"A cafeteria" (20 Gemini)
and "Men cutting through ice" (20 Sagittarius)

Aspect: Quintile.
Quality: Creative genius.
Shared motifs: 'Food as a social catalyst,'
'warmth while eating in common.'

"A cafeteria" is an image of a highly systematized way of serving food to many people. The genius of "a cafeteria" lies in the efficiency of keeping hot dishes warm, fresh foods cool, and serving large numbers of people. The creative systems serve to keep things warm efficiently in order to serve many in a short time. This can lead to factory-like processing in order to serve food and move people along. The cafeteria system of serving food has the potential to offer a wide variety of cuisines offering an international selection, making everyone, in some small way, feel at home.

"Men cutting through ice" is an image of thought for a future season. "Cutting through ice" harkens back to earlier times when it was necessary to carve blocks of ice from a frozen lake in preparation for the hot summer. Blocks of ice were stored in ice houses, houses covered with sod in order to preserve the frozen ice through summer. The icebox, a precursor to the refrigerator, was kept cool with blocks of ice as needed. "Cutting ice," therefore, is creative thought for the future, pragmatic thought of a seasonal, cyclic sort. Cutting through ice is a hard task, like attempting to get a date with someone very cool toward you; however, the communal chore was often augmented by a wee dram or two in order to keep the spirits warm and help matters along.

Thought for efficiency in a cafeteria can have people lining up with trays making selections from whatever is served up. Ice cut in winter can be efficiently hauled on a skid with runners over the ice and snow. "Breaking the ice" derives from breaking harbor ice to allow ships to come and go, hence, to dispel social stiffness and reserve. In a cafeteria, diners are all the same, eating common food in a communal fashion. Despite the cool manner of service, there is plenty of food available. The ice cutters perform a service dealing with cold things in a warm way. This service-task allows for the preservation of plentiful food throughout a season when the rate of perishing is normally fast: creatively slowing decay; stretching the life of perishables.

Apply this degree-pair with a mind for service genius that skillfully handles issues of hot and cold; creating an atmosphere that encourages future communal gatherings; creating a sense of welcomeness and belonging. Watch for ice sculpting; food display and presentation; get-it-while-it's-hot immediacies. Be alert for attitudes of acceptance where differences cut little or no ice; that regard social and cultural differences in the context of being one big family. Consider efficiency, smooth delivery especially as a vocal manner, sliding things along, ice skating; using food to break the ice, to develop relationships; balancing ideals with day-to-day practicalities of sustenance.

"A labor demonstration" (21 Gemini) and "A child and a dog with borrowed eyeglasses" (21 Sagittarius)

Aspect: Conjunction.
Quality: Focus.
Shared motifs: 'Magnifying perspectives,'
'Looking at things in new ways.'

"A labor demonstration" is an image of a practical exhibition or explanation intended to transmit know-how. Imagine a father showing his young son how his reading glasses magnify the print on the page in order to aid his reading capabilities. A labor demonstration may be a show of discontent on the part of workers, laborers, who might march "en masse'" in public to bring attention to their views. However, a "demonstration" is not a "strike." It does not bring the wheels of industry to a grinding halt. "To demonstrate" is to express or show some matter: feelings; opinions; usage; political views. The mood of the demonstration is an open question. The focus within this symbol is on the "how to," on proving something, on magnifying how one feels about such and such.

"A child and a dog with borrowed eyeglasses" is an image of a playful situation between child and dog that puts a whole new perspective on things. "Borrowed eyeglasses" are glasses temporarily acquired for some purpose, the intention being, as with all things children borrow from their parents, to return them in good order. Imagine a boy who has placed his father's eyeglasses on his dog, speaking with authoritative sincerity about how everything will look better. The dog looks hilarious to an outsider, and one can only wonder what the world looks like from the perspective of a dog wearing eyeglasses. There you have it! A demonstration of the proper and effective use of eyeglasses for dogs!

A demonstration to show how something works magnifies the finer points of know-how. In a cafeteria, you might have to be walked through the routine: shown where you get your tray; the order of food and drink as it is laid out; and the position of the cashier where one pays for the meal. One might show, in exaggerated, slow demonstration, the steps to a dance being taught. A "demonstrative crowd" is one that is openly amplifying their feelings. Perspective is everything. The world, viewed through borrowed lenses, can shift assumptions, cause one to see things in a different light. It is perhaps worthy of note that the gardens with water lilies, viewed through Monet's exceedingly poor eyesight, led to some of the world's most beloved paintings.

Apply this degree-pair with a mind to know-how exhibited, explained, and transmitted to others. Watch for magnified feelings, details, skills, and procedures; demonstrative self-expression. No need to belabor the mood of the matter: a tumultuous demonstration about inequities, or a hilarious glimpse of the world through another's spectacles. Issues of focus, blurred perspectives, poor eyesight, improving vision: all can manifest whenever two differing views interact. Consider self-deprecation through an awareness of different ways of seeing life: through a child's eyes; through the eyes of a dog; through the eyes of laborers, scientists, logicians; the ability to show, to teach, to demonstrate with humor, these very different perspectives.

"A barn dance" (22 Gemini) and "A Chinese laundry" (22 Sagittarius)

Aspect: Opposition.
Quality: Awareness of.
Shared motif: 'Double-standard communication.'

"A barn dance" is an image of an informal social gathering for country dancing. Social gatherings within a barn centered on dances: square dancing, line dancing, circle dancing. Couples would move together or separately according to calls or cues, sometimes forming straight lines or woven queues. In a "square dance," partners interweave with three other couples, taking steps in unison and exchanging partners in a series of called moves: dos à dos; à la main left. Missing your cue can really mess up the queue in hilarious ways. Imagine ending up with the wrong partner after a series of miscues, missteps. A most enduring impression of barn dances and square dances is the inordinate amount of time devoted to explaining the calls.

"A Chinese laundry" is an image of taking on work that gains a foothold in a social economy. This symbol is an historical reference to Chinese immigrants striving to find ways to make a livelihood in a foreign, often intolerant, land. Chinese laundries arose in North American urban centers in the nineteenth century as a means to gain entry into the local economy, to get a foothold in a foreign society. "Laundry" derives from the Middle English *lander*, the French *laver,* to wash, and ultimately from lavender, a sweet aromatic shrub. The function of the laundry is to take in what is soiled and send it out clean; the soiled clothes are from those who can afford to have someone else, in a manner of speaking, do their dirty laundry.

At a barn dance, people come to a not-so-clean barn dressed in their finest, clean dancing duds. After a long night of dancing, people might take their soiled clothes to the Chinese laundry. Communication, in both scenarios, can be strange, like "Chinese whispers," a party game of relaying whispered messages to each participant in turn, ending in a distorted communication at the end. Understanding a square-dance caller is a little like trying to follow a strange code. Working in the close quarters of a laundry must have been very much like a square dance: everyone has to move properly and efficiently in order to iron out the wrinkles.

Apply this degree-pair with a mind to an awareness of a foreign perspective; of misunderstandings about others that are passed along; misunderstandings that perpetuate divisions. Watch for entry-level jobs or services; working in pairs; efficient moves in close quarters. Listen for the cues, foreign-language influences, cross-cultural slang. Be alert for social perceptions concerning being clean or being soiled; for being stuck with someone else's dirty laundry. Consider stepping to one's own tune; resenting stepping to someone else's tune; dancing shoes; gaiety; nosegay; lavender; receiving what is dirty; giving back what has been cleaned; braided hair, pigtails, pleats, and plaits; weaving dance steps; perceiving others to be out of place; stepping on others' toes out of misunderstandings and misapprehensions.

"Three fledglings in a nest high in a tree" (23 Gemini) and "Immigrants entering" (23 Sagittarius)

Aspect: Trine.
Quality: Maintaining.
Shared motifs: 'Harbingers of a passage in life,'
'trepidatious excitement.'

"Three fledglings in a nest high in a tree" is an image of young birds not yet ready to fly, in a safe, secure home, high in a tree. A "fledgling" is a young bird whose feathers are still forming. "Feathering," in this case, is about growing into one's abilities and capacities, rather than making something comfortable. Imagine birds just before taking their first flight: a tenuous, trepidatious moment; "Ready, set, not quite go!" A "nest high in a tree" is a place of safety and signifying familiarity with a well-rooted home. The young birds sing, or squawk, loudly whenever the parent birds fly near with food. A bird's song expresses identity and a kind of bravado: "This is who we are, our clan, our family, and we are safe high in our tree!"

"Immigrants entering" is an image of the moments before setting foot in a new land, a new home. Like immigrants on ships viewing the Statue of Liberty while approaching Ellis Island, there is an intense sense of expectancy: a symbol of being one step away from freedom and independence. Imagine the feelings: the pain of having left one's homeland; the excitement of the possibilities that open up after taking the first step in a new land. Immigrants must exercise patience while waiting for the process to take its course, and intense impatience to get on with it.

Little birds sing the tune of their family or species. Having voracious appetites, they sing for their supper with competitive insistence: "Me first!" Immigrants may sing or hum songs of their homeland. New tunes lie ahead. Fledglings are impatient to leave the nest; immigrants have left the nest, but have not yet set foot on the new land. Fledglings have yet to stretch their wings in flight in the open air; immigrants wait to stretch their legs on firm land. The new world lies ahead; the old world lies behind. Immigrants may carry a "nest egg," money laid aside, an allusion to placing a china egg in a hen's nest to encourage the laying of eggs. Without a "nest egg," a new immigrant could be "up a tree" or "out on a limb" in a new land.

Apply this degree-pair with a mind to attempting to remain rooted in one's sense of home while being faced with resettlement; the moment before a new independent life takes off; trepidatious excitement; impatient waiting; attachments to the security of home. Think of transition points in life: the passage to a new life, a new level of maturity, conflicting emotions about what lies just ahead but is still out of reach. Listen for songs of home and nationality, the voice of insistent impatience; naively giving away your identity and location; singing for your supper because you are not yet ready to fly for your own. Consider trembling in the face of being received; eagerness to leap into freedom; having to sublimate the sense of home or the nesting instinct to a higher level.

"Children skating on ice" (24 Gemini)
and "A bluebird standing at the door of the house" (24 Sagittarius)

Aspect: Square.
Quality: Challenge.
Shared motifs: 'The challenge of getting out into the world,'
'the promise of rewards that await outside.'

"Children skating on ice" is an image of unsteady legs trying to move forward on un-familiar terrain. "Skating" is a slippery affair: getting used to standing on a slick sur-face; taking new steps to move forward. Children exemplify these tremulous mo-ments of motion when they first step onto an icy surface with their first pair of skates, like immigrants taking their first steps on land after a long journey. It may take a while to find one's legs. "Ice" is a surface of frozen water over which one can potentially glide with grace and ease. There may be concern over whether the ice is thick enough to support one's weight.

"A bluebird standing at the door of the house" is an image of beginnings that bode happiness, and fortunate possibilities just outside the door. When fledglings leave home, they are outside the door, into the wide world of their own. When immi-grants set up a new home in a new land, they can sense the promise of good things that may lie ahead, just outside the door. Imagine the mixed sense of a sad, blue, longing for the homeland, and the possibilities for happiness that the new land por-tends. The cheerful call and warbling song of the bluebird is a harbinger of the ap-proaching spring, the symbol of new life, promise, and regeneration.

Imagine children skating on a frozen pond and their shouts of vigor and joy. The better skaters glide gracefully, having found their legs. The less adept skaters wobble and are possibly frustrated by their struggle to push off, to make some headway. The world awaits outside one's door: it sings alluring songs of rewards; it bodes dangers and frustration as well. One may be skating on thin ice when an alarming "Crack!" is heard. One may fall hard on cold, harsh realities.

Apply this degree-pair with a mind to the challenge of stepping out onto the ice of a new life; finding one's legs in a new world. Look for outlooks of optimism, hopefulness, cheerful eagerness, mixed with apprehension about the solidity of one's foundations. Cheerful rewards that await one may be pure happenstance: to be in the right place at the right time. Or they may be rewards for hard effort that eventually makes things glide more easily. Listen for bright, cheerful calls; warbling, songlike voices; halting voices. Consider all things blue: the blues, nostalgia for home, happiness, blue skies, blue blood, blue from cold, blue baby, blue powder for laundry, lavender, blue-collar worker, blue-rinsed hair, open seas, blue moon, blue movies, out-of-the-blue good fortune.

"A man trimming palms" (25 Gemini) and "A chubby boy on a hobbyhorse" (25 Sagittarius)

Aspect: Quintile.
Quality: Creative genius.
Shared motifs: 'Victory in the palm of one's hand,'
'finesse, fineness, and flourish.'

"A man trimming palms" is an image of grooming, cultivating growth, and putting a personal finish on a personal victory. A "palm tree" is a tree without branches having a mass of fan-shaped leaves high at the top. The palm frond is shaped like the out-spread human hand, hence it is associated with the palm of the hand. A symbol of victory or excellence, palm fronds were awarded to victorious Roman gladiators and strewn along the path as Christ triumphantly entered Jerusalem. "Trimming" means to make neat or add a touch of fineness to something. One may cut away old growth from a plant in order to show it in its best light. "Catching a fair breeze" means in nautical terms to possess good sailing skill for trimming one's sails.

"A chubby boy on a hobbyhorse" is an image of a child playing with a toy horse. "Hobbyhorse" refers both to a stick with a horse's head, and a rocking horse. By extension, anything that was a favorite pastime of amusement became one's hobby, one's preoccupation or favorite topic for conversation. "A chubby boy" is an over-weight boy, thick and round: well-fed. A horse is a symbol of power. Placing the head of a horse on a stick gives one the idea of power. The "hobbyhorse" derives from the traditional English "Morris dance," performed during May Day pageants celebrating the return of the "green man" and the verdant season of growth.

"Trimming palms" would appear to be a matter of tidying up since the palm tree has no branches, its crown being elevated high on top. The head of a horse affixed on top of a stick adorns or embellishes one's amusement. Rocking to and fro recalls skaters gracefully striding across a frozen pond. The instrument used for trimming, and the hobbyhorse, are held in the palm of the hand, suggesting situations that are in one's own control.

Apply this degree-pair with a mind to a creative ease that trims away the old and celebrates the new; the sense of getting a hold of one's power; having a happy read of one's situation. Watch for crowning achievements won by one's own hand; personal touches; the height of personal amusement; or matters coming into hand. One might be going back and forth over the same ground or obsessing over the refinement of a singular pursuit. Consider the "Rocking Horse Winner": imagining victory until it is a reality; equine affinities; the rocking motions of procreation; swaying back and forth; phallic symbols; emerging sexual awareness; palmistry; a fascination with the care of the hands and nails; a knack for imagining what is true; rehearsing things over and over; cheerfully going back and forth while refining one's position in the world; optimism; sharing success with others easily.

"Winter frost in the woods" (26 Gemini) and "A flag bearer" (26 Sagittarius)

Aspect: Conjunction.
Quality: Focus.
Shared motifs: 'Finding warmth in cold exposure,'
'high standards that can melt away.'

"Winter frost in the woods" is an image of entrancing beauty where the fingers of frost spread to create a world of glimmering, glowing light. "Winter woods" are bare of leaves in a barren season. "Frost" is frozen water vapor that forms in clear, still weather on vegetation. The atmosphere of a winter frost in the woods seems to echo with hoary antiquity, hence hoar frost and the white beard of "Jack Frost." To be cold with frost is, strangely enough, connected with warmth: frost-bitten fingers have a tingling sensation that feels hot and itchy. A solution derived from "witch hazel," also called "winter bloom" because the plant blooms in the winter months while the twigs are bare, is an astringent used to alleviate itching. Walking through a frost-covered woods can be a bewitching, spell-like experience.

"A flag bearer" is an image of one who carries the flag of his troops into battle. Although it is an honor to bear this responsibility, the flag bearer is defenseless against attack while openly carrying a prize the enemy is keen on taking away. A "flag" bears one's colors much like winter bears its colors with frosted trees. "To bear" is to carry, withstand, stand under as in under a load. For advancing troops, the flag is always a focal point, and a reminder of that for which they fight. One might get the chills of pride while bearing the standard, or a chilling sense of being in a perilous situation while leading troops into the heat of battle.

The frosted branches of trees are stiff and brittle, suggestive of frosty human behavior such as a stiff handshake or an unfriendly reception. A forest covered with frost can arrest one with fascination in its beauty. White, frozen crystals of ice intensify light, creating an aura of magic and ice-blue wonder. A flagpole must be stiff enough to bear the flag, like the stout character of the flag bearer, upon whose courage and self-sacrificing uprightness the collective depends. The flag itself creates an aura of honor associated with collective past and tradition. One could easily find oneself under the spell of something greater than oneself: a national campaign; a corporate flagship; an obsessive itch or deep, wanton desire. "Breaking the ice," socially speaking, may depend on the colors of one's flag.

Apply this degree-pair with a mind for transforming the world, transforming life, through inspiration and crystalized standards of integrity. Watch for gray-white hair; cold, hard, or brittle standards to live up to; May-December relationships; a crystalized focus on goals; obsessions with experiences that burn like ice. Consider Ice Queen coldness; casting spells of a prurient nature; personal accents like frosted hair, rosy cheeks; a cool social demeanor; burning intensity within, aloofness without; branching out to try new talents, to try old talents kept in cold storage; enchanted by impersonal intimacies; receiving a frosty reception.

"A gypsy coming out of the forest" (27 Gemini) and "A sculptor" (27 Sagittarius)

Aspect: Opposition.
Quality: Awareness of.
Shared motifs: 'Flexibility and hardness,' 'leaving one's mark,' 'sang-froid: cool and collected under pressure.'

"A gypsy coming out of the forest" is an image of a member of a wandering people leaving the wilderness of the woods. The life of a "gypsy" is characterized by wandering, passionate music, an aura of knowing the future, and a said propensity for swindles and fraud. The "Gypsies," or "Romany," came by their name from a mistaken belief that they derived from Egypt. Historically, wherever they have migrated, they have been met with a frosty reception of suspicion and persecution. "Coming out of the forest" suggests emerging into an open vista where field meets forest.

"A sculptor" is an image of one who carves, who gives shape and form to a base material. A sculptor's medium may be a number of substances: wood, metal, plaster, clay. Thought of in terms of human character, giving shape to or forming character assumes the awareness of the possibilities that lie before one, like a sculptor with a vision of the possibilities contained in a block of wood. The sculptor, in one sense, releases the form of beauty from the uncarved block. The gypsy is, perhaps, releasing himself or herself from a life in the forest wilderness.

The sculptor's eye is on the lookout for pieces of wood holding interesting potential. The fields beyond the forest may be carved by the farmer's plow, suggesting a path to follow, a route carved toward a town or village. A gypsy leaving the forest suggests leaving the wilderness, the life of wandering. What lies ahead is still an unshaped mystery. Perhaps one has been out in the cold and is now headed toward the warmth of human habitation. Perhaps one wishes to leave one's mark in the world, like a sculptor carving lines into stone. The wanderer cannot be brusk in manner when entering a new community. Caution and gentleness are called for when one is a stranger in a strange land. A wanderer's stay may be temporary, a sojourn, yet still attract suspicion. Sculpting requires a gentle, penetrating regard for what shapes lie within an uncarved block. Heavy-handedness may ruin delicate potential: one must go with the grain.

Apply this degree-pair with a mind to character formation: oppression and suspicion may test one's character; the carving of a work of art must be in harmony with the material at hand, suggesting the exercise of character. Watch for wanderers; appearing like a gypsy; carving out new paths; an ability to finesse something out of raw material. Look for traits such as quietly infiltrating; secreting away; heavy-handed impositions that leave a scar; visions and ideals that are carved into stone. Flexibility of character, or the lack of it, suggests a gentleness, or the lack or it, through which to shape one's life. Consider a sense of feeling gypped; suspicion that may project ingrained bias onto others; an entrenched position; the outlook of one of no fixed abode.

"A man declared bankrupt" (28 Gemini)
and "An old bridge over a beautiful stream" (28 Sagittarius)

Aspect: Trine.
Quality: Maintaining.
Shared motifs: 'Solving or bridging a situation,'
'Though manmade structures become old and collapse,
life flows on like a beautiful stream.'

"A man declared bankrupt" is an image of an open proclamation of financial failure, an inability to carry the weight of obligations. "Bankrupt" is a term deriving from medieval Italy where moneylenders used a small bench, Latin *banca*, bench, in the marketplace to conduct their business. Should the moneylender's business fail, they were required to break their benches: hence *banca rupta*. To be "declared" is to be openly proclaimed, made known formally, emphatically. Declaration makes matters completely clear: calling a spade a spade. Someone is "declared bankrupt" by a higher authority issuing a decisive stroke of judgment. Sometimes such charges are all trumped up, mere rubbish or trumpery.

"An old bridge over a beautiful stream" is an image of an ancient structure that carries a path, a road, over a stream, from one bank to the other. "Bridgework" can cover the gap in the road, bear the weight of having to cross to the other side, trump a difficult situation by means of an overarching structure or power. A "stream" follows its course between two banks. One might choose to ford a beautiful stream on one's own. "An old bridge," however, is made of old planks, also used to make benches, arranged in a line, suggesting walking in the footsteps of those venerable ones who have gone before. Should the bank dissolve, an old bridge may become insolvent, and collapse.

Imagine a sculptor, with one decisive stroke of his hammer and chisel, rupturing his work of art. At first, all seems lost, unless he can pick up the pieces and start again. Imagine a gypsy walking a path that comes to a stream difficult to ford. Perhaps he can not afford the toll being exacted, or he is being declared morally bankrupt by someone in a position of authority. Both sculptor and gypsy look for ways to solve the difficulty. Life flows on like a "beautiful stream," ever affording new ways to bridge problems that arise. Insolvency can lead to bankruptcy, which, ironically, can release one from, solve, a lot of problems. A bridge is a solution to crossing a stream unless the banks weaken and dissolve. There is a natural flow of a beautiful stream: one can choose to go with the flow or against it.

Apply this degree-pair with a mind to solving difficulties in effective ways; bridging life situations; getting beyond apparent irresolvable difficulties. Watch for ingrained ways of doing things, ingrained beliefs that make a situation seem worse than it is. Failure in an everyday sense of life can bring release into a higher stream, therefore watch for struggling against the flow, or a natural sense of ease in crossing to another shore. Listen for social/political planks; emphatic attempts to shore up old beliefs or projections; using one's trump card to overrule; trumped-up charges in order to maintain the old ways. The issue is one of attitude: a sense of affording to trust in life, or feeling resourceless, always having to shore up, truss up, old broken ways.

"The first mockingbird in spring" (29 Gemini) and "A fat boy mowing the lawn" (29 Sagittarius)

Aspect: Square.
Quality: Challenge.
Shared motifs: 'Harbingers of new beginnings,'
'efforts in unfamiliar arenas.'

"The first mockingbird in spring" is an image of being alerted to the first signs of spring. The "mockingbird" is so called for its ability to mimic the songs of other birds, suggesting that one never really knows if what is heard is what it actually is. The first bird song of spring may be a sham, not the real thing, a mere imitation. When something sounds like something else, one can hear assonant connections, such as the first sounds heralding spring. Spring is the season when things begin to grow, the first stages of new vegetation, suggesting resilience: the natural ability to spring back to life.

"A fat boy mowing the lawn" is an image of a person unaccustomed to labor cutting down grass in an open area. "Mowing" is an activity associated with harvesting, reaping: the opposite of sowing, scattering seeds about. An overweight boy may benefit from the exercise of cutting down the grass. It might be the first bit of exercise in a long time, much like the first day of jogging, the first workout. In northern climates, it can be humorous to see how early people get outside to mow the lawn, so glad are they for the approaching spring. "Lawn" derives from glade, an open clearing in the woods. One might be glad to hear the first robin of spring, even if it turns out to be the mimicking mockingbird.

Although one may be happy to hear the first signs of spring, the challenge lies in correctly identifying what, or who, has been heard. Reaping rewards from hard labor seems an uncomplicated, good thing. One might be challenged by mocking ridicule at first: "Hey, fat boy! Hurry up with that lawn before winter comes!" As one crosses over to a new land, or into a new season, there is a sense of uncertainty, awkwardness, regarding what is realistic. One might bust a gut by prematurely striving for what is really beyond one's reach or capabilities; or, bust a gut with laughter or merriment. The question is: what tips the scales from working out, to overwork; from laughing with, in joy, to laughing at, in ridicule?

From the sounds of things, many assumptions can be made. A sharp "Crack!" from a plank on an old bridge or bench may alert one to an impending collapse. A certain bird song can alert one to an impending change of season. Loud grunts and groans while mowing a lawn may signal that one is not in physical condition for the task at hand. The situation calls for a realistic assessment. The question is: are these glad tidings of spring that inspire renewal or cruel mockery; do the efforts of glad perspiration in unfamiliar toil, promising rich rewards, put a spring in one's step, or unrealistic, insubstantial expectations of achievement?

Apply this degree-pair with a mind to new beginnings that are in process; sounds that herald a new season or area of activity; situations that call for a discriminating awareness; struggles to begin a new phase. Look for the initial stages of efforts that hope to reap the rewards of seeds that are sown. Consider issues regarding laughing, mimicry, mocking, ridicule. One may have an ear for harbingers of coming times, or an ability to identify who or what really cuts sway: a sense of the feasible, realistic greatness.

"Bathing beauties" (30 Gemini) and "The Pope" (30 Sagittarius)

Aspect: Quintile.
Quality: Creative genius.
Shared motifs: 'Giving an audience,' 'the eye of blessing.'

"Bathing beauties" is an image suggesting a public display of beauty with the intention of being seen. Imagine a fashion runway where the standards of beauty walk in the latest beachwear. Imagine a popular beach where large crowds of people gather, many of whom are alert for a good look at passing bathing beauties. "Bathing" is an act of cleansing, such as washing in water, hence, the beauties may be nude, free from all artifice. A truly beautiful sight commands all eyes and attention; a disappointing show leaves one feeling all washed out.

"The Pope" is an image of the human and worldly representative of the divine, the head of the Roman Catholic Church, the sovereign or supreme Pontiff. "Pontifex" and "pontiff" refer to the supreme Father of church hierarchy, who is characterized as being spiritually infallible. To "pontificate" is to pronounce dogmatically with an attitude that may be, in lesser mortals, pompous. "Infallibility" suggests a genius for speech or action that is sure to succeed. Poetically, the pontiff is the bridge, the link to the divine. A primary function of the Pope, as spiritual father, is to bless. When the Pope gives audience to crowds of the faithful, he is there to see and to be seen, as in the Dharsan tradition in the Hindu and Buddhist religions.

Bathing beauties are dressed in order to be looked at, appreciated, smiled upon. Every human being appreciates being appreciated, being bathed in a kind regard that blesses. Most bathing suits are worn to be seen, rather than for actually swimming in water. In a social arena, bathing beauties vie for recognition and attention. A blessing from the Pope is akin to the act of "beatification," making blessed, sanctifying: the sacral equivalent to profane pleasing or smiling upon. A beatific smile exudes happiness and success. One feels blessed by another's smile, kind words, generous acts. It is like being washed clean, refreshed and cleansed in the eyes of another.

Apply this degree-pair with a mind to the ancient sense of audience: a hearing; the importance of seeing and being seen. Think of gathered assemblies of listeners or spectators where what is heard and seen brings joy and happiness. Watch for a creative flair for the right word, the right look, which is both pleased and pleasing: a knack for evoking the sought-for response. Consider ostentatious displays of fashion or style as opposed to expressions of natural beauty; dogmatic inflexibility as opposed to freely given approval. Consider an ease of gesture without any sweat; an uplifting tone of voice or looks, which do not mock; a sense of raw, naked, and open exposure, which radiates either success or pompous show; radiant moments of recognition and appreciation.

1. In his book *The Sabian Symbols in Astrology,* Marc Edmund Jones replaced the original word on the notecard, "orating," with "haranguing," cf. Diana E. Roche, *The Sabian Symbols: A Screen of Prophecy* (Victoria, B.C.: Trafford, 1998) p. 107.

2. M. E. Jones wrote and circled "early A.M." on the notecard, later changing it to "sunrise," cf. Roche, p. 291.

—⌒—

CHAPTER FOUR

CANCER-CAPRICORN

**"A furled and unfurled flag displayed from a vessel" (1 Cancer)
and "An Indian chief demanding recognition" (1 Capricorn)**

Aspect: Conjunction.
Quality: Focus.
Shared motif: 'Power going up and down a flagpole.'

"A furled and unfurled flag displayed from a vessel" is a twofold image of flying a symbol of one's colors, one's allegiances. A "furled flag" is one that is wrapped up, or bound, as in being tied to a mast. An "unfurled flag" is one that is unfolded, unrolled, allowed to hang freely. If a flag is "furled," it is not displayed, not flying: present, but not available for public view. "A vessel" is a container that can float in water, capable of transporting a cargo in its hold, or a "canal" that allows the flow, the transport of fluid. In a spiritual sense, man is a vessel capable of receiving, containing, and delivering the flow of life energy. The image suggests a twofold capacity of human endeavor: a double career, a double talent; two distinct stages of life, one replacing the other.

"An Indian chief demanding recognition" is an image of a show of personal power. A "chief" is someone who normally does not have to demand recognition, which suggests an emergent power. Claiming one's place, one's power, implies recognition from others. "Demanding recognition" suggests boldness and an authoritative manner, one that preemptively eliminates dissent. A "demand" can be a question, asking for something, with little or no room for alternatives, or it can be an authoritative, insistent claim.

Flags are raised on flagpoles or masts to the maximum height. An "unfurled flag" is surely at its peak or, at least, on the way up. If an "Indian chief" is on his way up, he may have to contend with his elders, to win their respect and recognition. A flag under wraps is one that cannot be recognized, since it cannot be seen. "To be recognized" is to be acknowledged: even the everyday greeting or salutation may be demanded. Imagine a claim to power that displaces the old power structure, such as a young Arthur pulling the sword from the stone. The other chieftains may object, protest, refuse acknowledgment. Since Arthur bursts onto the scene, an unknown contender, he must win recognition. Stepping down from power in a natural succession is like folding up one's flag, creating space for new colors to be flown.

Apply this degree-pair with a mind to issues of personal power and the dynamics of the process between furling and unfurling. Think of power potentials under wraps; bold displays of power. Look for changes of course in life; potentials that flap at the mercy of the breezes that blow. A demanding character may yet have to prove itself. Worthy vessels carry greatness to great heights; unworthy vessels may flounder from an inconstant or flagging sense of purpose. Consider shyness within, bravado without; tied-up or inflexible within, free-flowing and adaptable without.

"A man suspended over a vast level place" (2 Cancer) and "Three stained-glass windows, one damaged by bombardment" (2 Capricorn)

Aspect: Opposition.
Quality: Awareness of.
Shared motifs: 'The dangers inherent in the transition of power,' 'suspended animation.'

"A man suspended over a vast level place" is an image of uncertainty or indecision: being hung in suspension over an immense horizontal plane. An unfurled flag raised atop a flagpole is suspended over the level ground. "A man suspended" suggests being barred from where one belongs. Perhaps one has been promoted to chief but has to wait for a period of time, like a president-elect. "A vast level place" suggests an immense horizontal position. In human terms, everyone is said to be equal, to be on a level playing field. Leveling everyone down to the lowest common denominator is one thing; finding one's level relative to everyone else, one's position in a vertical dimension, is another.

"Three stained-glass windows, one damaged by bombardment" is an image of uniquely colored windows that have been subjected to an attempt to level them. Raising one's flag, claiming a high position, exposes one to challenges. Rivals may seek to tarnish your reputation; to fire off charges of a stained character; to point out character flaws. "Bombardment" is an attack with a number of bombs, or being bombarded with a flurry of persistent questions. "Bombs" can raze, such is their explosive power, entire cities, let alone damage a window. That one window is damaged suggests narrowly avoiding total destruction by a razor's edge.

"Three stained-glass windows" recall a common rose window or rosette pattern often found in cathedrals. Only one window is damaged, letting in unfiltered light, suggesting an open moment of opportunity, a moment of clear sight. Sacred space cannot be destroyed. Though bombs may level the stone cathedral in a worldly sense, there is ever a sense of renewal within the symbol of the sacred rose. Human eyes must, of necessity, filter the bombardment of sensory stimuli. However, the eyes are said to be the windows of the soul, the unfolding of which is the flower of mankind. King Arthur, presidential candidates, supreme court justices: all are subjected to extreme, potentially damaging, challenges to their claims. Demanding recognition upsets the equilibrium, challenges the status quo. In musical terms, a suspended chord is a prolongation of cadence, creating dissonance before resolution. The process of individuation sounds very much like this. Should one raise one's flag too high, almost certainly someone else will fire a few cannon shots to knock you down. The issue touches the primal rules of which one must be aware: Who is the king of the castle?

Apply this degree-pair with a mind to awareness of challenges to one's claim to personal power; windows of opportunity that may be dangerous; suspense while waiting for a resolution. Watch for perceiving things as if through rose-colored glasses; light filtered through colors; personal attacks that are like being bombarded; tendencies to distance oneself from the fray; a knack for narrowly escaping serious loss. Consider a penchant for suspense; a tendency to be hung up as if suspended in time; critical times within the transfer of power, passages of life; choosing oneself or joining the crowd.

"A man all bundled up in fur leading a shaggy deer" (3 Cancer) and "The human soul receptive to growth and understanding" (3 Capricorn)

Aspect: Trine.
Quality: Maintaining.
Shared motifs: 'Bundling as creative exploration,'
'the base and the sublime tied together.'

"A man all bundled up in fur leading a shaggy deer" is an image of rugged individuality in a cold environment. To be "bundled up" is to be sensibly wrapped in warm clothing or furs against the threatening cold. "Bundling" is also an old American custom of sleeping in the same bed, partly or fully clothed, to keep warm in winter. The "bundle" or bundling board was a barrier, placed between the individuals, a long leather bag or hard cloth pillow, acting as a sexual speed bump, as it were. Deer are shaggy when their hair is rough, which suggests the molting season: the shedding of one's coat of hair. Although all bundled up, it is told that many couples shed their clothes to pursue other means of keeping warm: hence the slang term "shagging."

"The human soul receptive to growth and understanding" is an image of the character of openness, expressive of the deep nature of human being. "Soul" derives from the Greek *psyche* and is closely linked with *spiritus* and *anima*. To be animated is, in contrast to being temporarily suspended, to being shell-shocked by the bombardment of sensual impressions the soul is open to, active rather than passive. Anyone all tied up hardly seems open to new experiences. Ironically, tying up, as when two people are bundled up together for warmth, may animate the situation greatly, providing an enormous amount of stimulus through which to grow and understand. Receptivity is deeper than mere inquisitiveness: it addresses something primal in human beings, touching what it means to be human: openness.

The "man all bundled up in fur" is like Santa Claus leading a reindeer loaded with gifts from the North Pole: the spirit of giving warms hearts with gifts from a cold clime. The giving of gifts presupposes receptivity. A "human soul" suggests the relationship between ego awareness and the deeper source of life and spirit in the human psyche. The sense of one's identity, the ego structure, is described in Buddhist psychology as being made up of heaps or bundles from the Sanskrit *skandha*, bound together, forming a containment vessel through which the sense of existence is created. In other words, the soul can grow and understand only through the bundled vessel of the self. Receptivity, however, is not passive. It is the openness of human exploration, like that of an arctic explorer traversing a vast, open landscape.

Apply this degree-pair with a mind to the rugged, exploratory nature of human experience; a character of openness to new experience; the creative potentials that cook within. Think of forming a sense of personal identity that is at once between the perils of experience (Latin *ex-peritus*, arising out of peril) and the soul, understood as that which cares exquisitely for the self. Watch for shaggy appearances; towing baser instincts to higher, more refined levels; life passages; tying together life experiences in order to untie knots of human worry. Consider weaving; knitting/ knotting; leading; gaining understanding through tying things together.

"A cat arguing with a mouse" (4 Cancer)
and "A party entering a large canoe" (4 Capricorn)

Aspect: Square.
Quality: Challenge.
Shared motifs: 'The scent motivating instinctual actions,'
'rationalizing base instincts.'

"A cat arguing with a mouse" is an image of the power differentials between instinct and reason. Under what circumstances does a cat argue with a mouse? Cats are excellent mousers, possessing natural abilities to walk softly, pounce quickly, and move with agility, grace, and ease. "A cat arguing" echoes the question-and-answer form of instruction of catechism. "A mouse" is a common small rodent, but is also, in nautical terms, a knot or knob on a rope to prevent it from slipping. The term "mouse," like the rodent itself, has been around since early antiquity all around the world, bearing kinship with musk, a secretion with a penetrating odor extracted from the sac of the musk deer. "Mouse" is also connected with the Sanskrit *mushka*, meaning scrotum and vulva.

"A party entering a large canoe" is an image of a group of people boarding a primitive vessel carved or fashioned out of wood. While canoes are admired for their capacity to move swiftly and gracefully through the water, they are also notoriously unstable, especially when loaded with many passengers. "A party" can be a group of people, or a symbol of a shared philosophy or common sense of purpose, as in a party platform, a social gathering for fun. Issues can be divided along party lines, sometimes even when everyone is in the same boat.

"Arguing" is a quarrel offering reasons to support or contend an opinion or stance. A rational argument attempts to prove a position. Related to *argent*, silver, "arguing" makes clear by shining a light upon a matter. As a human characteristic, to be argumentative is to be just plain quarrelsome, or shrewd, subtle. Playing cat and mouse can be a trivializing refinement, toying with matters within extreme power differentials. A cat on the hunt for a mouse calls upon instinctual nature. A cat on the prowl may caterwaul, the cat howls of being in heat, which sound like a noisy dispute.

Apply this degree-pair with a mind to the challenge to find one's place between the instinctive animal urges and the sublime natures of being human; calling for order while entering an unstable circumstance; having to patiently fit in, wait one's turn. Watch for penetrating scents that trigger instinctive responses; entering into debates along party lines; rationalizations of all kinds, but especially those that smell fishy. Think of sexual politics, the politics of sexuality; divine creation versus down and dirty. Look for hidden motives beneath the artifice of well-reasoned positions; caterwauling and little peeps; positions that rock the boat. Consider the shrewd ability of knowing when to pounce; a tipsy manner of reasoning; quick, corrective changes in direction of thought, strategy, and movement; the thrill of the hunt; not rocking the boat.

"An auto wrecked by a train" (5 Cancer) and "Indians rowing a canoe and dancing a war dance" (5 Capricorn)

Aspect: Quintile.
Quality: Creative genius.
Shared motifs: 'Evoking power through rhythm and motion,' 'guerilla tactics in love and war.'

"An auto wrecked by a train" is an image of a collision between the lesser and greater powers of manmade vehicles.[1] "Auto" derives from the Greek element meaning by one's self, suggesting one who acts on his own authority: drives one's own car. "A train" is a much larger, more powerful vehicle for the transport of many people. Hence, there is a power clash between the individual, who drives where he pleases, and the collective, which follows along the tracks laid out. "To wreck" is to destroy or ruin. A person in ruins might be said to be shipwrecked. To be shipwrecked on a desert isle is a classic image of being stranded all alone, left to one's own devices, apart from the human collective and social means of support.

"Indians rowing a canoe and dancing a war dance" is an image of a group working together for forward progress with an energizing preparation for a specific mission. A "canoe" is one of the most archaic of water vessels, originally a hollowed-out tree trunk. The birch-bark canoe of the North American Indians is a much lighter craft, which when handled with skilled efficiency, is an excellent means to traverse shorter spans of water. A skilled team of rowers can maneuver a canoe to practically any place they wish to go, even against strong headwinds or currents, by traversing a zigzag line. "To portage" literally means to carry one's vessel between two navigable waters.

An automobile is wrecked by a train when there is a collision. A "collision" is a violent impact between two objects, or a clash of opposing interests or considerations. A ship run aground can wreak havoc, even destroy the vessel. Ironically, it is the popular proliferation of the single-owned automobile that has brought trains, as a means of transportation, to the brink of obsolescence. When many hands row together, even lightweight vessels can outmaneuver heavy, cumbersome, if powerful, vessels of war. Consider the ruin of the Spanish Armada against the lightweight British naval force in 1588.

"Dancing" has long been recognized as an effective means to move the social dynamics of love further along, as well as a means to psyche up warriors before battle. Dancing suggests lithe, graceful moves, like those of a cat. Rhythmic dancing can evoke sexual energy like the clicking of a railroad track, the powerful swaying of the train traveling through the night. Dancing a war dance brings the warriors together in an intensely felt union for a common purpose, like a team getting pumped before the big game.

Apply this degree-pair with a mind to creative and skillful means to navigate extreme differences in power, guerilla tactics against a powerful foe; issues of being swept away by prevailing currents, or ingenious ways to maneuver on one's own course. One can drive one's own car, but when love happens, love drives *you*. Consider popular songs, especially blues and rock, about love, cars, and trains: hearing the lonesome train whistle blow; the love train; "Mustang Sally." All is fair in love and war: the issue lies in what strokes of genius one brings to navigating that which is deep and powerful.

"Game birds feathering their nest" (6 Cancer) and "A dark archway and ten logs at the bottom" (6 Capricorn)

Aspect: Conjunction.
Quality: Focus.
Shared motif: 'Obstacles along the path to comfort
and security.'

"Game birds feathering their nest" is an image of finishing refinements for comfort regarding home security. "Game birds" are the quarry of hunters. Anyone thought to be fit for ridicule or criticism is said to be fair game. Regarding human character, someone who is "game" is ready and willing for anything. "Feathering their nest" suggests prosperity accumulated through tending to one's property or with thought to one's future comfort. "Game birds" feather their nests with breast down to soften the long periods of hatching their eggs. One can hatch a plan for future comfort or pad one's nest with finery and showy decoration.

"A dark archway and ten logs at the bottom" is an image of an entrance or passageway with unwieldy objects upon the threshold. An "arch" is a curved structure spanning an opening. An archenemy is one who is the principal foe or opposition, possessed with characteristics of cunning, roguish wiles. "Logs" are the heavy cut portions of timber from the trunks of a tree, such as from the featherwood tree of Australia, which is likened unto hickory hardwood. "Ten logs at the bottom" suggests a formidable obstacle on the threshold. Ten logs at the bottom of an archway may be arranged in a variety of ways. Visualize the logs in one's mind. See how it is with them, assessing their position relative to the ease or difficulty for one to pass through the archway.

One might need a hatchet to cut through the logjam that blocks the way. Being at loggerheads with someone can bring a sharpened edge to a dispute. Rowing a canoe calls for feathering the oar: turning the paddle blade horizontally as it is carried back to the fore position. "Feathering" a blade, like an arrow or propeller, is to adjust the pitch such that the leading edge is directed in the line of flight, suggesting quickness, haste to pass through. When an arrow strikes a log or a tree, it stops dead in its tracks, so to speak.

A swift canoe slices through the water like a hot knife through butter until they run up against fallen logs in a narrow waterway. Such obstacles call for a more refined strategy to get through. One can sit in a cozy nest and preen before one's eggs are even hatched. One can be stalled in forward progress by massive foreign objects and stubborn objections, or one can finesse the situation to one's advantage.

Apply this degree-pair with a mind to an urgent sense of making progress; hatching one's eggs; a sense of frustration with obstacles; of becoming stuck on one's path; or the elegance and finesse to realize one's goals. Visualize how the logs are arranged: corduroy; crisscrossed; blocking; adorning. Watch for arch factors that plague one's path, then revisualize the situation. Watch for a sense of urgency that finds patient, slow growth a foreign quality, a hard nut to crack. Consider unnecessary duplication of work limiting output; overrefinement of strategies; game natures clashing with ponderous delays.

"Two fairies on a moonlit night" (7 Cancer)
and "A veiled prophet of power" (7 Capricorn)

Aspect: Opposition.
Quality: Awareness of.
Shared motifs: 'Showing and veiling,' 'hiding one's light,'
'seizing and imaginative releasing.'

"Two fairies on a moonlit night" is an image of rarified, supernatural energies on a night illumined by the light reflected by the moon. "Fairies" are beings of subtle energy and presence, such that they are usually hidden from human sense perception, hence, called "imaginary beings." A "moonlit night" is a time normally so dark that one cannot see except by the reflected sunlight from the moon. The emphasis is on the otherliness of the situation bathed with luminous lunar light: light twice shone and two shining presences. When the mind is affected by lunar influences, when one is struck by the moon, it is said to be lunacy, a term reflective of when the imaginations of lovers and poets are flooded by the same lunar light.

"A veiled prophet of power" is an image of covered light that sees through divine eyes. "Veiled" is a covering, usually a veil of cloth draped across the face or over the head. If the light is overpowering, a protective veil may be required. "Power" is just power: it is neither good nor bad. What man brings to the expression of power colors its estimation. A "prophet" is regarded as a person who can interpret or channel the will, light, and power of the divine. A hierophant is one who shows or interprets esoteric or sacred mysteries. A hierophant may be seized by the energy of the divine in much the same way that seizures may be induced by the influence of the full moon.

When something else takes you over, a higher power, an emotion, a sudden insight, it is as if one has been seized or possessed. One might be arrested by imagining obstacles in one's path to prosperity and comfort, or bring imagination to a situation to creatively see things in a different light. Looking directly at the sun can blind human eyes, a situation calling for a protective covering or a means to reflect safely on an intense, overpowering reality. The veil between the worlds, like that between the fairy realm and human reality, can at times be thin. It is a thin veil that also separates imagination and reality. The lunatic may be a divinely inspired poet; the "prophet" may be a lunatic in disguise.

Apply this degree-pair with a mind to the awareness of other realms; realms of power and imagination, insights that shed a different light on the matter. Think of revelations that leave one moonstruck; that reflect the extraordinary. Watch for seizures of all kinds: captivated by silvery shining light; epilepsy; seized with emotion; possessed by a sense of the other; a rigid mind. Consider hiding oneself as a clever, protective measure; altered states such as those induced by moonshine; reflecting on strange possibilities; allowing that there may be factors that one does not understand; wearing clothing that veils or hides; keeping something aside in order to evoke a sense of mystery about oneself; having an intense awareness that appearances are not everything, that nothing is as it seems.

"Rabbits dressed in clothes and on parade" (8 Cancer) and "Birds in the house singing happily" (8 Capricorn)

Aspect: Trine.
Quality: Maintaining.
Shared motifs: 'Keeping up appearances,'
'happy with one's lot.'

"Rabbits dressed in clothes and on parade" is an image of anthropomorphic imagination paraded for public view. "Rabbits" are creatures that tend to hide timidly from human eyes. It is dangerous to be openly exposed in the wild. "Dressed in clothes," rabbits are like the Beatrix Potter characters: Peter Rabbit, Flopsy, Mopsy and Cotton-tail. "Rabbits on parade" would be, like Peter and his fine blue jacket and shoes, dressed for a public procession, perhaps to display their fine clothes. Recall that it was his fine coat that got Peter caught up in Mr. McGregor's garden. To be caught up in public appearances suggests a nature willing to passively conform rather than fight against prevailing social expectations.

"Birds in the house singing happily" is an image of creatures known for flying freely in the wild in a cheerfully domesticated situation. A bird is a feathered vertebrate with wings that is usually able to fly. Kept within a house, birds are denied the ability to fly freely, yet they still sing "happily." Birds in full song sound like birds in fine feather, in good spirits. To be in full feather suggests being well equipped, in full force, and therefore fully dressed. Birds primp and preen, tidy their coats of feathers with their beaks. "To preen" is to dress or adorn, often associated with to pride or congratulate oneself.

One's home and apparel are matters of pride: clothes make the man. Cloth is a woven fabric used to cover, dress, or adorn the naked body. "Clotho," one of the three fates, or *moirai*, spins the thread of life. To be dressed for parade suggests being in one's finest garb, cheerful and proud to display oneself publicly. Rabbits, almost totally silent creatures, are known for their large ears and keen hearing capacity. Birds are loved for their musical songs. "Rabbit ears" is an expression suggesting reception, while singing like a bird suggests a proclivity to tell everything. One might dress in a manner that conforms to the surrounding circumstances, or dress a domesticated bird, such as a chicken, by trimming and cleaning in preparation for cooking: two senses of being fully dressed for dinner.

Apply this degree-pair with a mind to the human characteristics of birds and rabbits: extremes of timidity and boastful display; alert listening; overly chatty or rabbiting on about something; domesticated sensibilities. Think of clothing as adornment rather than covering; one's house as a show of decor, pride, and security rather than as a cage or shelter. One may be hung up on keeping up appearances or show a flair for well-maintained beauty. Consider big ears, chatty, informal styles of expression; melodious voices of birdsong nature; timid compliance; doing the best with what one has, within realistic limits; accepting the status quo; putting the best face on the situation; adapting to social realities.

"A tiny nude miss reaching in the water for a fish" (9 Cancer)
and "An angel carrying a harp" (9 Capricorn)

Aspect: Square.
Quality: Challenge.
Shared motifs: 'The naked truth,' 'sublime messages,'
'surprise catches.'

"A tiny nude miss reaching in the water for a fish" is an image of guileless innocence attempting to grasp what is elusive. "A tiny nude miss" is a young, unmarried girl or woman, without any clothing suggesting one without guise. "Reaching in the water for a fish" is an act that attempts to grasp what is slippery. Getting a hold on a fish is especially difficult since the actual position of the fish is distorted by the refraction of light as it passes from the element of air to water: the fish is not where it appears to be. Fishing for something, a compliment, the truth, is an attempt to find indirectly what one seeks. A Roman fable tells of Truth and Falsehood bathing. Falsehood came out of the water first and dressed herself up in Truth's garments. Unwilling to wear the clothes of Falsehood left behind, Truth went naked: *nudus veritas*.

"An angel carrying a harp" is an image of a sublimely beautiful and innocent messenger bearing a triangular stringed instrument. "Angels" are the attendant spirits that may guard and protect, or are the bearers of something: the angel of death; the angel of mercy. "A harp" is a triangular-shaped stringed instrument that is plucked by the hand held in a clawlike fashion. "Lyra" is a constellation containing the bright star Vega: the falling vulture, and the Ring Nebula: a cloaklike surrounding cloud. Lyra is named for the lyre invented by Hermes, the messenger god. A "Harpy" is a winged woman, or a bird with a woman's face, from Greek mythology. Harpies are rapacious monsters who seize victims in their talons, carrying off the souls of the dead.

Not to harp on the matter, but winged women with talons tend to grab one's attention. "Talons" are sharp, slender, pointed projections of a bird's claw. A "tine" is a small, slender projection of a larger thing, such as a fork or a barb on a hook. Getting your hooks into the mouth of an angelfish is a hit-or-miss proposition. One might harpoon a whale, or harp on a story about the one that got away. What is being transported or conveyed is not necessarily what is being reached for: having the pluck to reach for what you seek meets the clouded uncertainty of what is born to you. Free of ulterior motive, one's reach is often rewarded in unexpected ways. All one has to do is reach.

Apply this degree-pair with a mind to the challenge of innocently reaching into realms of powerful potentials; of discriminating between sublime messages and pointed barbs. Look for tiny pointed instruments; stringed instruments; angelic affinities; a tendency to harp on about something. Watch for naked honesty and the refusal to wear Falsehood's clothes. Consider triangular shapes; clouds of confusion; attempts to shroud the truth that miss; lyrical voices or sensibilities. What you seize upon may be sublime good fortune or a storm cloud with which you are carried away.

"A large diamond not completely carved" (10 Cancer) and "An albatross feeding from the hand" (10 Capricorn)

Aspect: Quintile.
Quality: Creative genius.
Shared motifs: 'Adamantine resolve,' 'grace in the rough, refined gracelessness.'

"A large diamond not completely carved" is an image of a clear, hard precious stone in the process of refinement.[2] "A large diamond" may be a major mining discovery, or the central playing field in baseball. A diamond shape is a rhombus: a four-sided shape with oblique angles and equal sides. "Not completely carved" suggests being in the process of being cut, shaped, refined. The diamond, therefore, shows some facets of a classic shape, but is not yet finished either by design or because it has not yet been fully attended to. In baseball, this would be analogous to being stranded at third base, without making it all the way home.

"An albatross feeding from the hand" is an image of a large, sometimes awkward, sometimes graceful bird, bestowed with the gift of nourishment. The "albatross" is a seabird with the widest known wingspan of any bird. Often associated with Samuel Coleridge's *The Rime of the Ancient Mariner,* an "albatross" has come to mean an encumbrance or source of frustration. Indeed, the large bird is renowned for being clumsy, has been given disparaging names like "stupid gull" and "gooney bird," and is known to be hardly able to fly at all without a wind. "Alba" means white, but "albatross" is actually a corruption of the Portuguese *alcatraz*, also the name of a prison island on which one would rather not be stranded.

Diamonds are renowned for their hardness and clarity. "Diamond-like wisdom" is a Buddhist reference to a discriminating awareness that cuts through obscurities and shines with limpid clearness. Because of their hardness, diamonds suggest that which can cut, but cannot itself be cut. Nothing can force the "albatross" from its nest, a characteristic suggesting an unshakable, loyal resolve for home. "Feeding" is to supply with food, the raw materials needed for survival. Hand-fed birds are thought to be healthier and happier. Diamonds may be a girl's best friend; a diamond ring, the modern symbol of marriage, may be the ultimate sought-for status. Then again, a diamond ring may be like an albatross around one's finger.

Apply this degree-pair with a mind to diamonds in the rough, marvelous in size, clumsy in manner. Think of gliding forever with a single flap of the wings; adamantine clarity without hardly lifting a finger; graceless efforts to bring it all home. Allow a lot of room for a wide span of creative capacities; soaring talents that are still taking shape; fierce, unbreakable determination to stay in one's ways, one's nest. Consider loners; one-of-a-kind qualities that would be ruined if further refined; cumbersome steps yet graceful flight; a genius for balancing conformity with creative independence; being dressed well enough so as to not stand out; having enough rough edges so as to not quite fit in; a knack for seeing the beauty in the journey, in what is not yet complete; the genius of unshakable resolve that transcends mere stubbornness, soars freely without obstacle.

"A clown making grimaces" (11 Cancer) and "A large group of pheasants" (11 Capricorn)

Aspect: Conjunction.
Quality: Focus.
Shared motifs: 'Painted faces,' 'the loudness of mime,'
'the great pretender.'

"A clown making grimaces" is the image of a buffoon, professional or by nature, making faces expressive of pain, disgust, or fright. "A clown" derives from a derogatory name for a rustic, or a farm peasant, so called for their clumsy manner when exposed to city society. "Clowns" can entertain by acting the fool, by zany antics meant in jest. "Fool" derives from the Greek *follis*, meaning windbag or bellows. A court jester or fool serves the royal monarch by deflating pomp, often appearing foolish while being cleverly wise. "Making grimaces" is distorting facial expression to either show disgust or to amuse. The art of a clown is to show an exaggerated expression of an obvious nature through a painted face.

"A large group of pheasants" is an image of long-tailed, colorful birds. "Pheasants" are so called for being discovered by the Greeks near the river Phasis, which flows to the Black Sea, and perhaps also for their colorful appearance (Greek *phasis*: show or appearance). Ring-necked pheasants, common to North America, have wattled heads, a colored head and neck of dark iridescent green, a red face, and a white ring around the neck. Associated with high aristocracy, the pheasant relates to giving oneself airs: pretentious and affected manners. Associated with vulgar manners, a pheasant relates to bellowing, as in the "Billingsgate Pheasants": shouting fishermen trying to attract attention and vend their fish.

"Fools" are often thought to be windbags, full of hot air. The function of the royal fool is to deflate the grandiosity of the king and his court. A famous painting of Henry VIII shows him with a fine pheasant feather stuck in his cap; his longtime fool, Will Somers, is also portrayed in this fashion. "Clowns" can, by intention or by naïveté, poke a hole in a windbag with a mere facial expression. Exaggerated expressions and mannerisms say one thing; behind a painted face, who is to know? Perhaps one comes face to face with the great pretender: loudness disguising fright within, or silent mime disguising confident character; coarse manners disguising quiet within, or putting on airs of finery disguising petty conceit.

Apply this degree-pair with a mind to a need to cleverly camouflage oneself and the question "Who's the fool?" Look for exaggerated differences of social position and mannerisms; inflated or deflated character; painted faces to show off or show up. Watch for what lies behind a brave face, a frightened face; mannerisms that conceal inner realities; game for any occasion; game humor, whoopee-cushion humor. Consider wattled necks; beards; humorous barbs; fashion finery; rubber faces; mimicry; blushing; having an impact on others that uplifts; having a felt understanding of the sharp edges of reality, of the inner emotional impact of brilliant ideas; a knack for infusing cold thought, pristine ideals, with a human element: the artistry of the wise fool.

"A Chinese woman nursing a baby with a message" (12 Cancer) and "A student of nature lecturing" (12 Capricorn)

Aspect: Opposition.
Quality: Awareness of.
Shared motifs: 'Learning and teaching potentials,' 'strange elements in getting one's point across.'

"A Chinese woman nursing a baby with a message" is an image of a strange awareness of wisdom from an unexpected source. Imagine dismissing someone as a fool, as a shallow, loquacious show of cosmetic intelligence, only to discover a great source of nourishing wisdom in that very same person. "A Chinese woman" is a woman from a strange and foreign land. "Nursing" is to feed, sustain, and nurture. "A baby with a message" is an unlikely source of knowledge or information. Nurturing a child's potentials arises from a tacit recognition of human potential. If an infant child speaks to you, you are apt to be fully attentive.

"A student of nature lecturing" is an image expressing the natural process of all learning: the true teacher is ever a student, guiding others to learn how to learn. "A student" is one who is basically on the way regarding the process of learning. The study of "nature" requires an openness to the natural world as it emerges and appears. "Nature" derives from *physis,* the Greek word for "being" in its enduring power. "Lecturing" is engaging in a discourse that provides information or knowledge of a subject matter. Should a student lecture his professor, he would be exuding an arrogance of knowing more than the teacher. However, a student lecturing may be a wonderful, if surprising, source of newly perceived information, information gathered through fresh eyes.

A child's place in the world is often dismissed as "to be seen but not heard." A "baby," as yet unconditioned by the prevailing social take on things, sees the world, nature, through fresh, newly opened eyes. "Lecturing" can mean assuming a position of authority, pontificating, the final word on the matter, or scolding, reprimanding. Like a young child's baby-babble, a lecturer may babble on in an incomprehensible manner. One may not be willing to brook the babble. In its highest expression, the pursuit of knowledge is an ongoing process, open and responsive to innovative insight while honoring and transmitting that which is already known.

Apply this degree-pair with a mind to an awareness of messages, knowledge, wisdom from unexpected sources; nurturing potentials in others; magnanimous grace to step down and let others have their say. Listen for hints in "pidgin English": a language with no native speakers, combining distorted English with words from other languages and Chinese constructions, which often effectively gets the message across; technical language or jargon, argot, or special vocabularies unintelligible to outsiders. Be alert to personal investment in one's own responsibilities, achievements, discoveries; tendencies to chatter incessantly; extremes of speech ranging from a mere murmur to bellowing infallible truths. Consider a knack for understanding incomprehensible mixtures of languages; getting right to the point while distorting the usual perspective; innocent innovations that convey meaning and insight; the love of learning.

"One hand slightly flexed with a very prominent thumb" (13 Cancer) and "A fire worshipper" (13 Capricorn)

Aspect: Trine.
Quality: Maintaining.
Shared motifs: 'A personal imprint regarding a view of life,'
'devotion to a way of living.'

"One hand slightly flexed with a very prominent thumb" is an image of a physical gesture using the fat, protuberant, opposable digit found only in primates, or, in less impressive terms, sticking a thumb out while slightly bending the hand. Imagine a lecture coming to an end. This is a moment signaling a show of approval or dismay about what has been said: thumbs up or thumbs down. "To be flexible" is to be able to bend: pliancy; adaptability. One's hand gesture may indicate an inflection of superlative import, for example, thumbs up meaning "Bravo!" "Prominence" suggests a protuberance, a swelling out beyond the surrounding surface, like a bulging knob. As with a mime clown and a baby, communication is achieved without recognizable words.

"A fire worshipper" is an image of one who pays homage to the element of fire. "Worship" is homage paid to, or devotion for, something, someone. A mother adores her baby, sees and hears all things angelic and sublime in the child's little hands and gesticulations. "Fire" is the active phase of combustion and symbolic of passion and spirit: the fire within. One may passionately disapprove of someone or something, and consequently, fire off a gesture of rejection. One may passionately approve of someone or something and feel really burned about those who do not share the same belief. The flame of spirit burns brightly for one who worships, containing an inner combustion, as it were, in a religious sense: *religio,* binding again.

Sticking your thumb out may be an attempt to hitch a ride, seek to go along for the ride with someone else at the wheel. One might join a crowd in a shared expression of support, or show a devotion to the applause of one hand clapping. It depends on your bent: thumbing your nose, yet another human protuberance, or being under the thumb of a particular binding belief or opinion. One might be inclined to be flexible in matters of spirit or intellect, or all thumbs when it comes to building a fire.

Apply this degree-pair with a mind to the distinctive human attempts to get a grasp on matters of spirit; emphatic gestures of approval or disapproval, burning devotions that really stick out. Watch for silent gestures, impassioned, loud gesticulations; getting burnt by one's beliefs. Be alert for a willful insistence regarding what counts as correct expression; proper speech; true belief. Look for characteristics of resolve, conviction, inner strength; or inflexibility; unyielding in one's stance; fixed in one's belief. Consider Promethean gifts of fire and spirit; passionate shows of defiance; well-thumbed books to which one is devoted; being bound to attitudes for or against a set of beliefs, which can leave one inflexible; willpower; Agni; Zoroaster; a torch-song singer; the spiritual significance of the opposable thumb.

"A very old man facing a vast dark space to the northeast" (14 Cancer) and "An ancient bas-relief carved in granite" (14 Capricorn)

Aspect: Square.

Quality: Challenge.

Shared motif: 'An intensified sense of existing as opposed to being defined by one's beliefs.'

"A very old man facing a vast dark space to the northeast" is an image of solitude and aloneness as one faces one's own goodnight. "A very old man" is a man who has nearly run his course in life. The "space to the northeast" is associated with stillness, the deepest personal inwardness. As a temporal image, the "northeast" refers to the time of dreamless sleep, a time when the ego structure dissolves completely into the transpersonal realm. This space and time stands in relief from the social realm. While "facing the northeast," one is all alone. The I Ching associates this time and direction with a vast mountain, standing still, its peak reaching high toward heaven. "A very old man" faces, with heightened awareness, the issue of his own being against the "vast dark space" of all eternity.

"An ancient bas-relief carved in granite" is an image of a carving in very hard stone where a figure stands in slight relief from the background. A "bas-relief" is a type of sculpting that carves figures lifted out of the background. "Relief" may mean a release from the weight of duties or responsibilities, or to bring something into prominence by contrast. "An ancient bas-relief" suggests that the same issue faced our ancestors: a truth of human existence carved in stone. "Granite" is a rock suggesting great hardness and endurance. Such stones are commonly used to mark the resting place of the dead.

Regardless of the views championed throughout time, enduring and inflexible facts define human existence. One can give an emphatic thumbs-up to a particular view: conservative over liberal, members of the church of one's philosophy as opposed to the infidels. There are times, however, that sharpen awareness, challenge the individual to define himself, like a personal distinguishing relief, carved in hard stone, against the background of being as a whole. Such times cut through even beliefs carved in granite.

Apply this degree-pair with a mind to challenging tensions of human existence; heightened awareness of transient existence over and against the background of all that is. Be aware of issues of what is flexible or inflexible; solitude and social identities; religious stripe and pure spirit. Watch for loners; chiseled faces; principles carved in granite. Be alert for existential intensifiers; gloomy dispositions; Amor fati: saying yes to life even in the face of Atropos: the Sister of Fate; the Inflexible one who cuts the thread of life. Consider relief found in solitude; stoney silences; wakefulness in the dead of night; affection for the winter season; reading by touch; braille; the Mayan calendar; temporal relief from the cycles of Venus; slight elevations that make a world of difference.

**"A group of people who have overeaten and enjoyed it" (15 Cancer)
and "Many toys in the children's ward of a hospital" (15 Capricorn)**

Aspect: Quintile.
Quality: Creative genius.
Shared motifs: 'Hospitality,' 'stewardship';
'Amor fati: the love of life.'

"A group of people who have overeaten and enjoyed it" is an image of a hospitable situation where pleasures are indulged and enjoyed. On special festive occasions or at celebratory parties, a little indulgence is acceptable, since it does not reflect an everyday practice. However, there are responsibilities for the host. When Aunt Betty pushes yet another piece of cheesecake at one, she does so out of generous hospitality: "Oh, go on! One more piece won't hurt!" Eating and drinking to excess on a regular basis leads to a deterioration of health. One may end up in a hospital ward. On the other hand, consider "Eat, drink, and be merry, for tomorrow we die," an expression celebrating the transience of human life.

"Many toys in the children's ward of a hospital" depicts a situation where young, and therefore innocent, children require focused attention for some malady, through no fault of their own. "Many toys" are in the children's ward as a way of relieving the strain of illness, balancing the sense of seriousness with playful elements. Children's illnesses are not the result of habitual patterns in everyday life. When illness strikes a child, one's heart naturally seeks to reach out with an abundance of care, gifts, toys, any measure that encourages the more positive attitude possible for the recuperation of the child.

"Toys" are objects of amusement that stand in relief from the serious illnesses one might find in a hospital. Lifting the spirits of a child with mere amusing trifles is an action that seeks to soften potential extreme outcomes. Feeling alone and isolated in a hospital can lead to excessive anxiety or worry: not the best disposition for a happy recovery. A "hospital" is an institution where the wounded and ill are cared for. Such a place for the terminally ill is called a "hospice." Such a place in the human heart is called "hospitality." Skill in alleviating the impact of the hard facts of human reality, having the right touch, one that does not seek to avoid, but rather, one that comes from a generous heart of compassion, is the trait of a fine host or hostess.

The term "ward" derives from guard, protect. "To ste*ward*" is to care for and nurture, a protective overseeing. If one has been drinking excessively, others must oversee safe arrival home. Although one's destination in life is ever *toward* one's own end, one can take care to enjoy life along the way. The manner in which humans travel their paths to their destinations is not ruled by hard and fast strictures, but by the care emanating from the heart, which guides and guards against harm along the way.

Apply this degree-pair with a mind for the genius that appreciates the difference between hard rules and guidelines; has a deft touch of knowing when to bend the rules; has a heartfelt sense of when and where to uplift the situation. Watch for avoidance of life issues through indulgence in trifles; masking reality with a glut of trifles. Look for a talent to guard the joy and pleasures of life without straying into repeated excess; the joyful wisdom to smile at overly serious philosophies.

"A man before a square with a manuscript scroll before him" (16 Cancer) and "Boys and girls in gymnasium suits" (16 Capricorn)

Aspect: Conjunction.
Quality: Focus.
Shared motifs: 'Decoding,' 'preparation in suitable garb,'
'one step removed from the bare facts.'

"A man before a square with a manuscript scroll before him" is an image addressing the interpretation of a symbolic fourfold representation of the cosmos, the world, life. A "square" is a four-sided figure, the fundamental shape of a mandala. Standing before a square is like standing before a city square with a city map in your hands, or reading the rules for a board game spread out before you on a table. A "manuscript" is literally a hand-written document. In "scroll" form, a manuscript may be an old document. This suggests a process of reading and interpretation: a manuscript holding the keys for understanding the meaning of the square.

"Boys and girls in gymnasium suits" is an image of being dressed and ready for gym activities. "Gymnasium" is a Greek word literally meaning to train naked, as was the way in ancient Greece for men to physically train. "Gymnasium" also means preparatory schools for university entrance in various European countries. "Gymnastics" has come to refer to developing or displaying physical agility and coordination, a task that calls for suitable clothing. Being dressed in gym suits is still today, especially in high schools, close to being naked.

Both a mandala and the gymnasium address the wholeness and wholesomeness of life. An interpretive appreciation for a symbol of a well-balanced whole, the mandala expresses the need to focus upon that which addresses the nurturing of all facets of being human: physical, emotional, intellectual, and spiritual. "Training in gym suits" suggests being appropriately dressed for activities that prepare one for the fulfillment of potentials as a whole. In addition to forming a foundation of physical health through wholesome activity, gymnastics calls for flexibility, coordination, and the mastery of oneself through exercise and discipline. "Boys and girls" may approach this training with exuberant excitement: the din of excited voices in a cavernous hall. "Din" is a loud, protracted, and distracting sound, often heard in high school gyms, however "dinning" means to learn through repetition.

Apply this degree-pair with a mind to a naked approach to life as a whole; wholesome training for future potentials; flexibility and fitting attire for what one wants to master. Think of code books, road maps, interpretive work involving texts or language, blueprints, deeper readings (hermeneutics) of something that is symbolic of the whole. Watch for fresh approaches, repetitive exercises, dressing to code, uniforms. The game court is a mandala-like area wherein a demonstration of skills used for specific achievements is exercised. The game is known by the dress and social focus for accomplishment, whereas the square is known by the kind of code book that unlocks hidden meaning.

"The germ grows into knowledge and life" (17 Cancer) and "A girl surreptitiously bathing in the nude" (17 Capricorn)

Aspect: Opposition.
Quality: Awareness of.
Shared motifs: 'Organic unfolding,' 'cautiously wading in,'
'tender penetrating roots.'

"The germ grows into knowledge and life" is an image of the germination of a seed, organically unfolding its potentials. A "germ" is a portion of a microorganism that possesses the capacity to grow into a new seed. A mature germ cell able to unite with another in sexual reproduction is called a "gamete," from the French and Greek *gamete,* wife, and *gamos,* marriage. Imagine the boys and girls in gym suits getting together to sport and gambol, as the old Celtic folk songs would express. What allows a germ to grow is a deep inner coding that enables the fully grown tree to exist in potential within its seed.

"A girl surreptitiously bathing in the nude" is an image of a naked approach to experience, to experiment with life without clothing, adornments, or code books. The raw and naked experience of wading out from shore into deeper waters speaks to a simple and authentic manner of growth. Getting wet is clearly an image of embracing the emotional waters of life. Still, bathing "surreptitiously" is to bathe in secret, by stealth. The au naturel approach is not a full-blown public display. It is done precisely so others may not see. Private and personal, this is an image of quiet daring, not that of a person performing a cannonball while skinny-dipping.

Embryonic ideas are original ideas, like an elementary principle upon which entire edifices of knowledge and life can unfold. Stripped down to its essentials, a seed-thought can quietly, tentatively, grow to maturity. "Achievements in principle" are those that are not yet fully developed, and therefore call for tentative, cautious advancement. If one has a great idea in principle, one would perhaps rather not let anyone have a look at it prematurely. It might be like a young poet: one must be careful about whom one shows one's poetry to. It would be like exposing the tender new roots of a plant to the harsh light of the sun: one can be burned. Modesty is the way of treading one's path that forms the basis of character. While the principle of modesty holds true throughout life, at moments of tender beginnings its importance becomes magnified.

Apply this degree-pair with a mind to the tender beginnings of germination, delicate roots that penetrate the earth and carry mature potentials. Think of life organically happening, unfolding on principles of its own; tender roots that gently penetrate the hard earth; gentle breezes that find their way everywhere, around all obstacles. Watch for a sense of propriety, shyness, modesty, but also secretiveness and caution. Consider wading out into emotional waters, learning by privately trying something new, the mysteries of sexual union; shyness; inhibited caution; the wisdom that in a harsh world it is wise to step gently at first; tribulations regarding coming out; silently getting around obstacles.

"A hen scratching for her chicks (18 Cancer) and "The Union Jack" (18 Capricorn)

Aspect: Trine.
Quality: Maintaining.
Shared motifs: 'Transmitting identity,' 'clan colors.'

"A hen scratching for her chicks" is an image of the care for maintaining the healthy growth of the young by transmitting the instinctual means for survival. The earlier stages of life call for guidance and wise alertness to the incredible difficulties of keeping the young ones alive, of finding enough nourishment for the now well-formed but still young creatures. It is a down-to-earth enterprise of the everyday provision for life and further growth. This does not require a code book, nor does it simply happen. Providing for the young takes a concerted and an everyday, earth-focused effort. The hen is teaching the young how to grow into independence. Something instinctual and essential for survival is being passed along.

"The Union Jack" is an image of an emblem that confidently announces identity. The "Union Jack" is the name of the flag of the United Kingdom. The flag represents a union of the differing stripes or crosses that form a whole: the crosses of patron saints, Saint George, Saint Andrew, and Saint Patrick, combined to signify the union of England, Scotland, and Ireland. The "union" is about identity: ethnic, cultural, and historical. It is showing one's colors, like waving a pennant: "Go, Yankees, go!" It is about filling the air with a certain color or stamp, like that of the once glorious British Empire, hence suggesting imperialism. It covers the world with a family or tribal imprint. It says, "Jack was here!" or "Oh, bloody hell! Here comes Jack and his fellows!"

The Union Jack passes from generation to generation, expressing an intangible identity. Having an emblematic identity helps Jack know to what people he belongs, but it can feed him only indirectly. A chick without a mother hen to pass on the ways of the world may not be able to survive on its own. Having enough scratch, money or resources, helps one get on with life and living. Jack may know how to take what he wants, what he needs from others; the hen knows how to give to her chicks what they need to live on. Jack sees beyond the horizon as somewhere to conquer and explore; the hen may be a little chicken about straying too far from the coop. The mother country, like any mother, responds without hesitation when it perceives a possible threat to its young. It is a mistake to assume that a mother lacks the courage to defend her young.

Apply this degree-pair with a mind to showing one's colors, one's heritage, the sense of owned tradition. Watch for an alertness for that which one is prepared to fight for, work for, or defend. Consider tattoos, any manner of showing one's stripes, female domesticity, ruling the roost, and actions that come home to roost. Consider issues of having enough or having it all; handwriting that looks like chicken scratch; bold in the world, henpecked at home; bold at home, but chicken in the world; scratching one's name on something or planting one's flag.

"A priest performing a marriage ceremony" (19 Cancer) and "A child of about five with a huge shopping bag" (19 Capricorn)

Aspect: Square.
Quality: Challenge.
Shared motifs: 'Marrying and synergy,'
'carrying huge responsibilities.'

"A priest performing a marriage ceremony" is an image of a ceremonial act of uniting two people together in marriage. "Ceremony" is suggestive of the forms of convention and conformity within prevailing socioreligious norms. If the ceremony is mere empty form, then conformity triumphs over the sacred. If the ceremony is performed with a genuine feel for ritual process, then the priest, who is the substantiation of higher, divine energy, truly weds two individuals into a greater whole: synergy. The arithmetic of marriage is ever ruled by the principle that the whole is greater than the sum of the parts, for example, one plus one is ever "about" three or more.

"A child of about five with a huge shopping bag" is an image of a young child carrying responsibilities beyond his years. "A huge shopping bag" suggests a big curiosity about the world. Potentially, if you have a big bag, you can put a lot of stuff into it. The supermarket view of the world reduces experience and growth to the concept of "shopping": a big-box store calls for a big bag. Perhaps, in a little girl's world, she is shopping for agreement, for approval or recognition from others, out of circumstances that have placed big responsibilities in her hands. If the bag were to be filled, there is a question of whether one "of about five years" could carry the load.

The global cultural/intellectual/creative/spiritual marketplace has much to offer. The question is: Is there enough maturity to carry the load? The adult variation of this question is: Are you acting immaturely with regard to shopping for your perceived needs? Perhaps the supermarket view of the world comes with considerable baggage. Perhaps the responsibility of marrying others together, of marriage in general, is a heavy load. When life thrusts adult responsibilities upon the very young, inevitably there is a long silence before their voices are heard, before their experience takes on an effective role in the wider world.

Apply this degree-pair with a mind to marrying youth to adult responsibilities, wedding young hands to big loads. Be aware of the arithmetic of the situation: Does it all add up? Is it only "about" right? Or does wedding together two human factors always mean the whole is greater than the sum of the parts? Watch for a missed childhood due to circumstances concerning the welfare of others: incapacitated or absent parents, caring for siblings. Consider consecration, uplifting relationships, elevating status, marrying youth with age, wedding maturity with youth; adult children; childish adults; learning how to put bread on the table early in life; quietly assuming responsibilities of others out of a perceived necessity; patiently waiting one's turn to sing one's own song.

"Gondoliers in a serenade" (20 Cancer)
and "A hidden choir singing" (20 Capricorn)

Aspect: Quintile.
Quality: Creative genius.
Shared motifs: 'Floating voices that move one along,'
'singing like nobody's listening.'

"Gondoliers in a serenade" is an image of being moved along by enchanting song. "Gondoliers" are the oarsmen of gondolas, flat-bottomed boats with high ornamented stem and stern posts. One is reminded of J. Offenbach's *The Tales of Hoffman:* the "Barcarolle" opens a scene in the Grand Canal in Venice with an exquisitely beautiful and seductive love song in the night. A "serenade," like the "Barcarolle," is an intoxicatingly sublime love reverie sung at night, especially under a lover's window. A slightly less dignified example of serenading is the unabashed bacchanal: a wild and drunken revelry associated with Bacchus or Dionysus.

"A hidden choir singing" is an image of many voices raised in song, but hidden from view. To be "hidden" is to be out of sight. Usually associated with church music and cathedrals, there is a suggestion of celestial, sublime music in celebration of divine love. A "chorus" is a group singing in unison. Often choirs lift their voices together out of view from the gathered assembly. Perhaps one can hear a choir rehearsing in passing. Singing in unison while in visual seclusion is suggestive of a cloistered choir. Cloistered choir meets roisterous street song.

Imagine the many instances of hidden voices singing in unison. After a big sporting match, home-team revelers stream through the streets, intoxicated with joy while singing the team song. One might awaken to an exalted love song that seems very much like sweet dreaming. One might have a sense of a choir of angels whose sublime singing uplifts the spirit. A siren song can cause ruin: Odysseus had his crew put wax in their ears to prevent them from being wrecked on the rocky shores, while he himself was lashed to the mast of the boat so he could hear the irresistible song. Consider the confidence of voice while singing in a shower, under the assumption that no one can hear; or singing in a boisterous group where the quality of one's own voice is no longer an issue, therefore an uninhibited vocalizing of joyful song. There is a Confucian dictum that goes something like this: "While alone, act as if you are in the presence of others; while with others, act as if you are alone."

Apply this degree-pair with a mind to the hidden, alluring powers of sublime singing. Think of the blissful joys and destructive potentials of intoxicating reveries and revelries; alluring temptations that promise comfort and joy; sirens singing sweetly or sounding an alarm to head for hidden shelters. Think of floating along propelled only by something or someone standing behind, out of view; of a church choir hidden above the nave; of roguish knaves roisterously singing below your window. Consider songs any Jack might sing, but also sublime voices and songs of unearthly beauty; a genius to hear the music in all things; to make even the everyday and the ordinary sound good.

"A prima donna singing" (21 Cancer)
and "A relay race" (21 Capricorn)

Aspect: Conjunction.
Quality: Focus.
Shared motifs: 'Focal point of attention,'
'the scepters of artistry and competition.'

"A prima donna singing" is an image of the first lady of song in an opera. The floodlights focus on the principal singer on center stage, relaying the story of her character in song with sublime power, beauty, and technique. As the principal singer in an opera company, a prima donna plays a focal role, is the object of focused attention, but is by no means solely responsible for the overall production. The opera company, the singers, the orchestra, the behind-the-scenes crew: all must pull together to stage a triumphant show. Operas can be lengthy. A prima donna must pace herself, to be ready, for example, for the difficult passages within a well-loved aria.

"A relay race" is an image of a team effort focused on the passing of the baton to the next runner. A relay team calls for each individual to exert their best at the appropriate time within the lines that define their lane. Little separates team members in status. It is crucial that each help the other in a smooth exchange for maximum team success. While a relay race is run, the crowds cheer their vocal support. There is a strong focus on athletes excelling in a cooperative competition: the merging of power and precision in the running of the race; the spontaneous orchestration of the crowd at each interval; the groans of a thousand voices when a baton is dropped; the crescendo of delight at a smooth pass and a burst of speed.

While the prima donna sings, the audience is in rapt attention. Applauding during an aria is like crossing the lanes or taking off too soon in a relay race. "To relay" is to convey, to pass on, as one would convey a message. Imagine the Pony Express, which depended on having fresh ponies in reserve in order to deliver the mail on time. "Relay" also means to keep in reserve, to allow for, to let something happen again. While the conductor holds the baton that leads the orchestra, it is the singer who must keep in reserve enough energy to run the full race of the entire opera. Prima donnas are often associated with temperamental airs of self-importance. Their role, however, is demanding, requiring enormous stamina while displaying ease and grace to the audience.

Apply this degree-pair with a mind to the extraordinary focus in performance that commands attention; the technique and ability that ever allows for power in reserve; an intense alertness to the faux pas. Listen for the interrelationship between audience and performer; the passing of the symbolic baton; the expectation of, or the winning of, loud approval. Watch for swinging batons: the staff of authority or privilege. Consider wands that energize, excite, and empower; being at the center of focus for the benefit of others; being at one's best so as to not let others down; standing in reserve in case you are needed; feeding off the crescendo of applause and excitement for a well-timed finish; counting on others to back you up.

"A woman awaiting a sailboat" (22 Cancer)
and "A general accepting defeat gracefully" (22 Capricorn)

Aspect: Opposition.
Quality: Awareness of.
Shared motifs: 'Acceptance of one's lot in life,'
'harmony of heart, action, and life.'

"A woman awaiting a sailboat" is an image of expectancy that can only be fulfilled through the favor of wind. "Awaiting" means to be ready for, in store for, to watch for. Imagine a woman attentively watching the horizon for the sight of a sail rising into view. A "sailboat" is a watercraft that relies on wind power to propel its motion across the sea. It is not within the scope of human capacity to rule the winds: one can only harness the energy of the winds that grace our world. "Awaiting" is not mere empty hope. Human longing reaches beyond the horizon of apparent prospect, bends over the horizon in anticipation of something more: a fair wind to fill our sails.

"A general accepting defeat gracefully" is an image of a display of admirable character acting in harmony with the prevailing winds. "Grace" applies to movement as a harmony of motion and is distinguished from "beauty," which applies more to appearance. "Defeat" is to fail to accomplish, to be vanquished, to frustrate victory of one's purpose. "To try" or "to attempt" something ever admits of possible greater powers that lie in reserve to overcome human attempts. It may be maintained that to say "I am" is nobler than "I tried," but the exultant glory of the moment of victory still bears a questionable transience when held up to a noble and graceful defeat.

Wind seems to wander aimlessly, to change direction without apparent reason. A "wand"—the conductor's baton, the royal scepter, the magician's wand, the warrior's sword—is a slender stick used to canalize energy, to direct focused energy for human purposes. A general symbolically acknowledges defeat by surrendering his sword. Handing over one's sword symbolizes relinquishing all intention of directing an attack; disarming conflict. Favoring winds can convey one to one's destination. Catching a fair wind requires having a sense of the right time to hoist the sail. Catching wind of something puts one on the alert, wakefully on guard like a sentinel for the winds of destiny.

Apply this degree-pair with a mind to nobility of character, grand and fitting gestures; longing strengthened by divine influence. Watch for awareness of greater powers, patience for appropriate timing; knowing when to step down; regenerative capacities in the face of apparent defeat. Consider graceful movements; picking up a scent; respect for the winds of fortune, for one's lot in life (Lachesis, the second sister of Fate who measures the thread of life); being in the doldrums. Graciousness in defeat is a hallmark of greatness of character. To be defeated by a power far greater than oneself, the longing for love, the power of might, is a victory of the inner spirit, not an achievement for public applause, but that with which every human spirit needs to wrestle in order to know their own invulnerable dignity.

"Meeting of a literary society" (23 Cancer) and "Two awards for bravery in war" (23 Capricorn)

Aspect: Trine.
Quality: Maintaining.
Shared motifs: 'Special-interest motivation,'
'agony and ecstasy.'

"Meeting of a literary society" is an image of a gathering of persons with a shared love for literature. "Literary" refers to a broad range of books or written composition valued for quality of form or style. A "literary society" gathers men and women of letters whose interests may welcome all forms of literature or focus on areas of specialization. Literature tends to be prized for the quality of beauty of language or by the effect upon the emotions, the way a good book or poem may inspire others and live beyond its author.

"Two awards for bravery in war" is an image bestowing honor, reward, or recognition for courage displayed while at war, win or lose. "Bravery" is the display of courage in the face of danger, a resolve to follow through to the end, setting one's personal safety aside in favor of completing the task. A warrior sacrifices his personal well-being to get the mission done. Receiving awards after wartime service is not dependent upon having won the war. Individual displays of courage are recognized even if the war or mission was a failure.

"Ward" means to watch, to guard. An "award" is a token of recognition deemed due or bestowed for actions or efforts in a contest of some kind. All contest is a struggle: *agon* is the name of the ancient Greek competitions or games from which the Olympics derive. "Agony" is intense suffering of body or mind in the face of stiff competition or violent struggle. A general may receive awards even in defeat. A woman watches the horizon for a sailboat that may never appear, yet receives respect for her constancy in longing. A good book about bravery in war may be highly appreciated by a literary society. What is to be awarded, to be recognized and appreciated, is not immune to special interests with a common purpose to vouchsafe those interests: awards, like swords, can have two edges.

Apply this degree-pair with a mind to the internal struggles and agonies within both the world of art and beauty, and that of the battlefields of war. Think of protecting, watching over, in terms of both self-sacrifice and the guarding of self-interest. The question is: What moves, what motivates, the awarding of recognition? Consider bestowal by grace or bestowal by the machinations of special interest. The intellectual and emotional fray of a gathering of men of letters is not all that far from the daunting battlefield. Watch for tokens, two-faced badges of courage; romantics versus might is right; favoring dignity or lobbying for favor. Consider those who watch over past neglects; who honor the greatness of those who fly beneath the public's radar; gatherings of unknown people who appreciate your efforts; quiet, anonymous cheering sections; receiving acknowledgments from surprising sources. Remember that the pen is mightier than the sword.

"A woman and two men on a bit of sunlit land facing south" (24 Cancer) and "A woman entering a convent" (24 Capricorn)

Aspect: Square.
Quality: Challenge.
Shared motifs: 'Facing the full light of day,'
'withdrawing from the fray.'

"A woman and two men on a bit of sunlit land facing south" is an image of a classic love triangle: the challenge of choosing personal affinities born of the heart. The I Ching says of this situation: "When three people journey together, their number decreases by one. When one man journeys alone, he finds a companion."[3] "Facing south" is an archetypal expression of sacral kingship. It refers to seeing things in the clearest light, contemplating the forms of reality, while directing sacral energy through the scepter of the royal couple guided by the ancestral rulers associated with the north. "A bit of sunlit land" suggests a small issue that is highlighted, such as a conflict focused upon for consideration. A woman may have to choose between two very different kinds of men: an artist or poet and a warrior; a lover and a man of action; an intellectual and a man of status or authority.

"A woman entering a convent" is an image of choosing to leave the profane world and seeking refuge in a cloistered world. The world of human society is filled with turmoil and struggle. One may choose a spiritual path, sacrificing worldly pleasures and achievements for the pursuit of religious devotion. It is as if the intense pressures of having to choose in matters of love and life motivate a third course: withdrawing from the fray. A "convent" is a community of like-minded people who live in quiet seclusion from the outside world. A cloistered existence is one that is covered, guarded, protected from worldly temptations.

The sun illuminates the world. Metaphorically, the sun brings to light every issue of human existence and the fact that the issue of human existence is having to choose. One may retreat from the world, confining oneself to a simpler way of life: escape from life in favor of spiritual upliftment, or escape from confinement to embrace life as a whole. One might run away to a desert isle only to find oneself facing difficult choices anyway. One may escape spiritual peril by cloaking one's life in spiritual seclusion.

Apply this degree-pair with a mind to the challenge of choosing one's path in life; having to choose between two worthy options; finding oneself in triangulated circumstances no matter where one goes. Think of protective covering in terms of both focusing light on a matter and avoiding the issue. Watch attempts to guard and protect under cover; withdrawal to contemplate or focus upon important choices; feelings of being confined in the world. Consider the world as a prison; confinement as spiritual freedom; forfeiting emotionally charged decisions; withholding one's favor, as in toying with the hearts of others; never having a relationship that just involves two; finding that even the love of God involves a third party; feeling stuck in what seems like an eternal threesome.

"A dark shadow or mantle thrown suddenly over the right shoulder" (25 Cancer) and "An oriental-rug dealer" (25 Capricorn)

Aspect: Quintile.
Quality: Creative genius.
Shared motifs: 'Bold choices,' 'covering and revealing,'
'every orientation casts a shadow.'

"A dark shadow or mantle thrown suddenly over the right shoulder" is an image of displaying a definite choice and shouldering the full consequences of that choice with a flourish. "A dark shadow" is that which is cast by a definite stance: the sun shines on the southern exposure of a river valley while the side facing north is obscured by shade. "A mantle" is a covering or cloak, usually sleeveless, that is thrown over the shoulders. When thrown "over the right shoulder," a mantle suggests a powerful showing of one's self that both reveals and cloaks. Imagine a Roman senator, suddenly throwing his mantle over his shoulder in a show of decisive affirmation or rejection. The right shoulder is covered, the left exposed.

"An oriental-rug dealer" is an image of one who trades in floor coverings, suggestive of how one enters and walks through life. A "rug" covers the floor, that upon which we stand. A "standard deal" is a fir or pine plank measured three inches thick, nine inches wide, and twelve feet long. An "oriental rug" is usually a hand-knotted covering, the making of which recalls Moira or the three sisters of Fate: the spinning, allotting, and cutting of the thread of life. "Oriental" means of or pertaining to the east. An oriental rug is often an elaborate geometric pattern like a mandala, an expression of life as a whole upon which we stand.

Taking a strong, decisive stance is a quality to be admired. It is like showing your face to the world much as the sun breaks over the eastern horizon, illuminating, as it were, a course through life for a destination to the west. One orients oneself in life relative to a vast array of possibilities. Choosing one's path in life is an "oriental" matter: emerging suddenly in the east while journeying west; guided from the north while facing south. To "shoulder" something is to support, bear up, carry one's own load: shouldering both the burden and the blame. A soldier shoulders arms; a mission is completed by people working shoulder to shoulder. Taking a stance, making a choice, is like being illuminated by the sunlight. Since one's body intercepts the light, there is ever a shadow cast by one's choice.

Apply this degree-pair with a mind to the human creativity to stand decisively, to shoulder one's identity with a flourish; accepting being partially vulnerable while claiming one's power; accepting one's deal as the best one can get. Think of that upon which humans stand; a sense of the whole relative to personal choice; choice and consequence; being straightforward about where one stands. Be aware of shadow dynamics: covering over; hiding or half-revealing; standing tall, therefore casting a shadow. Every choice, every stance, throws a shadow. Consider a confident bluff; a defiant stance; a clever cover; a well-woven position; standing up for new influences; tossing off insignificant matters; the dignity of boldly standing one's ground.

"Contentment and happiness in luxury, people reading on davenports" (26 Cancer) and "A water sprite" (26 Capricorn)

Aspect: Conjunction.
Quality: Focus.
Shared motifs: 'Enticing excess meets spiritual ecstasy,'
'that which casts no shadow.'

"Contentment and happiness in luxury, people reading on davenports" is an image of sustained feelings of satisfaction from an understanding upon which one rests. "Contentment" means a satisfaction that is free from worry, held together within comfortable bounds. "Happiness" is a sustained feeling of aptness about something, like a happy choice of words. "Luxury" pertains to pleasure that lies outside the bounds of life's necessities. A "davenport" is an American term for a sofa, often also used as a bed. In Britain, a davenport is a small writing desk. "Reading" suggests understanding, taking to mean something, in this case, being satisfied and comfortable regarding one's take of the world, lying in the bed of one's choice, so to speak.

"A water sprite" is an image of a spirit with an affinity for water. Water is a necessity of life. It is symbolically, and often naturally, a clear liquid. A "sprite" is a disembodied spirit, that is, one that casts no shadow. Often associated with elves and fairies, a sprite can be a fanciful product of the imagination, or an invisible, if almost tangible, sense of spirit: esprit de corps. "Water sprites" are also water nymphs (naiads, nereids, and oceanids), feminine divinities often associated with youth and enticing beauty. A water nymph can allure hapless young men to their doom, or effect a mania of the same name. The story of Hylas and the water nymphs is a case in point. Hylas left his traveling party to fill a jug of water from a nearby spring inhabited by water nymphs. He did not return. It is not known whether he went to his death or to his ecstasy.

Satisfaction that surpasses the limits of reason is a divine ecstasy. When luxury is ecstatic, it is extravagance: wandering outside normal limits or beyond moderation. Luxuries, since they are beyond the necessities of life, can be indulgent and rare, and usually come with a cost. One comes to learn that the deluxe model comes with all the unnecessary bells and whistles: really more than you need. In a spiritual or sexual sense, ecstatic bliss is without blame. Still, it is a delicate point: spiritually pure, or excessively indulgent. Does spirit cast a shadow? Ultimately, such questions turn upon how one reads the situation.

Apply this degree-pair with a mind to the inclination to recline in contentment as opposed to a sprightly or spirited manner; extravagant layabout as opposed to a quick and agile nature. Watch for quick learners; the insensible apprehension of spirits; a fascination with the perils of ecstasy; happiness or hapless fortune. Look for alluring qualities; a penchant for divans, long, low, armless sofas, rooms used for councils, smoking and drinking; reading and writing poetry; poetry of spiritual or sexual ecstasy.

"A storm in a canyon" (27 Cancer)
and "A mountain pilgrimage" (27 Capricorn)

Aspect: Opposition.
Quality: Awareness of.
Shared motifs: 'Ecstatic peaks,' 'scaling steep heights,'
'bent on passion.'

"A storm in a canyon" is an image of a violent or energetic disturbance in a deep valley. "A canyon" is a geological formation, often with a river flowing through a deep valley with steep, clifflike walls. "A storm" is a disturbance in the atmosphere, or a violent outburst of excitement or passion. One can storm a fortress with a vigorous, rapid assault, or have a tempestuous character. Storms are measured on the Beaufort scale: an "eleven" on the scale of wind velocity. The "elevenses" is a name for a break for tea at about eleven AM. The "Eleventh Commandment" satirically reads: "Thou shalt not be found out."

"A mountain pilgrimage" is an image of a journey that climbs a sacred mountain. "Pilgrimage" derives from "peregrine," meaning to travel or wander. A pilgrim is one who makes such a journey to a sacred site, coming from a foreign region with a specific motive and goal in mind. "A mountain" is a natural elevation on the earth's surface, typically with steep sides and a narrow summit. Scaling steep mountain walls is an arduous affair, often exposing one to precipitous cliffs. Perhaps one is steeped in religious motivation to reach the highest peak, or saturated with desire for peak experiences.

"Steeping" has to do with extracting the essence of something, the way a tea bag is steeped in hot water. A cup of tea is unsatisfying if it is steeped too long, or not long enough. "Steep" is also the name of a liquid for fertilizing seeds. Paradoxically, a pilgrim climbs a sacred mountain with an attitude of stooping or bowing low before the divine. If it is not stooping too low, "schtooping" is a slang expression with a sexual connotation much like a passionate, rapid assault of a storm in a canyon. Bending low for higher pursuits; rising high to enter deep: one is aware of the stark contrasts in elevation.

Apply this degree-pair with a mind to an awareness of extremes of high and low, sacred and profane, disturbance and excitement. Watch for heightened awareness of the essence of an activity, deep inner meanings, scales of difference. Steep objectives often lead to strange journeys, ecstatic obsessions, being taken beyond familiar, ordinary realms. Be alert to being bent over by powerful forces, bowing to higher powers, an inclination to rush into, or to be excited with, great passions or goals. Always look for the underlying motives to get the bent on the situation. Consider highs and lows of moods and dispositions; obsession with reaching the top; obsessed inclinations to stay low; personal realizations that get one off the couch; external forces that force one to get up and look all around; a sense that something is brewing; making a pilgrimage for no apparent reason: just something irresistible steeping inside.

"A modern Pocahontas" (28 Cancer) and "A large aviary" (28 Capricorn)

Aspect: Trine.
Quality: Maintaining.
Shared motifs: 'How legends grow,' 'youthful diplomacy,'
'a rose by any other name . . ."

"A modern Pocahontas" is an image of a playful, perhaps wanton, little girl fascinated with the strangers from a foreign region. "Pocahontas," the daughter of an Indian chief, had a great curiosity for the white settlers in Jamestown, Virginia. Said to have saved the life of John Smith, Pocahontas eventually married the very religious John Rolfe, a man who was shipwrecked earlier in a tempest near Bermuda from where he brought tobacco seed to cross with the harsher Virginia tobacco, a hybrid upon which his fortune came to be based. Pocahontas sailed to England with her husband, where she died at the age of twenty-two.

"A large aviary" is an image of a contained space that houses many birds. When a large number of birds are gathered together, the bird chatter abounds. In a large aviary, there can be many bird species mixed in close quarters, their distinctive songs producing a din of either harmonious sounds or discordant cacophony. Imagine a group of people, united by race or religion, talking amongst themselves about another strange and foreign group with whom they share nothing in common, apart from the fact of being human. Stories build, probably rife with moral branding, bias, and projected fears. One group is seen as invaders by the other; the invaders see themselves as colonists bringing civilization to a savage people and land. Enter a young, spirited female, over whom, about whom, because of whom, diplomacy is initiated.

"Pocahontas" means playful one; little wanton, playful, frolicsome girl; naughty one. Her real name was Matoaka, but the Algonquian tribe believed it safer to be known by a nickname, as their enemies could do harm if they knew the real name. Note that the name "Indian" is itself a misnomer: Columbus assumed he had reached India in 1492. Pocahontas was all of ten or eleven when the now legendary events with John Smith took place. She was briefly married to an Indian warrior and played an instrumental role in helping the foreign ones. Eventually a white man offered to marry her on the condition that she convert to Christianity. Her name was changed yet again to Rebecca.

Apply this degree-pair with a mind to wanton, unrestrained, spirited capacities to cross barriers of sorts: social, ethnic, racial, religious, political. Think of the stories that are told and grow out of proportion by many chattering mouths. Birds-of-a-feather themes are challenged by spirited ones who easily come and go from other camps. Be alert to the need to tell a story to one's best advantage, to talk matters up to reinforce a prevailing version. Watch for uninhibited natures: sexual, social, moral, political, that shamelessly wander into foreign regions, dress in foreign clothes, pray to strange gods; bringing home an unlikely marriage partner; bridging worlds of difference with sprightly, unaffected resolve, despite being very much talked about.

"A muse weighing twins" (29 Cancer) and "A woman reading tea leaves" (29 Capricorn)

Aspect: Square.
Quality: Challenge.
Shared motifs: 'Leaves steeped in meaning,'
'an inspired or a blind sense of balance.'

"A muse weighing twins" is an image of thoughtful consideration given to the two sides of a matter. "A muse" is an inspiring spirit or power. In Greek mythology, "Muse" can refer to any of the nine muses presiding over the arts and sciences.

"Weighing" is also a careful consideration that seeks to measure the worth or advantage of a thing: to weigh a proposal, for example. While "weighing" suggests weight, it also refers to lifting or hoisting, as in to weigh anchor. A weigh scale or balance is used to estimate the relative weight or importance of a matter. "Weighing twins" implies a twofold situation, one that is, to the naked eye, almost equal, yet requires more careful consideration.

"A woman reading tea leaves" is an image of deriving a take, an understanding of something, through divinatory means. "Reading tea leaves" is done after the cup of tea has been enjoyed. The leaves have been steeped and the cup poured and consumed, leaving the dregs, which form a chance pattern in the cup. A "teetotaler" is one who abstains from all intoxicants, entirely removed from the teetering, seesawing, extremes of passion and excitement that tip the scales now this way, now that. Like a balance scale held up for objective estimation, a teetotaling tea reader seeks to apprehend the meaning of something twice removed.

Imagine the blindfolded muse, Astraea, holding up the scales of justice, signifying impartial judgment for opposing parties. Decisions in the name of justice are not always free of bias: consider the Native American descendants of Pocahontas being moved from their homes and placed on a reserve of unwanted, unproductive lands. Some might consider it poetic justice, unforeseen, well-deserved retribution, that the American Indian gift to the white man was the tobacco leaf. Reason is challenged to render fair reading of human issues that lie in the balance; muselike inspiration may assess the same issue of deserving in an entirely foreign way.

Apply this degree-pair with a mind to the challenge of apprehending matters objectively while still weighing just due; pondering weighty issues while reading between the lines; restraining natural compassionate urges for happy endings in assessing issues of deserving. Watch for a tendency to jump into a matter or a project without forethought or adequate preparation; a tendency to pursue dead ends or blind alleys that block successful completion or progress. Consider why justice favors a blind eye; turning a blind eye to a rigged balance scale; being eye-blinded yet seeing deeper truths; supreme court decisions that are still smoking issues; the blind leading the blind or the tendency to give advice when unsuited to do so; having a blind spot while attempting to be objective. Remember that the blindfolded goddess Astraea is the daughter of Themis, justice, not justice herself.

"A daughter of the American Revolution" (30 Cancer)
and "A secret business conference" (30 Capricorn)

Aspect: Quintile.
Quality: Creative genius.
Shared motifs: 'Healing dreams,' 'dreams that call for healing,'
'inheritance summits.'

"A daughter of the American Revolution" is an image of the aftermath of the colonization of the Native American homeland. The descendants of the American Revolutionaries who fought for independence inherit the balance of their ancestors' choices. The present is ever bent by, infused with, the events of the past. The "American revolution" is itself a symbol of freedom from unjust influence and stricture from a foreign homeland. "No taxation without representation" was a revolutionary cry that led to a very different cup of tea. The sentiments of "life, liberty, and the pursuit of happiness" continue to inspire a sense of rightness, a supreme self-evident principle. Americans are, however, also foreign intruders into a land with an indigenous population: this, too, is an inheritance.

"A secret business conference" is an image of a behind-closed-doors meeting where significant decisions are made. The North American Indian word for a conference or meeting is "powwow," which derives from the Algonquian "powaw," magician, medicine man, literally "he who apprehends by dreams." A "secret" meeting is one where what goes on in the meeting is hidden from all but a few. A secret can be a mystery, a valid but not commonly known means to apprehend the meaning of something. "Conference" derives from "confer," to grant, bestow, consult. "Business" is that which is one's concern, work, dealings involving trade.

It may be self-evident to most that the leaves in the bottom of your tea cup are just leaves; to others, there is more meaning to apprehend. The Boston Tea Party was a dramatic show of defiance toward a foreign controlling interest: the essence of a discontent that had reached the saturation point. Secret meetings are where important matters are sifted through, considered deeply. The weightier the issue, the more need there is for exemplary people to divine a resolution. Sometimes the issue is just a tempest in a teapot; sometimes it is remarkable how an infused drink meant for enjoyment can become the standard or currency, the measure of worth. In American history, the tobacco leaf was the first commodity to supplant the tea leaf as such a standard.

Apply this degree-pair with a mind to inherited issues decided behind closed doors, sifting through leaves of paper to find one's roots, trifles that become the fuse for dramatic, revolutionary changes. Watch for getting heads together for conferring, summit meetings, steeping oneself in the issues, feeling infused with pride or shame from the past. Issues decided by the few, behind closed doors, can affect everyone, can cast a long shadow. Consider a genius for magical apprehension of the truth; inherited abilities; ills; smoking issues; paper documents of historical importance.

---

1. In his book *The Sabian Symbols in Astrology,* Marc Edmund Jones replaced the original word on the notecard, "auto," with "automobile," cf. Diana E. Roche, *The Sabian Symbols: A Screen of Prophecy* (Victoria, B.C.: Trafford, 1998) p. 125.

2. M. E. Jones replaced the original word on the notecard, "carved," with "cut," cf. Roche, p. 340.

3. Hexagram 41, Richard Wilhelm and Cary F. Baynes, trans., *The I Ching or Book of Changes* (Princeton, NJ: Princeton University Press, 1972) p. 160.

CHAPTER FIVE

LEO-AQUARIUS

"A case of apoplexy" (1 Leo)
and "An old adobe mission" (1 Aquarius)

Aspect: Conjunction.
Quality: Focus.
Shared motifs: 'Sudden onset in a slow-bake oven,'
'being fervent at a slow pace.'

"A case of apoplexy" is an image of a sudden rush of color to the face. "Apoplexy" is the name formerly used for a "stroke": a sudden impairment of neurological function, especially involving a hemorrhage. To be "apoplectic," however, refers to any effusion of blood into an organ or tissue, an occurrence mirrored in human character by sudden fits of anger, rage, or embarrassment. One can be paralyzed with laughter, facial tissues flushing with blood and blush. One can be suddenly warmed with enthusiasm, which shows so readily in an excited face. "A case" refers to an actual circumstance or state of affairs. There are medical cases and cases about which one can be passionate, excited, dramatically blurting out "a case in point" or a demonstrative example.

"An old adobe mission" is an image of a sun-baked building erected for a specific purpose or cause in a foreign territory. Imagine a white missionary being sent to a burning desert area like Arizona, living in dwellings of sun-dried brick and sporting the sunburn of one unfamiliar with the prevailing clime. A "mission" is a site established to advance a particular cause. Christian missionaries travel to foreign places like the burning-hot southwestern states of the United States, bringing their religious perspective to those indigenous to the area.

Imagine the burning fervor of someone whose deep beliefs motivate a journey to foreign, even hostile, places. Perhaps decisions made behind closed doors of a committee meeting call for spreading the word from Virginia to arid regions of California. Fervent individuals strike out to establish ideas, inherited traditions, and beliefs in far-off places where, almost literally, everything is sun-baked. The quest to carry beliefs and views far afield exposes all concerned to the inadvertent spread of foreign disease: in this case even a kindly message can have striking repercussions. To be "casehardened" is to be callous, to develop a thick skin through repeated experience. One eager with enthusiasm may become flushed with impatience when one's point is not taken quickly. "Hard cases" often take time to assess, the way a thief might "case a joint" before acting to liberate a house or building of the valuables within.

Apply this degree-pair with a mind to focused enthusiasm eager to broadcast self-evident, universal truths; an intense desire to burst out of the mold; dramatic onsets of fever, feverish expression, or fervent belief. Watch for the sudden onset in each case. Look for red faces; the colors of excitement; passions that call for a new form of shelter. Watch especially for creating circumstances in which the unexpected can strike. Consider traits of enthusiasm, optimism, kindheartedness, willingness to go into hot spots; the willingness to take on hard cases, difficult circumstances; the tendency to become quickly impatient or frustrated regarding the pace of development; being exposed to differing cultural senses of the pace at which things proceed.

"An epidemic of mumps" (2 Leo)
and "An unexpected thunderstorm" (2 Aquarius)

Aspect: Opposition.
Quality: Awareness of.
Shared motifs: 'Infectious ideas and their aftermath,'
'unforeseen benefit or detriment.'

"An epidemic of mumps" is an image of a widespread occurrence overwhelming the normal abilities to use or reject. An "epidemic" is the widespread occurrence of disease in a community. "Mumps" is a viral disease of the parotid salivary gland located in front of the ear with ducts reaching across the face to the mouth. The common "mumps" manifest as red swellings on the face due to an overload of the glands. Glands function to produce something of use, or to reject harmful elements from an organic body. To have the "mumps" meant, in archaic terms, to be sulky, sullen, even resentful in a silent, aloof manner. "Mumping Day" in England was a day when the poor would go about "mumping": begging for corn or gifts near Christmas time.

"An unexpected thunderstorm" is an image of the rapid onset of something loud and violent. A "thunderstorm" is known for its loud resounding noises that follow a sudden flash of lightning. It is a dramatic disturbance in the atmosphere. Something is "unexpected" when it appears out of place, in unusual fashion, without previous anticipation of the event. Imagine an adobe brick building beset with violent rains and wind. The sun-baked bricks might be reduced to mud; buildings might dissolve and crumble.

Epidemics bring one face to face, or red-faced to face, with the widespread prevalence of a sudden and surprising manifestation. Schoolchildren may seem sullen at first when the mumps strike, but then rejoice at the unexpected school holiday. Anyone who has traveled to certain regions of the world will be familiar with Montezuma's revenge: the sudden onset of deep rumbling signaling the need for quick expulsive actions. This condition of discomfort is called a "revenge" because the arrival of conquerors like Cortés brought unexpected, widespread foreign diseases that wreaked havoc on indigenous populations. Good intentions sometimes bring unexpected results, making it no surprise to be received in sullen, resentful silence.

Apply this degree-pair with a mind to the sudden awareness of the full effects of what is enthusiastically introduced; of the downside to big ideas, profound messages. Watch for things that spread rapidly, upsetting normal expectations; chances to reflect on the aftermath. Something that seems too good to be true probably is. Watch for an ability to be immune to infectious fads; cathartic turns of events; useful quiet time; knowing when to be quiet. Every burning idea overheats the atmosphere in some way: dark, rumbling clouds are never far away. Consider issues of digesting what has been said, speaking but not listening; listening but not speaking, and red facial eruptions; sudden fame or taking by storm; to "steal one's thunder," to have one's original idea taken over by someone for their own advantage.

"A woman having her hair bobbed" (3 Leo)
and "A deserter from the navy" (3 Aquarius)

Aspect: Trine.
Quality: Maintaining.
Shared motifs: 'Bouncing back,'
'aptly leaving off or cutting away from.'

"A woman having her hair bobbed" is an image of hair being cut short or bundled into a manageable ball. To have "hair bobbed" is to have it cut short or bound up, as in a bun. "To bob" is to move quickly up and down, like the motion of a head expressing sudden agreement; to bounce back buoyantly, like apples being bobbed for; emerging conspicuously, as in bobbing back after an absence, defeat, or illness. A "bob" is also a short curtsy or a greeting out of courtesy. When one places a bet on a "bobtailed nag," one is choosing to wager on a small horse whose tail hair is tied up so as to not interfere with running. A "bobtailed flush" in poker is a three-card flush, worthless since it takes five cards to count.

"A deserter from the navy" is an image of suddenly leaving something behind. "A deserter" is one who abandons, gives up, detaches himself, or runs away. A "desert" is an arid barren land, a forbidding wasteland unsuitable for cultivation. "Navy," deriving from navigation and nautical themes, is also a deep-blue color used for naval uniforms. One may be deserting the blues, leaving behind a sullen mood. Curiously, "naval," "nautical," and "noise" are akin to nausea, or the loud noise of violent seasickness from passengers in turbulent weather. The Navajo Indians happen to live in desert regions like New Mexico, where the Spanish sailors first encountered them.

Women may suddenly become fed up with long hair and have it cut short in order to manage it more easily. "A deserter from the navy" may deserve a reward for leaving a barren situation, a mood, a nauseating situation behind. Sometimes it's better to leave long-standing conditions behind, to bounce back with a fresh look, a fresh take on things. Irregular motions and actions can shake off a detrimental situation, bringing about a much more manageable set of circumstances. Dissatisfaction about routine and prevailing conditions can nag at one until such changes are made. Bending a little in order to manage a situation is perhaps like "genuflection," bending of the knee in worship, which suggests flexibility rather than submission.

Apply this degree-pair with a mind to establishing new and easy conditions; bouncing back with vigor; purging in order to start afresh. Think of appearance like sensible hair, short or tied back; dry flyaway hair; the wet-head. Look for the return of cheerful moods; the courtesy to cut something short, forgive a situation, acknowledge an unintended entanglement. Be alert to times appropriate for an uplifting change; the gut feeling about aptly giving something up; navigating away from hairy disturbances. Consider having to cut one's losses; adapting a new strategy to stay in the game; feeling the need to try a different tack or a new direction altogether; feeling bent or humbled by arduous circumstances; having the courtesy to bend one's pride, allowing a relationship to be workable.

"A formally dressed man and a deer with its horns folded" (4 Leo) and "A Hindu healer" (4 Aquarius)

Aspect: Square.
Quality: Challenge.
Shared motifs: 'Anomaly and misnomer,' 'hart and hind,' 'double binds.'

"A formally dressed man and a deer with its horns folded" is an image of a man dressed up and a deer with an irregular appearance. "A formally dressed man" refers to how one is clothed, such as in evening attire, covered in dress appropriate for the occasion, perhaps signifying a status like a matador elaborately dressed for the bull-ring. "A deer with its horns folded" suggests an anomaly, something irregular or slightly out of place. "Deer" are, strictly speaking, any ruminant animals having deciduous antlers (usually only the male), which are annually shed. "Antlers" are, strictly speaking, not horns. A rhinoceros' horn is formed from the epidermis: really just highly modified hair. Horns are derived from keratin. Antlers are most often formed of bone. There are exceptions: the whole topic is a little bent.

"A Hindu healer" is an image of someone who has a rightful claim to the name "Indian" and who deals with health: wholesome well-being. Christopher Columbus thought he had landed in the East Indies when he first encountered the native Americans. His misnomer "Indian" still sticks. "A Hindu" is one who comes from India, deriving from the Persian *Hind,* which basically distinguishes a region of non-Muslim dwellers. A "healer" is one who makes whole, makes well, makes hale. "Hale" is sound and vigorous health, akin to "hail," to greet loudly by name, to salute or acknowledge where one hails from: these common words are cut from the same cloth in a wholesale fashion.

A "hind" is a female red deer. It would be highly irregular to find horns on a hind or on the hind end, whereas a "hart" is a stag with antlers and a symbol of exalted status, to which all give hail. It's a tricky dilemma, like taking a bull by the horns. "Lemma" are assumptions that, when presented in twos, form the horns of a dilemma. One can get stuck on such issues, which seem to defy a satisfactory solution. Imagine being asked, "Are you still sleeping with your neighbor's wife?" Logically, an answer either way, yes or no, will lead one into trouble. One might well want to give up, acquiesce in submission to a seemingly impossible situation, in the way one might "fold" one's losing hand in a poker game.

Apply this degree-pair with a mind to the challenge of confusions created by misnomers, of formal irregularities, of contradictory assumptions. Think of how names stick like trophies on a wall, how one can get stuck by words or choices made by ancestors. Watch for greeting situations in healthy ways, with a mind to healing. Consider not knowing which way to turn; attitudes that greet life as a horn of plenty or see life in terms of mutually undesirable alternatives. One may toot one's horn with foolish pride; lock horns over irresolvable issues; withdraw one's horns in order to greet harmlessly; or have a battering-ram approach to matters.

"Rock formations at the edge of a precipice" (5 Leo) and "A council of ancestors" (5 Aquarius)

Aspect: Quintile.
Quality: Creative genius.
Shared motif: 'Human existence as a hard precipice
over an open space of ancestral embrace.'

"Rock formations at the edge of a precipice" is an image of human existence as a purchase on the edge of a deep plunge. A "precipice" is a high vertical or overhanging face of rock, suggesting a perilous situation, like a cliff over which one might fall headlong. Imagine a bull, or any large horned animal, lowering its head to charge, inspiring unexpected haste in one's actions. This may precipitate one's having to suddenly leap headlong off a high ledge to avoid the impending danger. "Rock formations" are hard, large stones that, despite their massive size, may be teetering, rocking back and forth, on the brink of a deep fall. "Living on the edge" is an expression suggesting that life is a precarious position such that the slightest misstep could result in disaster. "Precarious" originally meant "to be obtained by begging," by prayers or request, hence precipitating uncertainty in one's sense of existing.

"A council of ancestors" is an image of an assembly of those who have gone before, the ancients, our ancestral predecessors. In ancient cosmologies around the world, the ancestors are associated with the north, midnight, winter, and the time of falling asleep. Sleep is necessary for every human being, signifying a time when the egoic sense of self dissolves. Sleep plunges individual consciousness into something deeper, falling like a waterfall over a precipitous cliff. It is as if one goes to meet, in the depths of the unconscious, the assembled ancestors, receiving counsel and guidance from their collective wisdom.

The waking state tends to dominate what is considered to be human reality, yet each night, the hard formations of who we think we are dissolve into a deep, mysterious realm of dream and dreamless sleep. One can only appreciate the remarkable human genius for dancing on the edge of an abyss, so to speak. It's like being between a rock and a deep space. Life considered as running along the edge of a precipice suggests a genius for recreating balance between the individual human ego, who we think we are, and the deep sources of the collective human ancestry, which guides and informs our world. Imagine sitting down with all the great grandmothers and grandfathers for their counsel based on their vast life experience. This most certainly would evoke a sense of respect and open appreciation regarding what the old ones have seen and learned: a reverential pause for reflection.

Apply this degree-pair with a mind to affinities for ancestral roots, cutting-edge sensibilities, an uncanny sense of ancient wisdom. Watch for unique appearances, striking poses or positions, a deep appreciation of the unique occasion of human existence. Be aware of abilities for entering into trance, delving deeply into consciousness, skillfully appropriating one's place in history. Consider attitudes toward life that thrill at being on the edge, or that freeze on the brink of a precipitous fall: vertigo or "Geronimo!"

"An old-fashioned woman and a flapper" (6 Leo)
and "A performance of a mystery play" (6 Aquarius)

Aspect: Conjunction.
Quality: Focus.
Shared motifs: 'Formal and fun,' 'stiff and nimble,'
'creating a flap.'

"An old-fashioned woman and a flapper" is an image of two generations viewing one another from their own perspectives.[1] "Fashion" is a mode of dress or manner that prevails in a society. Deriving from the Latin *factio*, meaning to form or give shape, fashion is old when it is out-of-date. A "flapper" is a term deriving from the Roaring Twenties, circa 1920, referring to a young woman attempting to appear sophisticated in up-to-date dress and behaving in a manner that stirs excitement. "Flap" is a word that echoes "flop" and "flip": ultimately, flabbergasting flippancy. A "flapper" wearing floppy clothes and hats is found at the center of lively excitement. Both a "woman" and a "flapper" dress in a manner conforming to what is suitable to their lifestyles and tastes. Most likely they are, on a deep level, intrigued with one another, perhaps flabbergasted at each other's appearance.

"A performance of a mystery play" is an image of the dramatization of an alluring unknown.[2] A "mystery play" is a medieval enactment of scriptural events or characters. Old stories conveying ancient wisdom become, over time, stiff and stale and call for rejuvenation in a lively, contemporary fashion. Medieval "mystery plays" were performed by laypeople or members of the guilds: the livery companies. "Livery" means "that which is delivered," deriving from a practice of clothes being handed down, delivered to the servant and working class. "Performing" is the action of carrying out completely, giving form and expression to something. A performance of a "play" may be playful, amusing, lighthearted, even flippant, yet still convey the original message.

Youth is nimble in body and mind, quick to grasp a new take on something old. Imagine a children's performance of a biblical story infused with frolic and life, much to the delight and joy of an adult audience. If a performance is too impertinent, it may be a flop. A "flapper" is likely to have a fun sense of fashion. She may glance at "an old-fashioned woman" with curiosity and share a deep sense of intrigue, or perhaps a mutually scornful regard. To the older generation, the dress and behavior of youth is often a matter of astonishment and mystery: it can flip both ways.

Apply this degree-pair with a mind to the focus on new forms of expression for ancient themes; lively and nimble enactments of classic formality; the wonder and mystery behind evolving fashion sense. Think of how the old informs the new while the new refashions the old. Watch for memories of youth: the days of free and fun personal expression; dressing like one's grandmother; conforming to the latest fashion; fun adornments from ancient fashion. Consider being stiff as opposed to being nimble; staid as opposed to sportive and playful; somber as opposed to frolicsome; a disposition for being at the center of excitement; reveling in causing a stir; flippant remarks; floppy apparel; waggish dramatics or an air of being scornfully aghast.

"The constellations in the sky" (7 Leo) and "A child born of an eggshell" (7 Aquarius)

Aspect: Opposition.
Quality: Awareness of.
Shared motifs: 'Identifying with distant ideas and patterns of behavior,' 'renewal of the old.'

"The constellations in the sky" is an image of the recognition of patterns emerging in the heavens above. A "constellation" is a group of stars forming a recognizable pattern, or more broadly speaking, any group of ideas, persons, emotions, tendencies: the organization of human personality as a whole. The "sky" at night is studded with stars. Names for patterns seen within the starry heavens are derived from ancient mythology, such as Leo the Lion or Aquarius the Water Bearer. Some may feel it takes great imagination to project such patterns onto the stars; others may sense wisdom in the dictum "As above, so below."

"A child born of an eggshell" is an image of creativity in the form of a cosmic birth. An "eggshell" is the remarkably hard, brittle covering of a bird's egg. It suggests two extremes of meaning: to be fragile and thin like an eggshell; to be unbreakable as when trying to break an egg end to end. "A child born out of an eggshell" recalls ancient cosmologies regarding the cosmic egg. For example, "Night's silver egg" laid in the womb of darkness is the silver moon out which Love, Eros, is born in the Orphic creation myth. Aphrodite, goddess of love and desire, arose from the foam of the sea riding on a scallop shell.

As life unfolds, one becomes aware of recurrent patterns, the same stories with a fresh individualized take. Ancient mythologies tell of fundamental motifs that are recreated, reenacted in contemporary guise. It is as if the human psyche is constellated in a collectively shared way such that one knows what it means to be, for example, born out of the head of one's father, as Athena was born out of Zeus' head. Despite the sameness of stories, there is ever renewal and regeneration, like recreating one's world in the morning after a night of sleep.

Apply this degree-pair with a mind to the awareness of recurring patterns that generate new life; rebirth through deeper understanding; seeing personal connections in transpersonal themes. Think of stars in the sky reappearing night after night; recreating one's self, one's character, on a daily basis; maternal capacities to generate new life. Watch for understanding that connects the dots, sees patterns, deals with identifiable complexes. Consider walking on eggshells; broken ideas that lead to hatching something new; waxing and waning phases of life; egging on or instigating creativity; an awareness of signs suggesting deep stirring of meaning; incubating new ideas or ideas for self-renewal; feeling delicate against an imposing background; a sense of being the product of greater forces; a sense of something lying behind appearances; emotional fragility regarding one's appearance: feeling like a mixed-up mess or feeling all aglitter.

"A Bolshevik propagandist" (8 Leo) and "Beautifully gowned wax figures" (8 Aquarius)

Aspect: Trine.
Quality: Maintaining.
Shared motifs: 'Shaping the message,'
'rigidity and compliance.'

"A Bolshevik propagandist" is an image of passionate provocations for social and political change fired by expectations from a personal perspective. A "Bolshevik," historically, is a revolutionary of the Social Democratic Party in pre-revolution Russia. The Bolsheviks became the dominant faction for shaping social and political change within what was to become the Communist party. To be a Bolshevik means to draw on power by virtue of belonging to the majority, *bolshe,* meaning "greater," through ideas shaped by a small elite. A "propagandist" is one who publicizes highly selective information and ideas.

"Beautifully gowned wax figures" is an image of establishing appearance shaped by expectations and personal perspective. "Wax figures" can be found in wax museums, which contain realistic images of famous historical personages, or in store windows, such as mannequins displaying current fashions. "Wax" is a moldable substance that becomes more pliant with heat. The waxing moon becomes larger, stronger, or greater: grows into a specific or dominant state or mood. "Beautifully gowned" suggests being adorned, dressed in a flowing garment having an appealing affect.

Molding a message for public dissemination begins with shaping ideas internally. The majority of the Bolsheviks were guided by ideas shaped by a very few inside the party. A wax figure is shaped first, then dressed, for public display. The former is inclined to revolutionary or burning ideas that stir up sentiments of change on a broad scale; the latter is inclined to influence by appeal and allure. How one expresses oneself publicly depends upon internal ideas or ideals, upon which star one fixes. Ideals are dressed in the words with which they are adorned. Fashion, the show of appearance and style, hangs upon the human shape, the body posture.

Apply this degree-pair with a mind to controlled shaping at work beneath the surface; emphasizing the surface while molding within; manipulating the art of affect. Watch for physical and theoretical postures; hot styles displayed in a cool way; cold hard ideas delivered in an impassioned way. Be alert to the interplay of compliancy within, stiffness without; rigidity within, inclusiveness without. Consider the effects of turning up the heat: the underlying substance may melt away, or the external demeanor may become bad-tempered. Look for hotheads, pushovers, Madison Avenue smarts, hidden social agendas; political self-righteousness in disguise; passing on knowledge of appearances, of past fashion; hanging on to what one can of the past.

"Glass blowers" (9 Leo)
and "A flag turned into an eagle" (9 Aquarius)

Aspect: Square.
Quality: Challenge.
Shared motifs: 'Animation,' 'reversible transformations.'

"Glass blowers" is an image of forging and forming that intensifies moments of pliability and brittle fragility. "Glass blowers" are artisans who work with intense heat to shape material that is hard in its natural form, turns pliable when heated, and hardens into a fragile form. Imagine the skilled, controlled movements of glass-blowers working together in front of a forge. Great care is taken in order to not interrupt the flow of production. The informing power comes from breath: blowing through a tube, while turning the tube into hot, pliable matter; bringing into form by the controlled infusion of air.

"A flag turned into an eagle" is an image of the animation of a symbolic object into a living ideal which soars like a majestic bird in flight. "A flag" is an inanimate symbol bearing an insignia that declares identity or an identifiable message. "An eagle" is a majestic bird of prey, such as the American or bald eagle, which is associated with pride, leadership, and nobility. To be "turned into" something is to be transformed, reshaped: metamorphosed. When a flag turns into an eagle, an idea or ideal is dramatically brought to life. One might possess revolutionary ideals for society and carry a flag that comes to be known for those ideals. Should the flag incite public passions to take action, the flag is infused with life, like heat applied to water that comes to a boil.

A challenge facing glass blowers is to bring their work to a finished form without blowing it out of proportion, or shattering the crafted glass object. A chief feature of finished glass, however, lies in its property of reversibility: if it breaks, it can be reheated and fashioned into a new piece. The challenge of bringing ideals to life lies in the underlying enduring power of the ideal. Ideas and ideals go through their own waxing and waning cycles: sometimes flagging, sometimes flying; now in widespread abundant glory, now extinct. The challenge turns on the temperature of the situation: knowing when to heat something to a higher degree of temperature; when to blow in order to cool or shape something; when to pull back when something becomes too hot; knowing when to start over.

Apply this degree-pair with a mind to the art of animating a base material into a living thing; turning failure to flying success and back again. Think of internal fires that inflame creations and make shaping and reshaping possible; the fires of renewal. Watch for down-but-not-out resiliency; back-to-the-drawing-board conviction; dauntless beliefs and passions; irrepressible adaptability. Consider the life-giving power of breath; delicate matters of new life; blowhards; rising fortunes as if lifted on an updraft; a deft turn of hand; affinities for forging and forges; working in close quarters; a tendency to bump into others, inciting heated situations; quick maneuvers with fragile matters; seeking to find the right temperature for one's ideas and ideals.

"Early morning dew" (10 Leo) and "A popularity that proves ephemeral" (10 Aquarius)

Aspect: Quintile.
Quality: Creative genius.
Shared motifs: 'A proving ground,' 'the fine point separating condensation and dissipation.'

"Early morning dew" is an image of a gentle precipitation covering the grass and fields of the earth. "Dew" is a form of precipitation that forms silently, often through the night on cold surfaces, leaving a thin blanket of moisture. "Early morning dew" refers to a brief window of time for experiencing dew, before the sun burns it off. Dew glistens in the early morning sun like stars or shining beads of teardrops refreshing an open field. The "dewpoint" in one's own life experience is the temperature at which intangible vapors, like personal ideals or archetypal motifs, condense into moisture: a beautiful covering like a bejeweled gown of ideas that is worn naturally, with ease.

"A popularity that proves ephemeral" is an image of the sure, but gradual evaporation of fame and fortune. "Popularity" is a condition of human fellowship whereby the people show appreciation, confidence, or favor to a person, idea, or thing. "Pop music" is music that appeals to a wide sector of the population, often enduring for only a brief while, then disappearing from the charts after a few shining moments. The poplar tree is derived from the Latin word for all trees, *populus*. "To prove" something is to test for authenticity, to show to be true or genuine. An honestly good pop tune will prove itself over time to endure the collective test of public approval or disapproval.

"Ephemeral" fame and fortune is transitory, like the motions of heavenly bodies charted for position and interval in an ephemeris. Some ideas and ideals suited to the intelligence and taste of the ordinary population live only a brief while, evaporating like the morning dew. Others come back into fashion, finding fresh favor while being brought forward again into public awareness. Many believe a little distilled drop of the dew instills confidence or acts as a purifying constitutional. "Popularity" can be an intoxicating personal experience that, while it lasts, seems much like a permanent condition until the morning after.

Apply this degree-pair with a mind to bringing a graceful touch or manner to the fleeting nature of popularity; a delicate sense of the point between approval and disapproval; a natural ease with which one wears one's ideas and apparel. Think of illuminated awareness of Distant Early Warning; knowing when to put one's face forward, and when to disappear. Be alert for gowns and glitter; grace and glistening moments; popular sensibilities or classically distilled tastes. Consider brief brushes with fame and fortune; comeback specialists; getting one's feet wet in a youthful manner; a genius for keeping a cool head about temporary fame and fortune; an ease regarding enjoying the good times while they last; confidence about fresh starts in a new day; understanding every day to be a fresh start.

"Children on a swing in a huge oak tree" (11 Leo) and "Man tête-à-tête with his inspiration" (11 Aquarius)

Aspect: Conjunction.
Quality: Focus.
Shared motif: 'The nuts and bolts of inspiration.'

"Children on a swing in a huge oak tree" is an image of youthful swaying under sturdy support. The "oak tree" is renowned for its strength and enormous mature size. Connected with sky gods from various traditions, the oak tree symbolizes endurance, protection, and inspiration. Since it is often the tallest tree in the forest, and therefore struck by lightning often, it symbolizes being struck by divine wisdom, hence Druids taught children under the oak tree. A "swing" is held at one end; hangs free at the other. "Swaying" is a motion of rhythmic oscillation having a decisive influence, even a spell-like hold: swaying an infant to sleep; swinging to music that gets one "in the mood."

"Man tête-à-tête with his inspiration" is an image of a private experience of being aroused to higher wisdom, knowledge, or creativity. "Tête-à-tête" means literally "head-to-head," a private, heart-to-heart conversation. "Inspiration" is an influence often considered to be from, or of, divine origin. Associated with sudden brilliant flashes of a timely sort, inspiration animates individuals, ideas, and creative activity. The "head" is suggestive of a guiding principle, the monarchal crown of a human being. Coming "head-to-head with inspiration" is therefore an inward experience of being influenced by exalted energy.

"Lightning" strikes from the heavens: the thunderbolts of Zeus and Thor. The huge crown of the oak tree tends to attract lightning strikes, yet is thought to be a protective shield, like an umbrella guarding against the full force of what precipitates from the heavens. When one is under the hold of divine inspiration, it is an entrancing moment: the inspired artist must, like the blacksmith, strike while the iron is hot. Unlike the softwood poplar tree, oak trees are pillars of strength, living, in many cases, for several hundreds of years. Having one's swing affixed under the sturdy oak lends a sense of security and confidence that rises above the ephemeral nature of life's ups and downs.

Apply this degree-pair with a mind to the focus of inner, personal reflection of an exalted nature; hypnotic rhythms of an uplifting nature; re-collecting oneself around a sturdy inner core. Think of swinging as creating a striking atmosphere; as being firmly affixed to one's polestar; as the freedom of uncensored inwardness: the innocence of infantile promiscuity. Consider all things having to do with "nut": Nut the Egyptian sky goddess of night; a kernel or seed idea; one's head; acorns hitting one on the "nut"; eccentric inner thoughts; being nuts or obsessive about something or someone; the rigid focal point upon which tension depends in stringed instruments; the tension between human and divine energy; being held under the sway of exalted, divine music, encouraged by such; being characterized by pluck.

"An evening lawn party" (12 Leo)
and "People on stairs graduated upwards" (12 Aquarius)

Aspect: Opposition.
Quality: Awareness of.
Shared motifs: 'Impending decision or choice,'
'core issues surrounding stepping up in life.'

"An evening lawn party" is an image of a social gathering for enjoyment immediately preceding some event. A "party," a word deriving from the French *partir,* to divide, is a social gathering or group of people gathered and divided along party lines. A "lawn" is a stretch of grassy land, usually cut grass in modern times, which archaically derives from "glade" or "groove." "Evening" is the latter part of the day coming before nightfall. It is the time associated with the three daughters of Night, the Hesperides, and especially Hesperus, Venus, or the Evening Star, hence Vespers: the singing of evening prayers.

"People on stairs graduated upwards" is an image of the hierarchical organization with a common population allowing for opportunity to rise upwards. "Stair" derives from the Old English *stigen,* meaning "to rise" or "to climb." "Graduated" also refers to steps or stages. "People" derives from the Latin *populus,* meaning the collective population. The overall image is of people rising gradually, taking their place, their position, hierarchically relative to everyone else. When one is stepping up in the social, political world, choices have to be made.

The Evening Star following the setting sun is said to reflect the time just before the death of the sacral king. Sunset is associated with the apple grove of Hera. The apple tree, sacred to Aphrodite, is colored like the evening sky: the reds, yellows, and greens of an apple tree in full bearing. An apple cut transversely, divided into two, reveals a five-pointed star. In Somerset, a county in southwest England, plots of land were once allocated by drawing an apple from a bag. The apples were marked to correspond with a particular plot or grove, hence are associated with a standard measure of land distribution, a party to land division. Picking an apple, therefore, came to mean having to choose from amongst equally attractive things. On the eve of a change in order, decisions must be made. Opportunities for rising up in position appear on the horizon of the evening sky: it all hangs like a fruit of opportunity available to all.

Apply this degree-pair with a mind to the awareness of choice; social advancement in the wake of an old order; opportunities for rising up while the prevailing order is setting down like the evening sun, coming to the end of its day. Think of natural hierarchies; divisions along party lines, even in the context of an enjoyable social gathering. Be alert to plots and plotting in what appears to be an equal-opportunity situation; a level stretch of lawn, an open playing field: the upshot of which swings in the balance. Consider the core motif of the apple: forbidden fruits; the garden of Eden; the Judgment of Paris, or apples causing strife; the Lady Ragnall; golden apples; evening song, evening prayer; choices ruled by love and desire; slicing up the pie; caesura: a point of division; awareness that stepping up often means stepping on someone else.

"An old sea captain rocking" (13 Leo)
and "A barometer" (13 Aquarius)

Aspect: Trine.
Quality: Maintaining.
Shared motifs: 'Predicting changes in atmosphere,'
'tact,' 'wise patience.'

"An old sea captain rocking" is an image of the relaxed swaying back and forth of an experienced head of command of a sea vessel. A "captain" designates a position of rank that, for sea vessels, is that of commander. "To command" is to master something, be in control or oversee. "Rocking" is a back-and-forth motion, as with a rocking chair, swaying with relaxed patience to the rhythm of the sea. "An old sea captain" suggests long experience in watching for the tenor of the sea, the tides and currents, in order to avoid being wrecked on the rocks.

"A barometer" is an image of an instrument designed to gauge changes in atmosphere. Atmospheric pressure is measured relative to the mean air pressure at sea level. "Baros" means weight; "meter" is that which indicates measure. A "barometer" is used for predicting weather changes, not for reading the current conditions. Changes in atmospheric pressure forewarn of a change in the weather. Falling atmospheric pressure precedes stormy weather; rising atmospheric pressure presages the approach of settled weather. It may seem counterintuitive, but the higher one is in elevation, the lower the atmospheric pressure: calm seas equal high pressure; high seas equal low pressure.

Imagine a sea captain reading the mood of the sea, the winds and the weather. Low tide may not be an opportune time to leave port: not a suitable time to float a ship over an invisible barrier reef. "Red sky in morning, sailors take warning. Red sky at night, sailors delight" is an archaic expression for predicting sailing conditions. The pervading mood of a social gathering can have a foreboding air, the tone changing like a tenor voice giving way to a baritone. A sea captain does not command the winds and weather. Mastery through long experience means to shift with the tides of change, to remain balanced no matter which way the winds blow, to be able to read those changes that carry weight: to be slightly ahead of oneself and the surrounding atmosphere.

Apply this degree-pair with a mind to maintaining poise while reading how the tides change; one's position relative to the peaks and troughs of the collective; knowing what is coming by sensing the prevailing mood. Watch for forecasting trends:

money, commodities, consumer, intellectual, social. Bc alert to getting too far ahead of oneself or the situation; of pride that rises before a fall; of things that glitter with phosphorescence; Phosphorus, the morning star. Consider baritone voices; low, hollow moods of depression between buoyant crests of two waves; tact: knowing when to tack into the wind; knowing when to ride with the wind; knowing when to drop sail and head for shore.

"The human soul awaiting opportunity for expression" (14 Leo) and "A train entering a tunnel" (14 Aquarius)

Aspect: Square.
Quality: Challenge.
Shared motifs: 'Readiness for favorable winds to enter port,'
'entering into a breakthrough situation.'

"The human soul awaiting opportunity for expression" is an image of spirit, the intangible realities of human being, awaiting in readiness for the opportunity to manifest. The Greek term for "soul," *psyche,* the goddess of life breath, is one of the most echoic words in our language; that is, "soul" closely echoes the words for "breathe," *psyche*; "spirit," *spiritus*; and "air" or "vapor," *atmos.* What "soul" means, and what the "soul" is, is therefore difficult to express. An "expression" is that which is distinctly shown: "press," to apply steady pressure, plus "ex," from out of. "Opportunity" derives from a nautical sense of a favorable time to enter port. Therefore, continuing the nautical theme, an inspiration of breath would bring to life an opportune time to come into harbor; an expiration, an opportune time to sail away from port.

"A train entering a tunnel" is an image of the efficient means to press forward through an opening or passageway. "Tunnels" are artificial passageways that pass under or through an obstacle. A "train" is a continuous line of railway cars coupled together and drawn along a track by a locomotive: an engine capable of moving by its own power. "Entering a tunnel," the train disappears from sight, until it emerges through the light at the end of the tunnel. One might have tunnel vision while being on track toward the light, that is to say, one might disregard objects not central to the field of vision.

The expression of the human soul in the physical world is, most distinctly, trained upon that expression's expiration: "human being" is ever on the way toward its own end. Conversely, the inspiration that precipitates creative expression awaits opportune times and conditions. While in training, one must wait for an opportunity to show one's stuff, to show what one can do. A well-trained body and mind is most efficiently ready to press forward effectively in the world. Putting ideas into action; following a train of thought or emotions; setting sail from port: to be born is a struggle; the challenge lies in the degree of readiness for an opportune time.

Apply this degree-pair with a mind to Hamlet's words, "Readiness is all"; the atmospheric tension that precipitates emergence into the world; the pressing issue of human existence to seize the moment, to express one's self. Think of the light at the end of the birthing canal; the light at the end of the tunnel in near-death experiences. Be alert to focused sensibilities of when to wait; when to press forward; of crowning moments; of times to assume command; a break or pausing manner in an imminent expression: caesura, the point of pausing or cutting. Consider a determined focus; an inadvertent disregard for others; an unawareness of what lies in the wake of pressing personal issues; the breaking of waters as being on the verge of birthing; caesarian births; inception; following in the train of a powerful natural force.

"A pageant" (15 Leo)
and "Two lovebirds singing on a fence" (15 Aquarius)

Aspect: Quintile.
Quality: Creative genius.
Shared motifs: 'The thin line between joy and struggle,'
'the uplifting flourish of waggery.'

"A pageant" is an image of a colorful procession, a spectacular show out in the open. "Pageant" derives from the Anglo-Latin *pagina*, a moveable stage or scaffolding, and relates to "page": that upon which one presses a pen in order to express oneself in writing. In medieval times, the "mystery plays" were performed on traveling wagons. The "wagon" was, itself, the stage for a "pageant," meaning a procession or cycle of processional plays, which parade, in a wagon-train fashion, past onlookers. A stage in the theater of life is an open platform for presenting spectacles to the public. A "wagon" is a four-wheeled vehicle with a platform, drawn by a means of locomotion, and is famous for its wagging motion. "Pageants," like a Mardi Gras, are carnival-like parades, with wags in exaggerated costume often behaving in a waggish manner, riding on a train of floats.

"Two lovebirds singing on a fence" is an image of winged creatures of affection in song on a barrier.[3] "Lovebirds" belong to the parrot family, possess high intelligence, and occasionally can be trained to talk. They are called lovebirds due to the apparent affection they express for their mates. "Singing on a fence" means, literally, sitting on a railing around an enclosed area while floating songs of buoyant joy and affection. The most common lovebird is known for its painted face.

A "fence" can be an intentional obstacle controlling an area: keeping someone or something apart from someone or something else: a degree of separation. An audience is normally kept in remove from the actors on moving stages. Actors strut their stuff across the stage, or float by on slow-moving ships decked in spectacular array. Occasionally, an actor will engage the "fourth wall," strip away the invisible barrier separating the performer from the audience, in shared revelry. An affectionate couple may whistle and cheer appreciation for the sumptuous procession from an observation point suited for a commanding view.

Apply this degree-pair with a mind to floating across the thin barrier separating seriousness and joy; uplifting moments of shared revelry; uninhibited expression that follows in the train of buoyant spectacle: *via exulter,* by way of exultation. Think of faces flushed with color; an infant's rosy cheeks; parents cooing in unreserved joy at a newborn child: being willingly foolish and affectionate. Consider slow yet colorful movements; wagging, rocking a child to sleep; glad tidings of the morning star, which heralds the rising of the sun; waggish, foolish behavior lifted by innocent affection; sharing in experience that poses no serious barriers for mutual enjoyment; possessing a natural feeling that all one's efforts have been worthwhile.

"Sunshine just after a storm" (16 Leo) and "A big businessman at his desk" (16 Aquarius)

Aspect: Conjunction.
Quality: Focus.
Shared motifs: 'Radiant breakthroughs,' 'solace for depressing times,' 'parting is such sweet joy.'

"Sunshine just after a storm" is an image of the first opening of cloud cover, allowing in radiant light and warmth, after a violent atmospheric disturbance. Storm clouds are dark coverings of the sky, which, when a slight hollow or rent forms, open, allowing the radiant rays of the sun to shine through. "Just after" suggests a heavy sky with a small fissure in the otherwise seamless cover. At these times, sunshine is a very cheerful, welcome sight as its rays flood through the clouds. It is like receiving a celestial blessing of warmth and light: an awe-inspiring lift of spirits.

"A big businessman at his desk" is an image of focused concern or responsibility with a wide scope. "Business" is an occupation, trade, or profession, normally of a commercial sort. "A big businessman" is one whose presence is formidable, or one whose range of influence is widespread, perhaps even creating a small depression from where he sits. A "desk" is a flat-surfaced table for writing or studying, or that over which affairs of a certain division of business are conducted. "Desk" derives from the Latin *discus* and is a doublet of "dais," "dish," and "disk." A "disk" is a flat, circular plate, like the appearance of a heavenly disk to the naked eye. A "harrow disk" is an implement to break or plow the earth. A "dais" is a raised platform on which a speaker may sit or stand. This is, therefore, an image of dealing with shining matters of importance, plowing through work that must be done with an eye to that which must be done first.

Imagine a man preaching from a church pulpit. His sermon may bring solace to those who have gone through dark and troubled times. He may conduct the choir in singing a song of praise for divine influence: "You are my sunshine . . .You make me happy when skies are gray." Sometimes, the sound can be a little flat: hollow rather than hallowed. Sometimes song is served up like a delicious dish: sumptuous rather than depressingly small. A choirmaster, with an expressive radiant manner, directs the choral parts in a manner evoking an overall uplifting harmony.

Apply this degree-pair with a mind to a big, cheery outlook; an influence that spreads from a brilliant, radiant core; a knack for parting curtains to focus the spotlight on the chief part. Watch for a warming to a sense of responsibility; bestowing glimmers of hope; evoking warm, courteous service. Be alert for shallow officiousness; hollow platitudes; George Psalmanazar, the pseudonym of a famous literary impostor. Consider lighthouses; guiding lights; rays of hope; slight or slim manifestations of light; parting happily; radiating influences: those that cause to spread out; those that highlight matters of the first order.

"A non-vested church choir" (17 Leo)
and "A watchdog standing guard" (17 Aquarius)

Aspect: Opposition.
Quality: Awareness of.
Shared motifs: 'Listening to the Master's voice,'
'vigilant inner spirit, casual outer dress.'

"A non-vested church choir" is an image of a group of singers of sacred song without the cloaks of ordained tenure. To be "vested," one must have the rights of tenure permitting no contingency; to be "non-vested" is to be not dressed in the robes of office. "Tenure" is the equivalent of a no-cut contract signifying the permanent status of one who cannot be fired. To be "non-vested" permits contingencies that leave one open to firing or open to losing one's hold or one's grip on something. A "church choir" is a group gathered to sing music suited to the vested interest of the church: music of an appropriate spiritual tenor. "Church" derives from the Greek *kyriakon*, ultimately, the house of the powerful Lord and Master.

"A watchdog standing guard" is an image of close and faithful stewardship. "Dogs" are renowned for their loyal faithfulness to their masters. A "watchdog" is a canine servant watching over the safety of people and property and monitoring the movements and procedures of others. "To watch" is to exercise vigilance, guarding over, caring for, stewarding someone or something. "Standing guard" suggests service that maintains a fixed, upright, and unimpaired position, such as a shift of standing at attention while on guard duty.

The conditions under which a church choir can be non-vested are many: tryouts for a new choir; a rehearsal; an informal modern church not requiring vestments; a choir in a nudist camp. Imagine a casually dressed choir singing "I Can't Get No Satisfaction." This may get the attention of the church warden, an elected lay officer, responsible for maintaining proper standards. Imagine the minor-key mood of *Kyrie Eleison* shifting to a major key with James Brown, the Father of Soul, shouting "Lord Have Mercy!" Sometimes a church shifts with contemporary moods: dresses up, or dresses down; sings contemporary hymns, or popular songs. Sometimes a shift in the church key leads to off-key spirituals, or losing a grip on traditional standards. Usually, this can only happen at the time of a shift in the guard.

Apply this degree-pair with a mind to an awareness of long-held traditions as opposed to new, unrestrained ways of doing things; precarious positions when the mood shifts; losing one's decorum while in exalted song as opposed to covering traditional tunes according to rule. Think about being overly fired up; prison warden vigilance watching new jailbirds; uncovering new keys for sacred song. Consider listening to the Master's voice: via church authority or via being flooded by raw, naked, intoxicating spiritual power. Be alert for signs of the Circe complex: an enchantment changing men into pigs or dogs; a dogged pursuit of standards; the ability to recognize someone after long years of absence; light sleepers; difficulty regarding learning new ways, as in "cannot teach an old dog new tricks." Shifts in key can be degrading or uplifting: it all turns on how one dresses a renewed sense of spirit; how one stewards the voice given to divine presence.

"A teacher of chemistry" (18 Leo)
and "A man unmasked" (18 Aquarius)

Aspect: Trine.
Quality: Maintaining.
Shared motifs: 'Seeking a comforting chemistry,'
'the face shown hides a deeper composition.'

"A teacher of chemistry" is an image of one who imparts knowledge regarding the inner structure, composition, and transformative properties of a substance. "A teacher" is one who instructs, trains by practice, or imparts knowledge of deeper principles. In Eastern traditions, the teacher is one who points the way, who transmits the foundations of knowledge, but is not himself the divine reality. "Chemistry" is the science that investigates the inner workings and properties of substances. Teaching may seek to transmit a held doctrine, or to encourage and guide inquiry into deeper, as yet not fully known areas of knowledge.

"A man unmasked" is an image of dis-covering the man, the person, within. A "mask" is a covering that conceals part or all of one's face. In a psychological sense, "mask" refers to the "persona": a necessary first showing of oneself that both projects personal presence in controlled, defensive ways, and filters sense impressions from the external world so one is not overwhelmed by it all. In a theatrical sense, a mask is used to assume a specific character or highlight a character trait. A "masque" is a sixteenth-century dramatic performance from which "masquerade" derives: a deception, disguise, false appearance, or a social gathering of enjoyment with masks and costumes.

Unmasking something or someone reveals or exposes that which was covered. *Aletheia,* the Greek term for truth, means disclosedness, uncoveredness. A chemistry teacher exposes or uncovers for the student the hidden composition and properties of a substance, such as the molecular structure of an element, the atomic properties that make up a molecule. One might reveal hidden transformative properties by splitting, for example, an atom of plutonium. A choir with good chemistry might reveal the deeper emotive power of a traditional sacred song. A choirmaster may be exposed for having a poor understanding of the inner composition of the music he directs, or a stiff adherence to music according to rule or doctrine.

Apply this degree-pair with a mind to the twofold truths regarding masks: highlighting features for effect; covering over more profound realities. Be aware of maintaining a show of a fragment of the personality as a whole for security or defensive purposes, or for effecting deception. Think of dominating principles or beliefs that stifle creativity as opposed to having the right chemistry, which reveals deeper realities. Consider the wisdom of hiding one's true face in a potentially dangerous situation; showing who you really are after getting to know someone, after becoming comfortable with prevailing conditions; masquerade as a creative expression of delight and joy, or a hollow means to fuel the fires of deception; a tendency to seek or attempt to maintain the right chemistry in relationships.

"A houseboat party" (19 Leo)
and "A forest fire quenched" (19 Aquarius)

Aspect: Square.
Quality: Challenge.
Shared motifs: 'Having to aptly cover burning issues,'
'floating amidst strangers.'

"A houseboat party" is an image of a social gathering on a keelless vessel suitable only for calm waters. A "houseboat" is a flat-bottomed boat used for recreation or as a dwelling and is not designed to travel on anything but calm water. A "party" is a social gathering for enjoyment where guests are entertained largely through social discourse with one another. A "flat-bottomed boat" is one without a keel, the backbone of a water-going vessel. Navigating a keelless boat is extremely difficult in turbulent weather or rough water. Equilibrium, to be of even keel, is managed only when conditions are calm: strong undercurrents and blustery winds can easily steer one off course.

"A forest fire quenched" is an image of a wild fire in untamed woods extinguished. A "forest" is an outdoor wooded area. "Forest" derives from the word "foreign," meaning outside, beyond one's own country, hence, wild. A "forest fire" is a wild, uncontrollable conflagration with an insatiable appetite for fuel worsened by strong winds. "To quench" a forest fire is to put it out, to cover it over in a way that denies fire the right chemistry of flame, fuel, and air.

Imagine a flaming left-wing liberal finding himself at a conservative right-wing party on a houseboat. It's a difficult situation calling for diplomacy and delicate maneuvers so as not to rock the boat. One might have to cool the wildfires of self-expression by masking who one really is, how one really feels: a guise of wise guile, so to speak. Social gatherings, often floating along in light ways, are not the platform to weather storms upon, nor the situation in which to get caught up in strong undercurrents: this is a ship with no depth to its keel. Perhaps one is in a foreign territory with strange gods toward whom one feels cool. It would not be inconceivable to find oneself playing fire warden to a fiery outbreak between donkeys and elephants who have quenched their thirst on some intoxicating, cool summer beverage.

Apply this degree-pair with a mind to the challenge of controlling the burning passions of belief in light social circumstances divided along party lines; stewarding combustible situations; keeping an even keel in potentially interesting times. Think of the twofold sense of "quench": to satisfy a thirst; to extinguish the flames of a fire. Be alert to encountering strange guiding principles; foreign gods; foreign camps of belief or philosophic outlook. Listen for songs of levity; a chorus of voices that puts a damper on an impassioned song; a knack for singing in a different key. A masquerade may bring satisfying relief to an uncontrollable conflagration; a guileful guise might keep one in calm waters. Consider floating about socially; the use of drink to soothe differences and party divisions; an uncertainty about where one belongs, which dock to tie onto; quick thinking in a potentially dangerous situation; suppressing one's words, passions, or beliefs.

"The Zuni sun worshippers" (20 Leo)
and "A big white dove, a message bearer" (20 Aquarius)

Aspect: Quintile.
Quality: Creative genius.
Shared motifs: 'Fire and water,' 'creative purification,'
'communing with higher realms.'

"The Zuni sun worshippers" is an image of veneration for the source of life by a small but remarkable Indian nation. The "Zuni" Indians are a tribe living in western New Mexico, whose church is the land or wilderness, and who especially worship the sun, equating "sunlight" with "life." "Sun worship" in an arid region is inseparable from the need for water, therefore the Zuni solstice ritual to the summer sun is intimately woven with the importance of rain. "Worship" is the devout reverential regard of human beings for divine energy. For the Zuni tribe, ritual process is of the utmost importance, after which follow the usual human concerns: food, shelter, security.

"A big white dove, a message bearer" is an image of a communication born by a creature of the sky: a peaceful message from a heavenly source. The "dove" is associated with peace, gentleness, and the Holy Spirit. "A message bearer" is one who carries a communication, an official dispatch, perhaps divinely inspired, which unites receiver and sender in communion. "White" is seen when light is reflected without sensible impression of the visible rays of the color spectrum. Politically, "white" is associated with conservative as opposed to fiery radical inclinations; spiritually, with purity, gleaming silver light.

The Zuni believe there are two types of men: sun-baked and un-baked. Curiously, Zuni is linguistically unrelated to any other North American Indian language. It is as if their language was created from divine communication. "Whitsuntide," or White Sunday, is a religious festival marking the descent of the Holy Spirit upon the apostles, and is associated with the white robes worn during baptism. "White hot" is the temperature at which a body becomes incandescent, yet "pure white snow" is the precipitation that replenishes the water table for the coming summer months. These symbols are replete with paradox: to some, so cool and refreshing; to others, something that really burns you up.

Apply this degree-pair with a mind to the genius that finds the sacred housed everywhere; purity regardless of color; gleaming, thirst-quenching water through communion with the life-giving sun. Listen for unique language, unrelated to any other; messages of relief precipitated by intense, burning reverence; unusual daily rituals of no apparent common source. Be alert for intense extremes: red-necked bigotry and angelic inclusiveness; white swine and red saints; fiery radicals and upright puritans. Consider affinities for a host of common world-religion motifs: Noah and the Ark; Zoroaster fire worship; baptism; white robes; white light. Consider feeling like one comes from another world, belongs to a strange tribe; a sensitive capacity to hear messages; feelings of stability; a capacity to listen carefully; a strong sense of community.

"Chickens intoxicated" (21 Leo) and "A woman disappointed and disillusioned" (21 Aquarius)

Aspect: Conjunction.

Quality: Focus.

Shared motifs: 'The perils and pleasures of ecstasy,' 'standing outside of oneself, with expectation, with excitement.'

"Chickens intoxicated" is an image of an uncommon state of being for the common domestic fowl. "Chickens" are usually the young females of the common domestic fowl. "Intoxicated" is a condition of being that can refer to having imbibed an intoxicating drink, or having been brought into an excited, ecstatic state by means of some energy or substance. "Chickens" can also refer to those lacking courage, easily frightened or cowardly by nature. "Chicken feed" is an expression that derives from the early American settlers, meaning grain unsuitable for human use, but small enough for the chickens to swallow. Should the feed be sour, due to a process of natural fermentation, chickens would exhibit extraordinary behavior.

"A woman disappointed and disillusioned" is an image both of frustrated expectations and of realizations that break a spell or misapprehension. "Disappointment" is the frustration felt when projected expectations fail to be fulfilled. To be "appointed" is to be selected, ordained, named for a position or role. "Disillusioned" means to be freed from illusions, to dispel enchantments like youthful, inexperienced illusions about lust and love. Intoxication tends to blur judgment and perception, an impairment that might lead to regrets, hence "disillusioned" can be a happy state of seeing things as they really are.

Intoxication can be induced by beverages derived from fermented grain, such as sour corn mash from which bourbon whiskey is distilled. "Intoxication" derives from *toxis*, poison, which is still heard in the expression "Choose your poison," as in choosing which drink, wine, beer, or spirits with which to fill one's cup. The Dionysian festivals, those of Bacchus, the god of wine and revelry, induced ecstatic states of revelry wherein all sense of constrained, morally upright behavior was dispelled. Drunken chickens may stagger about with false bravado, attempting, extraordinarily, to fly to great heights like other birds. A woman may be disappointed in herself for foolish behavior after a night of being in her cups. She may be disappointed about amorous advances made toward her by someone who had one drop of courage too many, only later seeing through the illusion.

Apply this degree-pair with a mind to the intoxicating nature of spirit; rushing into frenzied excitement of false expectation; dispelling notions of being the chosen one. Think of the potential effects of poison: in homeopathic terms, one drop of the right poison induces a healing crisis; too much of the wrong poison really takes the life out of a dream, and sometimes literally takes a life. Be alert for youthful, naive illusions; mature and sober perspectives; matters that turn sour; matters that soar beyond inhibitions. Consider sour grapes; "tart," the taste sensation, or "tart," the morally free, uninhibited young woman; tendencies to expect too much; tendencies not to expect enough.

"A carrier pigeon" (22 Leo) and "A rug placed on a floor for children to play" (22 Aquarius)

Aspect: Opposition.
Quality: Awareness of.
Shared motifs: 'On the importance of playfulness,'
'leaving and returning home again.'

"A carrier pigeon" is an image of a bird trained to carry messages attached to its neck or legs. A "pigeon" is a common bird that can be domesticated and bred for its ability to always fly home. The carrier pigeon's utility is one-directional: pigeons only fly home from a foreign point of release, not the other way around. "Pigeon" derives from the Latin *pipire*, meaning to whimper or peep like a young bird. The young of many species, not just birds, are well-known for constantly piping up with whining little voices. A "carrier" is one who carries or transports a message or small object. In chemistry, a "carrier" is the catalytic agent. The homing pigeon, another name for a carrier pigeon, can be the catalyst for taking action by virtue of bearing crucial information.

"A rug placed on the floor for children to play" is an image of a cover for comfort and safety spread over a level area intended for children's play. The nature of "play," Latin *ludere,* is to go beyond the bounds of normal containment. It is ludicrous to think that children will stay within the intended limits set for them: the sand has to get outside the sandbox or it is just not play. Parents may want to work, or have an uninterrupted time, while children play on the rug, but seriously, it is not long before a child crawls or toddles over to the comforting home of a mother's lap, usually with an insistent message that commands attention. It is much harder to train children to return to their designated play space.

While it is in the human nature of a child to wander, explore the world, beyond the limits set for them, they also have an unerring sense of where the security of home lies. If a pigeon is released from home, it may hang around, or it may fly away, never to return, but perhaps only after a long while. Raising the young to the point of maturity where they can safely leave home takes patience and, undoubtedly, a good sense of humor. One becomes aware that all hard-and-fast rules are only relative in the context of growing up. Leaving home and finding one's way back home again are lifelong themes crucial to the individuation process for all human beings.

Apply this degree-pair with a mind to the awareness of the relative nature of rules and boundaries; issues of safety and security regarding home and the world beyond; an unerring sense of homing in on what really counts. Think of the contrast between unbounded play and well-defined controls and limits; messages that accelerate developments; patience for the maturation process; impatience about growing up. Consider a chipper attitude, like a young, chirping bird; a whimpering attitude; an air of being swindled; an unerring sense of safe limits; complaints regarding safe limits.

"A bareback rider" (23 Leo)
and "A big bear sitting down and waving all its paws" (23 Aquarius)

Aspect: Trine.
Quality: Maintaining.
Shared motif: 'Bare facts, bears and beer: the unsaddled
condition humans are saddled with.'

"A bareback rider" is an image of riding a powerful force without a cushioning pad on which to sit. Riding one's horse is a symbol of taking hold of one's own power.

The Knights of Chivalry are so called for championing the right use of power: to show mercy and courtesy, never use arms of force unless for a just cause, and then only against an enemy who can defend himself and his cause. "Bareback" riding is to ride without a saddle, without a cushioning pad between the hindquarters of both horse and rider. Even though "saddle" is the name for the saddle-shaped lower back of a fowl, a knight cannot be chicken-hearted regarding the responsibilities with which he is saddled.

"A big bear sitting down and waving all its paws" is an image of a powerful animal on its hindquarters, with all four strong arms waving. "To bear" something is to carry or convey it along, having the strength to bear a weight or responsibility. A "bear" is a powerful creature, the might of which a man would not be able to bear. A burly circus bear might be trained to lie on its back clumsily waving its strong arms for an audience, where a Scotsman sits sipping stout made from *bear*, the Scottish word for barley. Perhaps he is a stout fellow known to John Barleycorn. This is a "knotty," like a burl, or "naughty," like a mischievous child, question that gives over to awkward pause: pun intended.

Imagine a stout burly man clumsily attempting to handle a delicate matter like a warrior knight lending a hand to a maiden. He might be ever so gentle, but the bare fact is that he still bears a lusty animal nature that is more inclined to rudely maul than master the finer points of courtesy: a bear on his back may seem harmless, but certainly not armless. A good-natured sort is often the butt of lame jokes. Mastery of issues that marry might and power with a gentle man are not impossible. Imagine the acrobatics of a bareback rider: the display of grace on a rough ride.

Apply this degree-pair with a mind to attempting to bring grace to raw power; bring beauty to the beast; rein in animal nature through practice and training. Chiron, the first centaur, was an immortal bareback horse and rider with his head and spirit above the belt: mature, well-integrated animal, human, and divine natures. The wild race of centaurs was known only for their rude lust for women and wine: immature, below-the-belt instincts causing harm. Think of trying to handle a fine crystal glass with a bear's paw; doing handstands on the back of a moving horse. Consider burly arms, barley beverages; acrobatic maneuvers; stout bodies; lust and courtly manners; a stout fellow; and what it means to be a gentleman/woman.

"An untidy, unkempt man" (24 Leo) and
"A man turning his back on his passions and teaching from experience" (24 Aquarius)

Aspect: Square.
Quality: Challenge.
Shared motifs: 'Man out of season,' 'master of one's vessel,'
'beyond the teeth of desire.'

"An untidy, unkempt man" is an image of an untimely man with a toothless comb. Being "untidy and unkempt" superficially suggests a messy person with no regard for personal appearance and demeanor, however, on a deeper level it speaks to the condition of being a stranger within societal conventions. "Untidy" means a lack of neatness or a disorderly disposition. "Tidy" derives from tide, the periodic rise and fall of tidal ocean waters as they appear on the shore, the intervals of which mark the flow of time. "Unkempt" means not combed, without polish or refinement. "Kempt," deriving from comb, is ultimately related to the teeth of a comb and the fleshy crest on the head of a fowl, or the disheveled crest of a wave.

"A man turning his back on his passions and teaching from experience" is an image of standing firm and erect in one's position regarding the overwhelming and turbulent waves of emotion, deriving and conveying wisdom from personal experience. The "back" is the location of the spine. To "turn one's back" suggests a rejection, but also implies a discipline of flexibility, like yogic practice. "Passions" are the overpowering emotions within human experience that can toss one about like an object caught in the teeth of turbulent waves. "Teaching from experience" suggests deriving understanding and wisdom from having seen and experienced much. An ascetic is one who turns his back on the ravages of strong feelings and desires, channeling those natural desires toward higher understanding.

Imagine a man finding himself out of place, out of season, with prevailing conventions such as how one combs one's hair. Social conventions are collective, silent agreements that are often just the flavor of the month. To turn one's back on convention simply means that one's identity is not caught up in the prevailing tides and currents of social custom. A yogic recluse, for example, does not reject emotions, but passionately pursues being the master of his own ship, rising above the turmoil of frivolous desires.

Apply this degree-pair with a mind to being true to oneself in the midst of current conventions; being the master of one's own ship as opposed to a coxcomb, the ostentatious conceit of a dandy; being on the crest of the wave of life rather than being swept away. Look for a confident but conventionally out-of-place appearance, demeanor, and practice. Think of standing tall with an erect spine; intentional, disciplined pursuits of spiritual intoxication as opposed to cock-of-the-walk conceits; spiritual erections that canalize desire for the purpose of enlightenment as opposed to rude erections to satisfy the tides of base desire. Consider hair like a rooster's comb; sorting with a fine-toothed comb; being led by the flavor of the month: Baba Choco-chip ice cream; "parting the waves" conceit; temporary thrills as opposed to enduring wisdom.

"A large camel crossing the desert" (25 Leo) and "A butterfly with the right wing more perfectly formed" (25 Aquarius)

Aspect: Quintile.
Quality: Creative genius.
Shared motifs: 'Refining balance through the whole spine,'
'beauty and the beast of burden,' 'balancing acts.'

"A large camel crossing the desert" is an image of a vessel with a copious capacity to traverse vast uninhabitable areas. Camels, renowned as the "ships of the desert," possess a large capacity to store water sufficient for long desert journeys. The camel's chief physical characteristics include long necks, padded feet on long slender legs, and one or two humps on the back. A "desert" is an arid region usually with inhospitable extremes of wind, heat, and cold. "Crossing the desert" requires uncommon capacities of endurance, especially while carrying heavy loads, large packs precariously balanced on the back.

"A butterfly with the right wing more perfectly formed" is an image of a delicate beauty that flutters due to irregular wing formation. In order to discern a slight anomaly in the perfection of the wings, a butterfly must be at rest or still, with its wings standing erect upon the back. Even then, slight differences in perfection are barely perceptible. The "butterfly" is a symbol of metamorphosis culminating in delicate beauty and fragility. With the "right wing more perfectly formed," the fluttering flight of the butterfly would be ever so slightly accentuated.

Poetically, a butterfly kiss, a butterfly song, the flap of a butterfly's wings, evoke images of tenderness, moments of exquisite delicacy and beauty: the heart fluttering at a tender embrace; the soft stroke of cashmere, camel hair, sending sensations that quiver up the spine. A camel may seem an indelicate beast of burden, yet the camel has the capacity to be trained to bear great loads on its back. The yoking of loads to the back must be almost perfectly balanced; the saddle for passengers well secured to stay in place through rocking rhythms of the camel's gait. It's all echoic of yoga, the practice of yoking the body in union with higher, divine energies. It is perhaps worthy of note that the Irish version of a common expression goes, "The feather that broke the camel's back," suggesting the delicacy of all things intoxicating: the one drop of difference between near perfection and toppling excess.

Apply this degree-pair with a mind to the genius for delicate matters of balancing energies; the ever so slight difference between divine perfection and overindulgence; marrying imperfect bodies with near-perfect ecstasy. Think of subtle touches with the spine; sufficient core strength to achieve delicate manifestations; ultrarefined sensibilities for moments of transient, indescribable beauty. Consider walking softly with a big stick; the beauty of slight asymmetry; padded shoes; long necks; peak experiences of tender erotics; the question "Does the flap of a butterfly's wing cause a tornado thousands of miles away?"

"A rainbow" (26 Leo)
and "A hydrometer" (26 Aquarius)

Aspect: Conjunction.
Quality: Focus.
Shared motifs: 'Suspended moments,'
'the measure of buoyant effects.'

"A rainbow" is an image of a celestial phenomenon of beautiful arching bands of prismatic colors that seem to hang brilliantly, suspended in the air. Iris, the Greek goddess of the rainbow, was an attendant and messenger for Hera and associated with being at everyone's beck and call. To see a rainbow is an uplifting experience; one's spirits are brightened with the sight of a divine message. Iris is depicted as a beautiful golden-winged goddess with long hair flowing in all the colors of the light spectrum. The white light of the sun is spread in an arching spectrum of color by means of refraction, reflection and dispersion of light through raindrops. The sun must stand behind Iris as she floats through the air, opposite the viewer on earth, in order for the rainbow to be visible.

"A hydrometer" is an image of an instrument for measuring the relative specific density of a fluid, usually relative to water, hence *hydro* + *meter*. A steel water vessel stood end to end in water will sink because the steel is heavier than water. The same ship will float when keel down in the water because the air it contains produces a buoyant effect: air is lighter than water. Hydrometers are used in the making of beer and wine, allowing for the precise measuring of specific density: ascertaining the degree of spirit in the spirits. Hydra, the many-headed water snake of Greek mythology, had a nasty tendency to grow back the head that had been cut off, suggesting, perhaps, a resurfacing regarding the right measure of intoxicants: after being subdued, it raises its head again.

No two people see the same rainbow, unless it is frozen in a photograph; no two people have identical irises of the eyes. The implication is that the iris of a person's eye reflects individuality, the way raindrops disperse white sunlight, revealing a full array of distinct colors. "Suspension," in physics, is the uniform dispersion of small particles in a medium: raindrops seemingly suspended in the air as a rainbow; a substance molecularly suspended in liquid form. Hopes and dreams cast over the rainbow can only be assessed in the full light of day as to whether they hold water.

Apply this degree-pair with a mind to the divine light behind appearance, the emotional water behind suspended substances; the aesthetic perception of uplifting experience and the precise measure and science of buoyancy. Watch for bright eyes; calculating eyes; bright dispositions; calculating dispositions. Be alert to the relative density of all matters: all wines, 11 percent alcohol by volume, are the same, yet no two wines are ever the same. Consider brightly colored hair; messages that bring relief; buoyant spirits; dangerous dragons that raise their heads again; brilliant displays, incandescent moments, that appear only at a precise angle of refraction.

"Daybreak" (27 Leo)
and "An ancient pottery bowl filled with violets" (27 Aquarius)

Aspect: Opposition.
Quality: Awareness of.
Shared motifs: 'Luminosity spreads, tiny stars of the
violet night fade,' 'a return that refreshes.'

"Daybreak" is an image of the moments of the return of luminescence. The ancient Greeks spoke of the golden-armed rosy fingers of dawn, Eos, which spread over the eastern horizon with daylight, dispelling the dark mists of night. Eos yoked the winged horses that drew the light of the day across the heavens, appearing with her many-colored broidered robe or her golden gown. "Daybreak" signified the regular return of a luminous glow after times of darkness, to which gods and men alike were subject.

"An ancient pottery bowl filled with violets" is an image of an archaic vessel adorned with delicate flowers. Ianthe, the mythological personification of the violet coloring of clouds, is associated with the promise of the return of spiritual energy. Having the highest frequency in the visible rainbow spectrum of light, violet was thought to be the transition to a higher octave of spiritual transcendence. A "pottery bowl" is a fashioned earthen vessel. "Pottery" is associated with cooking and with drinking vessels, hence "potage," soup, and "potable," suitable for drinking. One can distill whiskey in a pot, "poteen," or one can alchemically cook base materials into gold, a divine potion.

While the luminous light of dawn grows steadily with each moment, violets are associated with quiet, self-effacing manners like that of a shrinking violet. The tiny stars of night adorning the vaulted violet heavens fade like fragile touches of color as the luminosity of heaven grows. Placed in an ancient pottery bowl, violets bring a quiet, modest glorification to ancient wisdom of self-transformation, or a touch-up for what is old, humble, and worn. Think of the adorning effect of tiny blossoms in harsh elevated regions: alpine flowers; flowers found in the high arctic regions. In their season, such tiny petals remind one of the resilient return of life and sunlight, even in the harshest of conditions. For example, the commonly known children's verse "Ring around the rosy, / A pocket full of posy, / Husha, husha, / We all fall down" is really about a child's take on the Black Death in medieval times.

Apply this degree-pair with a mind to the awareness of a higher spiritual sense of the time of return and renewal; a sense of the slightest glimmer of hope and return.

Watch for modest honoring of archaic wisdom; subtle adornments that can turn night to day; an alchemical sense of common cooking; modest spices for common, communal soups. Consider delicacy in the shadow of the indomitable forces of life; refreshing touches that brighten old tradition; small offerings made with sincerity bringing supreme good fortune.

"Many little birds on the limb of a tree" (28 Leo) and "A tree felled and sawed" (28 Aquarius)

Aspect: Trine.
Quality: Maintaining.
Shared motifs: 'Suspended just over the horizon,'
'hesitation on the threshold,' 'thought for the future.'

"Many little birds on the limb of a tree" is an image of a cheerful gathering on the rounded edge of a branch well connected to the main body. The "World Tree" is a cosmological image of the central rootedness in the earth, a crown reaching to heaven, and strong limbs upon which the many creatures of this world sit. Collectively, all creatures are therefore out on a limb. "Limb" also means the curved edge of the sun, especially as it appears on the horizon, as if hanging there in limbo. "Birdlime" is a sticky substance made from mistletoe or holly and smeared on branches to catch small birds. "Hem" is an edge or border, as in hemisphere, defining half of a sphere. One might pause at the hem of a piece of cloth, hesitating before turning it over to sew it down, just as one may hesitate to step over a threshold into an uncertain realm.

"A tree felled and sawed" is an image of thought or provision for the future. Trees are a source of lumber and fuel. Cutting trees for firewood happens out of season, well in advance of the time of its actual use. Green wood needs to season and dry; sawed lumber needs to cure before being used for construction. To be "felled" is to be struck down: to cut down a tree; to finish a seam in sewing by folding under, joining edges together. An archaic sense of "fell" means cruel, deadly, as in a "fell potion," and from which the term "felon" is derived.

Imagine the curved edge of the rising sun as it breaks over the eastern horizon. The morning song of many birds welcome the new day as if encouraging the full return of the sun. The "horizon" is the threshold or limit that appears to bend under, suggesting something more, something hidden. Seeing the sun or moon rise is a sublime experience, as opposed to something clear-cut, hard, and wooden. A subliminal message is one that is perceived beneath the threshold of consciousness, the intensity of which is too low to form a clear thought, image, or impression. Still, one might, in the early spring, have thought for the future by cutting firewood for the far-off winter.

Apply this degree-pair with a mind to preparation for what lies beyond the horizon; thought for what lies ahead; wariness about stepping into the unknown; preparedness issues. Think of cheerfully welcoming what is to come; being trapped on the threshold of something; hesitation for no clear reason. Consider potions that effect a suspension in time and space; being deadly afraid of life; drinks that turn white in water; being controlled by subliminal messages; perceiving subliminal messages; being inspired by sublime messages; chatter; cutting remarks; far-reaching or sticky speculation through gossip; feeling caught out on a limb in conversation.

"A mermaid" (29 Leo) and "Butterfly emerging from chrysalis" (29 Aquarius)

Aspect: Square.
Quality: Challenge.
Shared motifs: 'Emergence,' 'tender newness,'
'feeling slightly out of place.'

"A mermaid" is an image of a state of anticipatory suspension, of a longing for fulfillment. The "mermaid" is a creature of fantasy at home in the great seas of emotion. She is out of place: in a situation of not quite belonging to either land or sea. Mermaids are thought to be seals, or kindred marine mammals, mistaken for sea nymphs with a fish tail by sailors. Seals lumber on land, dragging their tails in an awkward manner, but also exhibit deep feeling eyes and humanlike forelimbs. A mermaid emerging from the sea is an image of the fluid tides of feeling and emotion, propelled by longing, suggesting that the fulfillment and complete transformation of the mermaid into a "real" human is yet to arrive.

"Butterfly emerging from chrysalis" is an image of emerging from a chrysalis in a completely natural way, completing a cycle of transformation for which the butterfly is renowned. This cycle does not depend upon emotional longing, nor upon the transformation of the fantastic into the "real." "Chrysalis" derives from Greek and Semitic origins meaning gold or to be encased in gold. The timing for the emergence of the butterfly is entirely natural: emergence happens in its own time. One may have confidence and faith that all things happen in their own time or, like the butterfly that remains cocooned, be overly fearful and too timid to emerge into the world.

Imagine the newly emerged butterfly, its wings still wet with newness needing to be seasoned, to dry, before it can fly. Imagine a mermaid wet from the sea needing to dry before emerging fully human. One might feel stuck in a familiar tale, as a mermaid is with her tail, of unrealistic longing for one's prince to come, for one's dream to be fulfilled. Dreams of the heart are not always troublesome, rather they can unfold in their own time, perhaps passing through a challenging and awkward phase before being realized.

Apply this degree-pair with a mind to the tenderness and fragility of newly emerged realities; the struggle to shed an old skin; the challenges of showing oneself at one's best in a harsh world. Watch for an innate sense of positive unfolding; a deep sense of what is not yet; or hopelessly dreaming and waiting. Listen for tales of wondrous transforming; delicate songs of longing; a tender heart cocooned. Consider the good heart that longs to emerge and unfold its wings; transformation and courage; gold wrappings; golden dreams; selkie myths of the seal-woman who sheds her seal skin to become fully human; concern for the care of the very young; feeling too delicate for this world; having butterflies in one's stomach before every new venture; stage fright; innocent winning ways.

"An unsealed letter" (30 Leo) and "The field of Ardath in bloom" (30 Aquarius)

Aspect: Quintile.
Quality: Creative genius.
Shared motif: 'Ancient minds and meadows still in bloom today.'

"An unsealed letter" is an image of an enveloped message that is still open and available. "To be sealed" is to be closed, as in closing a seam, sealing an envelope to deny free access. A letter might be sealed with sealing wax, a pliable substance that can receive an impression when warm and that hardens when cool. "Seals" are signatures of authenticity and the means of maintaining mysteries. "An unsealed letter" suggests a message that is covered but not permanently closed, or unmarked for delivery. Mermaids, associated with the marine seal, are un-sealed when they shed their seal-skin.

"The field of Ardath in bloom" is an image of an open expanse flourishing with growth from an ancient era. "The field of Ardath" is a reference to ancient Babylon and a mystic meadow symbolizing the blossoming of a mystical brotherhood and its flourishing now as then. Since the fields of Ardath are associated with the "cradle of civilization," it is a meadow without specific identity or characterization: a symbol for all peoples in all times. "Ardath" is perhaps derived from the Zoroastrian term "ard," meaning good blessings or rewards. When a plant comes into full bloom, that is the culminating moment of growth and manifestation. A whole field in bloom suggests richness and bounty beyond estimation.

Imagine coming upon a letter to which no personal seal is affixed. There is an immediate sense of a message, however it is addressed to no one or to anyone. Its contents are a matter of mystery and intrigue. Imagine a butterfly, long encased in a golden sheath, emerging into the world in full bloom, so to speak. In an open field of flowers, there may be countless butterflies adding to the splendor of flourishing life. It is as if all the colors of the rainbow have manifested in a field of bloom, evoking a sense of a wonder of the world.

Apply this degree-pair with a mind to an uncanny sense of ancient civilizations; a vibrant sense of life open and immediately communicated though separated by a vast measure of time. Think of the time of birth as a moment open to ancient mysteries; a genius for the mystery and wonder of life as opposed to pragmatic attitudes ruled by reason; seemingly small curiosities that lead to wondrous discoveries. Consider creative energies that belong to no one, that are not owned, that are shared, like in an open mystery; unsigned messages; deep impressions with no apparent signature; signatures that leave an impression of an ancient past. Be alert to paradoxes such as being enveloped in open mystery, music on a harp unstrung; resplendent colors within pure white, messages that cannot be traced to any particular author.

1. In his book *The Sabian Symbols in Astrology,* Marc Edmund Jones replaced the original word on the notecard, "flapper," with "an up-to-date girl," cf. Diana E. Roche, *The Sabian Symbols: A Screen of Prophecy* (Victoria, B.C.: Trafford, 1998) p. 156.

2. M. E. Jones replaced the word "performance" with "performer," cf. Roche, p. 340.

3. M. E. Jones replaced the word "singing" with "sitting," cf. Roche, p. 349.

CHAPTER SIX

VIRGO-PISCES

"A man's head" (1 Virgo)
and "A public market" (1 Pisces)
Aspect: Conjunction.
Quality: Focus.
Shared motifs: 'The stamp of individuality and social identity,'
'character and the collective.'

"A man's head" is an image suggesting marks of individual character, the stamp of identity that would have one standing out from the crowd. A "head" is the chief thing, the uppermost part of the human body at the top of the spine. The head symbolizes consciously projected identity. Imagine a portrait suggesting a well-defined image of personal characteristics, much like a head shot reveals personality. In a caricature, the head is exaggerated, an overloaded depiction suggesting an inflated sense of identity.

"A public market" is an image of a locus for social exchange, the identity of which is determined by no one in particular. In the public market place, individuality leveled down to the lowest common denominator blends in with the crowd. Every market place has its own distinctive character: ethnic and multicultural markets can be readily found in the melting pot of the new world. The colorful character of public market places may be distinguished by characteristic facial features: Italian, Caribbean, Chinese, and so on. Within the thriving, buzzing public market, one must identify conscious affinities for belonging.

Consider the noisy trading floors of stock markets, which diffuse all semblance of individuality into a sea of uniformly dressed traders shouting and waving indecipherable scraps of paper into the air. There is an element of selling one's self for who or what you represent. In order to get a picture of the stock market, one has to get one's head above the flurry of activity taking place on the trading floor. The issue lies in trading on one's individual character or trading on anonymity. One can have a personal preference for one's market place of choice, a feel for how the market place works, an ear to the ground listening for market trends, or perhaps even a nose for bargains. Individuality and personal characteristics rise above the crowd, as in the expression "heads above the crowd." On the other hand, there is a danger of being lost in a crowd.

Apply this degree-pair with a mind to the distinguishing marks of individual and public character. The individual's task is to leave his mark on the market; the public's task, although the public is ever "no one," is to gather collectively for trade between individuals, thus establishing market value. Watch for traders, painters, photographers: any way of taking a snapshot of how something generally is; how identity is ascribed. Look for precision characteristics or the one thing that stands out.

"A large white cross upraised" (2 Virgo) and "A squirrel hiding from hunters" (2 Pisces)

Aspect: Opposition.
Quality: Awareness of.
Shared motifs: 'Elevated sense of choice,'
'good sense and discriminating awareness.'

"A large white cross upraised" is an image of lifting a decisive marker to a higher level: a crossroads decision. The crossroads motif appears throughout history and literature, touching core human issues: the crossroads scene in Sophocles *Oedipus Rex*, Hecate's crossroads, or Robert Johnson's blues classic "I Went Down to the Crossroads." A "white cross" is a divine marker guiding earthly footsteps. An upraised cross serves as a beacon signaling the way or ways one can go, a point of issue calling for guidance and a sense of "knowing which way to turn."

"A squirrel hiding from hunters" is an image of common good sense under possibly threatening circumstances. "Squirrels" are known for their deft quickness to avoid danger and their skittish nature, which appears to be like running scared. Knowing when to hide can raise chances for survival. The presence of hunters sharpens awareness of danger: the hunted display an alert attention for survival while staying out of the cross hairs of the hunters' sights. Perhaps there is an issue of being too timid, afraid of entering traffic. Even with a heightened awareness for survival, a squirrel might nervously dash onto a busy road, into the crossfire, and become road kill. Choosing a worthy yet feasible path is the issue: one may aim for the high road, or set one's sights too low.

Any crossroads decision marks deep and dangerous differences in power. While humans may come to a point along the road where there is a decision about which path to follow, squirrels show a natural, canny sense of knowing when to get off the road for one's own safety. These are not merely black-and-white issues, but issues that cut through what appear to be straightforward everyday matters, spanning animal instincts to divine guidance. The markers that come into view may have definite social and religious implications. Perhaps the market place mixes too many elements, compromising individuality, calling for a sensible need to scatter. White crosses on the tops of hills call up chilling visions of racial prejudice: marked men as opposed to beacons that mark the way.

Apply this degree-pair with a mind for an awareness of beacons, crossroads decisions come to a peak; markers for direction; seeking higher paths to follow. Look for themes of the hunter and the hunted, taking aim; cross hairs, crossfire, cross brows. Watch for signs of timidity as opposed to a focused, righteous pursuit of one's path; a superiority complex; an Oedipal complex. Consider nervousness about traffic; alertness for danger; a disposition toward leaving the rat race.

"Two angels bringing protection" (3 Virgo) and "Petrified forest" (3 Pisces)

Aspect: Trine.
Quality: Maintaining.
Shared motifs: 'The dual nature of rigid beliefs,'
'background presences.'

"Two angels bringing protection" is an image of protective background energies of divine stewardship watching over a person or place. "Angels" are spiritual presences, often depicted in human form with wings, that attend to and watch over humans with sublime care. An angelic character is one that is soft, gentle, virtuous: an almost imperceptible presence of quiescence. "Two guardian angels" suggests a twofold concern or matter for divine stewardship.

A "petrified forest" is an image of rigid pillars of what was once a vibrant stand of trees. "Petrification" is a process of fossilization that turns organic matter into a rocklike substance. A petrified tree cannot be cut down with ordinary implements: it would be like swinging an ax into a stone. Petrified pillars suggest near-eternal principles that stand reliably throughout time. In a negative sense, such pillars suggest inflexibility, stiff and ill suited for contemporary usage. Emotions can become frozen the way a squirrel may be petrified with fear having been caught in the cross hairs of the hunter's rifle scope.

"Guardian angels" harken from another kind of eternal presence watching over and protecting, for example, the struggle for a new life in the forest wilderness. Imagine a pioneering wilderness family inspired and guided by the lush foliage and tall trees out of which they are building their home. They may be attempting to carve a new life out of what is rigid and unyielding. The ambiance of petrification echoes in a forest bereft of leaves, suggesting the gray pallor of age and inflexibility. On the other hand, petrified trees may stand as beacons for a way that has, for nearly all eternity, withstood all manner of rot.

Apply this degree-pair with a mind to soft, imperceptible realities that stand guard; hardness that withstands the vicissitudes of time; beacons of unshakable faith. Watch for innovation frustrated by inflexible norms; a sense of being frozen in archaic beliefs fearful of softening with the times; flaky appeals to divinely guided new ways; hard realities that soften to the comforting call of eternity. The young may be unaware of unseen protective presences; the old all too aware of the "otherworldliness" that beckons at the end of a lifetime. Consider primal presences; moral rigidity; subtle and rarefied presences of protection; hardened pillars of time that echo ancient thoughts of eternity.

"A colored child playing with white children" (4 Virgo) and "Heavy traffic on a narrow isthmus" (4 Pisces)

Aspect: Square.
Quality: Challenge.
Shared motifs: 'The path less rigidly traveled,'
'a discriminating line linking to other peoples.'

"A colored child playing with white children" is an image of an atmosphere happily permitting of differences.[1] "Play" is an activity that blissfully ignores boundaries, rules, and narrowly drawn lines of convention and bias. A black child and a white child play together with ease and naturalness, oblivious to the "color barrier" that may define adult realities. Just imagine how an adult perspective of keeping the sand inside the sandbox plays in a child's world. For the child, sand outside of the sandbox is not a problem. In the world of child's play, stark, unsubtle differences blend harmoniously.

"Heavy traffic on a narrow isthmus" is an image of a well-defined sense of procedure that narrows into a bottleneck situation. To be "narrow" means to lack breadth, to be of limited scope with little margin for straying. A narrow-minded person is one rigid in his or her views, intolerant, prejudiced. An "isthmus" is a geographical formation of a narrow strip of land connecting two larger bodies of land. "Traffic" derives from carrying across for trade, as in from country to country. "Heavy traffic" is a public manifestation of busy trade or transportation.

Imagine a holiday weekend with heavy traffic heading down the narrow isthmus of the Florida Keys, or down a two-laned highway leading to cottage country, moving slowly, bottlenecked along a black, ribbonlike path. In this neck of the woods there is only one road, one rigidly defined way, that reaches the goal. Straying does not appear to be an option: passing on a solid white line would be dangerous, futile, and against the rules. Adults may become increasingly stressed in their journey toward a relaxing getaway location. They could pull off the road to play like children in the water, defusing a potentially strained situation, taking time to smell the roses.

Apply this degree-pair with a mind to the challenge of being tolerant while following a focused, narrow path to one's goal; crossing social and ethnic boundaries with childlike ease. Think of a capacity for seeing beyond appearances; playing with shadow and light (chiaroscuro); being happy with how things are. Be alert to narrowness: of vision, unable to distinguish between colors; of mind, unable to warm up to

other ways; of neck, unable to swallow the truths of others. Consider bottleneck issues slowing progress, making goals harder to attain; what is worthwhile is worth lining up for; needing to get away; funneling energy toward the key thing. Remember
Dorothy in *The Wizard of Oz* having been transported from a black-and-white world
to one fully colored, observing, "Oh Toto! I don't think we're in Kansas anymore."

"A man dreaming of fairies" (5 Virgo) and "A church bazaar" (5 Pisces)

Aspect: Quintile.
Quality: Creative genius.
Shared motifs: 'A powerful house for all things and everyone,'
'the all-inclusive dream.'

"A man dreaming of fairies" is an image of dreamlike sensibilities of other, non-human
realms. "Dreaming" can mean imaginative fantasy or reveries lacking proper perception of so-called reality. To "follow a dream" is to remain true to a vision that dares to
go beyond prevailing realities of the normal waking state. "A man dreaming of fairies"
signals affinities for other realms, the realm of faerie and fairy folk. One may have a
felt sense of supersensible realms, those not manifest, yet open to dream traffic.

"A church bazaar" is an image of a feast of spirituality open to all, regardless of
denomination. The word "bazaar" is one of the few that come to us from the Middle
East deriving from the Persian *bazar*, meaning a public market. Bazaars are distinguished by their wide variety of offerings: a colorful array of any and everything
from any and everywhere. "Church," deriving from the Greek *kuros,* power, and *ku-
rios,* master, lord, or king, thus is the house of the powerful Lord. Consequently,
under the roof of the house of the Lord, or divine presence, all peoples can find all
things openly traded without any membership qualifications.

The road that connects differing ethnic groups, religious and cultural orientations, may be long and narrow, like an isthmus linking two land masses and motivated by trade in an economic sense. Imagine a church bazaar where things are
bought and sold in the spirit of fun and wonder. There may be strange and unique
items from all over the world: books on angels next to angel food cake; Persian
lamps next to Delta Blues records; Chinese tea next to ruby-red slippers. The social
dimension is open, inclusive, and tolerant. The market dimension does not sell reli-

gion or identity with a heavy hand, but creates an atmosphere of appreciation of the vast array of diversity of this world with a light background sense of divine presence.

Apply this degree-pair with a mind to the creative genius to dream the big dream of inclusiveness; to experience the world in terms of richness under a single unifying roof. Think of fantasy that finds spiritual and cultural presence in every exchange, merely dreaming, disconnected from worldly realities. Watch for personal affinities for a church that lies in another, unseen realm; for an open-mindedness that diffuses apparent, irreconcilable differences. Consider the humor and welcoming sense of wonder that treats all manner of trade and traffic like a powerful stranger, an unseen presence of divine energy, sublimely housing all peoples of the earth.

"A merry-go-round" (6 Virgo) and "Officers on dress parade" (6 Pisces)

Aspect: Conjunction.
Quality: Focus.
Shared motifs: 'The wheel of life,'
'personal ambition defined by social circles.'

"A merry-go-round" is an image of cycles of merriment, cycles of ups and downs. Merry-go-rounds are found in parks and carnivals, in public circles. Those on the merry-go-round are in the spin of things; those who are not, merely onlookers or part of the passing world. Therefore, there is a sense of a well-defined social circle regarding who's on and who's off the merry-go-round. Going round and round may be a point of frustration, as depicted in the Buddhist Wheel of Life. There may be a sense of spinning one's wheels, never getting anywhere. No one is ever constantly at the top or at the bottom: status and hierarchy are constantly changing with gearlike precision.

"Officers on dress parade" is an image of an elite group of rank parading for public display. "Officers" are those elevated above the lowest station in an organization, possessing a rank of authority. The ranks are closed to the public, yet are paraded with all the dressed spit and polish for the general public to view. For military officers, status and position are more rigidly maintained as opposed to the common rank and file of soldiers or civilians. There is a sense of leaders in the making, a promise that, in order to be fulfilled, must "step in line," "keep in step."

Imagine a merry-go-round with delighted children riding on wooden horses. Parents and grandparents watch from the outside looking in at the spinning wheel. The whole scene is one of a casual carousel: an eye for amusement. Imagine a dress parade of officers displaying all the facial expression of wooden horses on a merry-go-round: the elite marching in straight lines, expressionless eyes fixed forward in strict attention. A "dress parade" really is not going anywhere: it is a show of form, precision, practiced polish. A "merry-go-round" is not really going anywhere: it is a show of merriment driven by precision gears and mechanisms dressed with colorful horses and decoration.

Apply this degree-pair with a mind to the illumination of the inner mechanics that drive social position; the roundabout nature of highs and lows in life. Watch for serious, at-attention facial expressions; wooden manners; rides of which one can't seem to ever get off; standing on the sidelines watching it all go around. Be alert to focusing attention regarding life achievement around social circles or issues of rank. Consider taking life as a ride as opposed to a focused intent; merriment as opposed to seriousness; lifeless eyes as opposed to lively colorful eyes; roundabout ways as opposed to distinction through what is uniform; attempting to get a head above others by belonging to a particular group.

"A harem" (7 Virgo)
and "A cross lying on the rocks" (7 Pisces)
Aspect: Opposition.
Quality: Awareness of.
Shared motifs: 'Cloistered comforts,' 'rugged adventure,'
'forbidding and forbidden paths.'

"A harem" is an image of forbidden quarters, especially those established for comfort and protection. "Harem" is an Arabic term meaning anything forbidden, such as the household apartments of women forbidden to strangers. A harem is a group that is in some ways privileged, while being cloistered, beyond public viewing. With privilege comes security and protection from public and social vagaries, however protection comes in exchange for service. Confinement and social insulation are two haremlike motifs that suggest an uncertainty about moving away from a comfortable existence, out into the wide world.

"A cross lying on the rocks" is an image of a marker or fallen beacon in a rugged terrain. "A cross" harkens back to the crossroad markers, such as the *herma* of ancient Greece, erect, pillar-shaped stones with the head of Hermes on top serving to interpret directions for the traveler at critical junctures. "Lying on" means to be placed in a recumbent position, upon or against a surface, especially horizontally. A cross lying on the rocks may have fallen, but more likely has been placed there due to the nature of the terrain: rocky, rugged, inhospitable, calling for a vigorous sense of adventure.

Imagine hiking through rocky mountain terrain. There are no maps or signposts, save for those that often are just painted on the rocks, markers indicating that one is still on the trail. Like an intersection where the street sign has fallen, it is difficult to know which way to turn. Imagine the comfort and protection of a well-sheltered, pampered existence. The great outdoors may seem too forbidding a place into which to venture. In order to traverse a rocky path, one must sacrifice a great deal of comfort with an uncompromising resolve. One might compromise oneself in order to remain in cloistered security.

Apply this degree-pair with a mind to the awareness of self-sacrifice; compromising oneself for secure situations; or an uncompromising sense of individuation within the world at large; forbidden areas of life experience. Watch for an insular approach to life; knowing when to retreat within a ring of safety and when to strike out over rough terrain; privileged and private groups. Be alert for being socially crucified for one's choice of path in life; cherishing that which must never be seen; trumpeting being the first to have seen the forbidden. Consider the difference between lounging in pajamas securely at home on soft, comforting pillows as opposed to ruggedly setting off on a rocky mountain trail with no guiding markers.

"First dancing instruction" (8 Virgo)
and "A girl blowing a bugle" (8 Pisces)

Aspect: Trine.
Quality: Maintaining.
Shared motifs: 'Safe arenas for personal expression,'
'accepted conventions for being in the hunt.'

The "first dancing instruction" is an image of attentive, if awkward, first steps toward self-refinement and social expression. "Instruction" is a manner of teaching that furnishes knowledge, a know-how of steps: in order to do this, first do this, then that. "Dancing" derives from expressions meaning to stretch one's limbs, to move here and there. The "first" instance of instruction is, depending on the natural disposition of the one receiving instruction, awkward, humorous, exciting, frustrating, as is the first attempt at any new endeavor. The student is molded by the instruction based on the transmission of accepted form.

"A girl blowing a bugle" is an image of a sharply sounded signal of attention. A "bugle" is a musical instrument named for the horns of animals of the bovine family and buffalo. A bugler sounded the hunt, hence "hunting horn." "Blowing" is to move air swiftly and strongly, but is also related to blooming, as when a flower blossom beyond its prime of freshness is said to be blown. A bugle blowing may announce the time for a dress parade, the post parade at a racetrack, the beginning of a trumpet lesson. A girl blows her own horn as a means of announcing individuality, perhaps expressing personal triumph. Sounding the call, which originates from the very young, can only be a call to rally around old ways of doing things: the girl is young and fresh; the sound she makes is derived from an inherited past, perhaps a little beyond its prime.

Social forms of grace are transmitted through tradition rather than innovation. A young girl announces innovation only in terms of personal potential. A dancing instruction is fully imbued with accepted, recognized, forms of dance expression: specific directions to "step, move, walk this way." The refinements of social expression, social graces, are contained within a controlled situation, such as a dance studio, yet ready the individual with anticipation of personal expression: corralling familiar resources of instruction with nascent personal potential.

Apply this degree-pair with a mind to acceptance of recognized primers for social expression; finding oneself in the moves and rallying calls of others; nervous first steps that promise refinement of personal expression. Watch for the appearance of promise within the socialization process; an openness toward inherited conventions; laying the foundations for developing personal potentials. Listen for calling to attention; calling attention to oneself; blowing one's own horn. Consider emerging awareness of being in the hunt for relationship, for love; stepping up socially; controlled and socially acceptable ways of stepping out of line; taking a bull by the horn.

"A man making a futuristic drawing" (9 Virgo)
and "A jockey" (9 Pisces)

Aspect: Square.
Quality: Challenge.
Shared motifs: 'Personal innovation,'
'drawing off the edge of the social page,' 'spurring on.'

"A man making a futuristic drawing" is an image of manifesting personal creativity in a way that goes beyond hitherto known expression. Artistic innovation is often ahead of its time, pushing the known limits of expression into new territory. A "futurist" is one who projects ahead, speculating on things to come: flying cars, space colonies, underwater cities, and so on. "Drawing" is the art of representing by line, usually delineated without color, or using a single color. "Making a futuristic drawing" is like dragging the prevailing styles of traditional and contemporary art into the future. The lamentably overused expression "think outside of the box" applies here.

"A jockey" is an image of a rider skilled in maneuvering power within a powerfully contested situation. Jockeys are professionally hired riders of thoroughbred race horses. Their job is to give the horse they ride, the horse power underneath them, the best chance at winning the race. "Jockey" derives from the diminutive for John, "Jock." A Scotsman may use "Wee Jock" as an endearing name for his dog, or as a euphemism for the distinguishing anatomical feature of the male gender, hence jock-strap. Jockeying for position means to place or guide oneself into an advantageous position. To jockey someone means to draw someone in or out by trickery.

Horse racing requires jockeys to be of diminutive stature, yet ride thousand-pound power animals using deft skill and cunning. Following the post parade, a jockey's real work is focused on a mere minute or two from entering the starting gate to the finish line. There are many tricks of the trade for gaining the best advantage over the competition. An artist, after years of traditional training, applies mastery of fundamental technique to innovative expression, draws upon inner resources and instincts that, like a jockey, deftly and quickly maneuver his instrument to effect the outcome, usually with a strong flourish at the finish.

Apply this degree-pair with a mind to the pushing forward toward the ultimate goals of social intercourse; disturbing contemporary paradigms in the rush for something new; creating excitement that spurs things on. Watch for a knack for accelerating creative interaction; deftly maneuvering or manipulating people and impressions; drawing people into something; drawing something out of people. Consider going a step beyond being merely in the hunt; spurring on or with appreciation; getting over and beyond social niceties; contesting the matter at hand with personal style, flourish, and intimacy; the shape of things to come.

"Two heads looking out and beyond the shadows" (10 Virgo) and "An aviator in the clouds" (10 Pisces)

Aspect: Quintile.
Quality: Creative genius.
Shared motifs: 'Looking ahead,'
'feeling out together what is to come,' 'flying on autopilot.'

"Two heads looking out and beyond the shadows" is an image of shared consideration for what lies beyond, what comes next. Perceptional horizons are constituted by light, color, hue, umbra: combining to give an almost compelling sense of something more. "Two heads," which are often said to be better than one, look out beyond "shadows" in an attempt to ascertain the object of perception, or clarify vision in a broader sense. A cooperative effort to see beyond might agree on what they see, or have a differing take on what lies ahead. "Shadows" suggest light cast upon something or forbidden actions that, having been done, cast a shadow of guilt.

"An aviator in the clouds" is an image of flying by the seat of your pants, or on autopilot. To "fly by the seat of your pants" means to figure things out as you go, without a plan, possibly having to change course in midstream. Before modern instrumentation, pilots flew their planes by feel, the felt feedback from the plane's reactions to the pilot's adjustment of the controls, the most sensitive contact being the seat area. Modern aviation can fly by instrumentation or through the autopilot control. "In the clouds" suggests being denied the vision to see ahead, consequently calling on trust or perhaps blind faith. One could have one's head in the clouds or wing it through instinct or gut feeling.

Imagine Adam and Eve sitting down together after having eaten the forbidden apple: "You know, I wonder if we shouldn't have done that. Oh well, it's done now. What do you think lies in store for us?" Imagine an airplane pilot making flight adjustments on the fly, not in response to what is seen ahead, but to what is felt through the course of the flight path. It's hard to have a plan in place when you cannot see all that lies ahead. Every perceptual horizon presents the same challenge: no matter how high you get your head in order to get a full overview, there is ever a suggestion of more, that which cannot be seen from where you stand. Imagine a young modern Adam and Eve coming home from the dance or a day at the races, saying, "Mom, Dad, Adam and I have something to tell you."

Apply this degree-pair with a mind to the genius for making plans on the fly; for feeling out the possibilities; getting heads together to ascertain a clear path. Watch for the knack of getting an overall, if indistinct, impression of what lies ahead; the tendency to panic when losing all perceptual, emotional, or social bearing. Consider the instinct to find one's way; whiteout circumstances; the pregnant pause; decisions in the wake of powerful consequences; overblown confidence and blind faith; trusting natures regarding how it will all work out; navigating uncertain social climates.

"A boy molded in his mother's aspirations for him" (11 Virgo) and "Men seeking illumination" (11 Pisces)

Aspect: Conjunction.
Quality: Focus.
Shared motifs: 'Being sucked into tradition,' 'waking to inheritance, but not yet weaned.'

"A boy molded in his mother's aspirations for him" is an image of exalted visions and ambitions transmitted from mother to child. "Molded" implies a pliable matter, which can be shaped, fashioned. "Aspirations" are desires for high goals, high achievements, often exalted visions of that which is beyond the reach of most, if not all, human beings. "Aspiring" derives from spirit in the sense of life-breath. A newborn child often needs to be aspirated, have the air passages cleared of mucus in order that the child can breathe freely on its own. An aspirator functions by blowing or by suction: blowing away minute obstacles, like dust, to free up function; drawing the mucus out in order to let breath in. Sometimes the aspirations others hold for one can blow one away, or suck the life-breath right out.

"Men seeking illumination" is an image of a conscious pursuit of a path of enlightenment, seeking light, clarity, and understanding. "To illuminate" is to shed light upon, to clarify something, to enlighten the mind. "Seeking illumination" comes about only when motivated by dissatisfaction. The frustration of not being able to

see clearly may motivate one to turn on a light: clouds may obscure a clear perception of something, shadows may hide, emotions obscure, guilt tarnish. "Seeking" is
fueled by the desire to find something, to reveal, discover, to realize something in a
higher sense. The thrust is toward seeing and understanding thoroughly as opposed
to a partial or incomplete understanding.

Imagine a newborn child in the arms of its mother. That most fragile and tender
of moments is fraught with deep feelings, hopes, dreams. It is natural for a mother to
have aspirations for the child, even indistinct goals wished for the child: health, happiness, to grow up to be a leader, an artist, a star athlete, and so on. The moments
following birth are powerful junctures where even silent wishes are transmitted from
mother to child, which continue to shape and mold as the child's life unfolds. Seeking
to realize aspirations may be a matter of attempting to fulfill ambitions, or to become
free from the projections others have had and held for you.

Apply this degree-pair with a mind to the focal point upon which all life journeys
begin and are shaped; the illumination of transmitted inheritance; the need to be
weaned from the mother's aspirations, the breast being the natural aspirator for an infant. Think of following a path others have illuminated for you; following a path that
seeks to transcend the influence of others; what motivates the desire to see the light. Be
alert for breathing problems; aspirants; aspirators; inspired ones, inspirations; breathing
on one's own. Consider a focus on determining one's own aspirations; finding oneself in
the midst of inherited obscurations; finding it difficult to own what has been cast ahead
for you; owning that you owe your path in life to the reach others have passed on.

"A bride with her veil snatched away" (12 Virgo)
and "An examination of initiates" (12 Pisces)

Aspect: Opposition.
Quality: Awareness of.
Shared motifs: 'A test at the juncture of stepping up on the
path,' 'scrutinizing the inscrutable.'

"A bride with her veil snatched away" is an image of a revelation at the point of an
elevating juncture in life. A "bride" is a woman who is either at the point of being

married or at the point of just having been married. The term illuminates a definite juncture along the bridal path. A "veil" is a covering, which, in the context of marriage, is a thin cloth worn over the head or face for concealment, ornamentation, or protection. That which is veiled cannot be examined or inspected. To have a "veil snatched away" is to have a covering suddenly removed, which implies several circumstances: hasty excitement of the groom to finally kiss the bride; a sudden exposure at a critical juncture; a surprising jest before the prescribed time.

"An examination of initiates" is an image of an open scrutiny or inspection of those who have commenced a specific course. "An examination" is an inspection or scrutinizing of someone or something. To be able to examine implies an availability or openness of that which is to be inspected, as well as a focus of light at a critical juncture along a path, the future of which hangs in the balance. Something that remains a veiled mystery is inscrutable. "Initiates" are those who are newly introduced to something: a path, a course, a ritual induction to a special membership. Ritual initiations suggest an introduction to secret knowledge, wisdom: an inscrutable source of illumination.

Imagine a bride, while walking the path to the marriage altar, having her veil snatched away. Perhaps this action strips away the mystery requisite for the marriage; perhaps it reveals one's true face, which may or may not show accordance with another's aspirations. Veiled heads and faces of women are common in some world cultures. A question open for scrutiny is: Does this protect a mystery necessary for spiritual ritual process, or does this merely cover the true face of the woman or bride? Critical junctures along one's path in life turn on an intense awareness of the scrutiny of others. A Zen koan asks, "Show me your face before you were born," to which might be appended, "Show me your face before and after the exam, before and after the wedding."

Apply this degree-pair with a mind to the intense awareness of critical junctures in life; points that put one's true self in the balance; pivots of exposure or revelation, hiding the truth or veiling mystery. Watch for tests of confidence: having one's life under intense scrutiny; fearfulness about being found out; nervousness about having the veil snatched away; being overly concerned about formalities, about credentials. Consider sudden surprises along the path; humorous, unpredictable actions; stepping up without hesitation; who you are after the wedding, after the exam. There is an elegance and dignity about that which is inscrutable: not revealing everything implies your truth, your genuine authenticity; revealing everything dispels the mystery.

"A strong hand supplanting political hysteria" (13 Virgo) and "A sword in a museum" (13 Pisces)

Aspect: Trine.
Quality: Maintaining.
Shared motifs: 'Drawing on inner strength to bring calm,'
'a discriminating sense of right order.'

"A strong hand supplanting political hysteria" is an image of taking a firm grip on a civic situation by tripping up emotional excesses. "A strong hand" suggests the capacity to have a firm grip, to handle weighty issues with authority. "Supplanting" is an action of displacing something or someone, uprooting or exchanging one thing for another. Deriving from *sub,* up from below, plus *planta,* the sole of the foot, the Latin *supplentare* means to trip up. "Hysteria" derives from the Greek *hystera,* womb, and has come to mean excesses of emotional extremes. A "political hysteria" is a situation where the social norms and controls inherent in any civic governing organization temporarily have lost their controlling effect.

"A sword in a museum" is an image of a weapon or symbol of decisive power preserved and displayed in the house of memories. A "sword" is a long-bladed weapon that can cut, slash, jab, or point. Symbolically, the sword signals confident, discriminating awareness: the ability to cut through obscurity. A "museum" is a place for preserving, named in the honor of the daughters, or Muses of Memory, *Mnemosyne.* The implication is one of an inspiring nature worth contemplating. While in a museum, a sword is not being used for battle, yet stands as a symbol of power worth drawing upon.

Recall the story of the "Sword in the Stone." The land was cast into a period of political hysteria as rival factions fought over who was to be High King, until a young Arthur drew out, with his hand, the sword in the stone. Imagine a wedding ceremony where some rascal trips up the bride, causing her to fall and lose her covering veil: an amusing prank to some or a cause for extreme emotional excitement for others; a deft action to deflate overseriousness or a scheming excess in need of check. Times of emotional chaos or excessive disorder call for one to draw upon inner personal power, like a sword from a stone, to stand strong, like the calming center of a storm. One does not have to wield a sword at all times in order to maintain order, but one does have to honor the capacity to do so when required.

Apply this degree-pair with a mind to maintaining order within chaos; taking matters into one's own hands; drawing on veiled powers at the right moment. Think of a sense of balanced awareness: when to diffuse unruly situations with humor, and when to diffuse with authoritative power. Watch for quiet confidence having no need to wave one's weapon around; a gathering of strength when things get out of hand; the ability to put a lid on runaway emotions; the capacity to not lose one's head. Consider claiming one's personal power; a cutting edge no longer in use; quiet stewarding of archaic values; defending tradition; a surprising source of centering power.

"A family tree" (14 Virgo) and "Lady in a fox fur" (14 Pisces)

Aspect: Square.
Quality: Challenge.
Shared motifs: 'Belonging,' 'cunning camouflage for family protection.'

"A family tree" is an image of the branching roots of heritage. Every human being stands in this world like a tree with deep roots, penetrating the unseen realm of both familial predecessors and ancestral affinities with no known biological ties. A "family" is a socially organized unit of belonging, usually including parents and children: a creative manifestation of descendants from an inclusive common source. A "tree" is a woody plant having nourishment-drawing roots that branch out under the ground, a strong, self-supporting trunk, and a crown of foliage reaching high toward the heavens.

A "lady in a fox fur" is an image of alert personal cunning able to blend in while quietly observing. The fox, as an animal totem, is associated with quickness of mind, vanishing capacities, and agility. The constellation Velpecula, Little Fox, was originally conceived as a fox with a goose in its mouth. A "vixen," the female fox, is a woman of villainous character and tempestuous temper. A "fox" is archaically a name for a sword, probably a small sword able to be concealed under a cloak, and a name for the sheath of a sword, echoing the covering theme. Although fox furs are highly prized as a symbol of fashion and status, there is an archaic association with hair falling out in clumps.

Imagine the boy Arthur, descendent of royal heritage, raised as an adopted child and serving as a squire to his less royally bred foster brother Kay. It was just clever good sense to hide his true heritage away from rivals for the throne until mature enough to claim his power and throne. Sometimes one has an uncanny sense of not quite belonging, descending from a foreign branch of the great family tree, a situation that calls for cunning, or reticence about revealing one's own heritage. A fox living amongst fowl may do well to conceal his cunning designs; a goose living near a fox's den would do well to think and act like a fox. The challenge is not to cause an uproar, concealing one's special heritage while maintaining a quiet, tempered sense of belonging.

Apply this degree-pair with a mind to the challenge of wearing one's felt sense of heritage well within the social milieu; individuality being made to fit family heritage; one's personal name supplanted by the family name. Watch for an aristocratic sense of style; wearing one's identity in style; being wrapped up in an animal totem. Be alert for a protective wrap; concealed power that, like a hidden sword, is nonetheless ready to hand; sly and clever minds. Consider trying to fit in; an aristocratic heritage worn with a wild, cutting-edge sense of fashion; a foxy lady; elegance and style covering a wild and uncontrollable sense of personal identity.

"An ornamental handkerchief" (15 Virgo) and "An officer preparing to drill his men" (15 Pisces)

Aspect: Quintile.
Quality: Creative genius.
Shared motifs: 'Passing on what one has seen,'
'personal refinements become the order of the day.'

"An ornamental handkerchief" is an image of power and rank embellished by beauty and refinement. "Ornamental" derives from the Latin *ordo*, meaning the order of the threads in a woof, hence a rank, an order or station, and is a variant of the Greek *arthron*, a joint, perhaps a joint upon which rank and order turns. A "handkerchief" is a piece of cloth having utility for wiping the face and nose, and embellishing capacities of an adorning accessory. A handkerchief can be used by one's own hand to cover the face as needed, hide a smile, cover embarrassment, or as an adornment signaling refinement.

"An officer preparing to drill his men" is an image of a person of rank readying his presentability as a means of transmitting noble refinements to his men. "To drill" others is to instruct, to train through repetition, the routines that must be rehearsed and learned inside out. "An officer" is a position of rank that carries responsibilities for a larger group. "Preparing" to drill is personal attention brought to readying for the training, the transmission order, ordinance, or the finer points and embellishments of an inherited comportment. Making oneself presentable is a preparation with a mind to the impression one makes in accordance with standards of high bearing.

Arthur won the rank of High King by right of blood inheritance and right use of arms. Although Arthur was heralded as the Flower of Chivalry, it was by ordinance of his Queen that the chivalric code was refined: a quest of ladies to be set on knights, to be judged while living with ladies; to fight for their quarrels, ever to be courteous and never to refuse mercy to he who asks for mercy. Knights, during tournaments, would accept the handkerchief of a lady as a reminder of the ongoing refinement of their oath. This is certainly not something to sneeze at, nor to allow to become a mere show of indulgent finery.

Apply this degree-pair with a mind to refinements of the right use of power; appearance projecting core beliefs; the genius for integrating one's own inheritance and carrying it well. Watch for preparing appearance as a matter of dignity and comportment, not mere apparel; making due with what one has at hand; disregard for a finished appearance as a matter of routine, or refined routines for making oneself up; getting ready with what you do not need, or creative readying garnering respect despite circumstances. Consider that an ornamental handkerchief was the best weapon in King Arthur's arsenal. Consider these most echoic words: *anthro,* man; *artho,* joint, which in weaving determines order; and *anthos,* flower; collectively flowing together in a high-ranking man: the flower of mankind.

"An orangutan" (16 Virgo) and "The flow of inspiration" (16 Pisces)

Aspect: Conjunction.
Quality: Focus.
Shared motifs: 'The raw flow of instinctual power,'
'the gold within.'

"An orangutan" is an image of the wild man within. "Orangutan" is a Malaysian word meaning wild man, or man of the forest wilderness. An "orangutan" is a large anthropoid of reddish yellow to brown color. The word for the color orange arises from the term *aur,* gold, and *naranga,* orangetree, in Arabic and Tamil. The orangutan mirrors for humans a primitive ancestral image, one that swings in the trees of the forest wilderness. Most humans never see an orangutan, let alone the wild inner primitive self, except behind bars in a zoo, or perhaps in bars that are like zoos, or when men who, having behaved like animals, are behind bars.

"The flow of inspiration" is an image of seamless inner connections with the source of life power. "Inspiration" is the infusion or arousal of energy that can lead to a creative action. "Chi" is a Chinese term, difficult to translate, meaning the flow of inherent life energy. To be in harmony with the natural flow of chi opens one to deep sources of vibrant power and well-being. "Inspiration" is an illuminating flow of divine energy, as in being inspired by one's muse. Muses, being the daughters of Memory, may call upon primal archaic memories of a more ape-like inheritance. Such a flow calls for an intimate inwardness. "Inspiration" is also to draw in fresh air in the process of breathing.

Civilized and refined manners not only shape socially acceptable expression to raw human energies, but can also separate a man from the deep, inner, instinctive source of power. "Iron Hans," a wonderful story collected and adapted by the Brothers Grimm, tells of an unruly wild man all covered in rust-colored mud, terrifying the forest wilderness. The story relays the unfolding of several motifs: encountering, capturing, and caging the wild man; liberating the wild man; relating to the wild man. Having made friends with the wild man, the boy grows into manhood, begins to get in touch with the gold, the power of his self, within.

Apply this degree-pair with a mind to deep inner sources of inspiration; almost compelling urges to act without thinking; the clash between wild inner instinct and tamed outer expression. Think of surges of sexual power; containing instincts, as a muse in a museum or as stifling wildness in a cage. Watch for red hair; matted hair, internal inflammations seeking external expression; creative strokes that shine like gold. Be alert for mirror images: revelations about human and ape-like affinities; raw, powerful expressions as opposed to mere emulation; refined social manners encroaching on one's inner wilderness; stark stripping away of social niceties. Consider pent-up forces that call for assimilation; malaise from feeling caged; a dexterity for getting the swing of things; breathing techniques for drawing on inner resources.

"A volcano in eruption" (17 Virgo)
and "An Easter promenade" (17 Pisces)

Aspect: Opposition.
Quality: Awareness of.
Shared motifs: 'The wild man in polite society,'
'the pace of renewal.'

"A volcano in eruption" is an image of an explosive force breaking free with uncontrolled displays of power. Volcanos are also powerful examples of containment: keeping a lid on things. One can live at the foot of a volcano for years, for centuries, unaware of the destructive power that, at any moment, may be unleashed. Although volcanos are thought of as being explosive expressions of destructive power, it is also true that, over time, they are the instrument of establishing new life: dramatic, primal expressions that bring about a new land, a new ecosystem, ultimately refreshing and renewing the lay of the land. "Eruption" is the breaking free of powerful inner resources of energy: molten hot; running wild.

"An Easter promenade" is an image of exhibiting oneself at a controlled pace within a social event inspired by feeling renewed, reborn. "Easter" is Christian celebration of rebirth and a time associated with the arousing, renewing energies of spring. A "promenade" is a casual stroll in an open social space. The "promenade" is at a walking pace, the word deriving from the Latin *prominare,* to drive cattle forward. On a beautiful Easter Sunday afternoon, all walks of life come together, dressed in their Sunday best. Rich and poor stroll along the promenade, casually enjoying the return of spring, watching and greeting one another.

Imagine an artist recently inspired by a terrible but powerful muse. He goes out on Easter Sunday to see the entire community moving along like a herd of cattle, driven, as it were, by social niceties and pretensions of importance expressed mostly through apparel. He might rush into the crowd like an explosive madman, violently disturbing the peaceful scene; he might suppress the powerful, tormenting urges, recognizing an impending disaster of showing himself at an inappropriate place and time; he might flee back into the wilderness forest. Just like a deep inner inflammation that rises to the surface as a hot, angry boil, the upsurge of raw personal powers cannot always be controlled. When the wild man, "orangutan," is freed from his cage, something in the human psyche, in the social world, has to give.

Apply this degree-pair with a mind to a sharp awareness of the appropriate expression of powerful inspirations; the urge to run furiously while everyone else strolls along; the potentially destructive forces of creativity. Think of demeanors that are hot within, cool without; explosive tempers just below the surface; cathartic eruptions that might rain on the parade of others. Be alert to the social capacities of acceptance and tolerance being tested by new, raw, explosive social expressions. Consider flare-ups of all kinds: boils, tempers, defiance; molten energies that flow with a mind of their own, take solid form only after long periods of cooling down, as opposed to the natural pace at which everyone shows themselves, their position and power, in a promenade.

"A ouija board" (18 Virgo) and "A gigantic tent" (18 Pisces)

Aspect: Trine.
Quality: Maintaining.
Shared motifs: 'Optimism doubled up for the extraordinary,'
'the role of moveable, temporary structures on the outskirts of town.'

"A ouija board" is an image of redoubled optimism in exploration of uncanny, extra-sensory communication. A "ouija board" is a device consisting of a board inscribed with an alphabet and other symbols, a point upon which two people gently place their fingertips while asking a question. The response comes through the uncanny motion of the pointer to letters, spelling out an answer. "Ouija" comes from combining the French *oui*, yes, and the German *ja,* yes, giving the impression of a double sense of optimistic, favorable answers. It takes two people to effect the movement of the pointer, neither of whom is to apply intentional direction or influence. The ouija response, therefore, implies a third, extrasensory component in communication.

"A gigantic tent" is an image of a moveable structure housing events, energy, and people. "Gigantic tents" are set up on rare occasions: a circus tent; a spiritual-revival meeting tent; a medicine show; a tent set up for disaster victims. A volcano, for example, may have destroyed houses and homes, calling for a temporary means of shelter. "Gigantic" derives from giant, meaning very large, of tremendous proportions. Ordinary everyday life is stirred with excitement at the arrival of the big traveling show, a huge spectacle passing through town. Whatever message is delivered under the tent covering, it is sure to be big: either of overblown exaggeration or of necessary serious import.

Imagine a traveling show setting up on the outskirts of town, sending ripples of excitement and curiosity through the community. In order to fully enjoy the show, one must temporarily suspend judgment and ordinary pragmatic reasoning. When a gigantic tent is set up, it is a temporary situation, one that will move on, and one that ever skirts the edge of town. A nursing tent at the fringe of a natural disaster; a political rally on the fringes of popular opinion; a dramatic show of spectacle: all call for a transient while of hope and belief beyond the ordinary. It's like ordering an ice cream cone with two scoops of optimism.

Apply this degree-pair with a mind to expansive attitudes needed to manage temporary situations; hope for relief; answers to prayers; signs of confirmation for that which lies just outside of mainstream belief. Think of boundless optimism; a willing suspension of disbelief; showmanship that is still searching for a permanent home. Consider situations that call for faith beyond reason; extrasensory perception; the ability to read each other's minds, think each other's thoughts; playing with something strange and more powerful than ordinarily expected; uncanny communication; reinforcing a shared secret realm; a mysterious third element introduced to discursive thought.

"A swimming race" (19 Virgo)
and "A master instructing his pupil" (19 Pisces)

Aspect: Square.
Quality: Challenge.
Shared motifs: 'On making headway in a foreign element,'
'plunging in and coming up for air.'

"A swimming race" is an image of a contest of dizzying speed in a foreign element. "Swimming" is an action of moving through water, being both immersed and buoyed at the same time. A "race" is any contest of relative speed, but also a swift channel of water, a current of accelerated motion when, for example, two tides collide in confluence. A "race" is echoic of "rase," as in to erase, wipe out, or scratch out. If one is caught in a racing channel of water, it may induce a dizzying sense of being flooded, and slightly overwhelmed. A flow of inspiration might have the same effect: a dizzying rush of fluid energy wiping out all sense of self-control.

"A master instructing his pupil" is an image of passing knowledge on out of a place of mastery. A "master" is one who is in control of something or someone, usually exhibiting a highly developed skill or artistry. "Mastery" derives from a confluence of "mister," an honorific designation, and "magistery," an alchemical agent or quality capable of transmuting other substances, implying capacities of greatness and dominating influence. A "pupil" is a young scholar whose eye, the pupil of the eye, reflects the guiding presence of a tutor. The pupil may feel overwhelmed by the dominating, overpowering influence of the master, or he may be doing just swimmingly.

The flow of inspiration from a deep and powerful source calls for a mastery of energies, of knowledge, and a skilled ability to transmit that knowledge. The challenge is to channel knowledge through fresh minds in a way so as to not overwhelm, but at the same time not to underwhelm: overdominating instruction works as poorly as watered-down instruction. Just as with a swimming race, it is good to have one's head above water at regular intervals along the course of the race; so too with learning, it is good to get your head on, assimilating the flow of knowledge as your own from time to time. If one is never one's own master, there is danger of being swept away by the strong current of someone else's take on things.

Apply this degree-pair with a mind to the challenge of diving into deep water while keeping your head about you; excitement about generous exchanges between unequals. Think of the twofold nature of water on a swimmer: buoyant and submersive; the sense of right proportion and right time: too much or too little of any ingredient ruins the stew. Watch for eyes that reveal being dizzied before the grandness of a master; eyes that water with overwhelming emotion; impatience about the pace at which others learn. Be alert to domineering tendencies buoyed by a sense of the right and true way; impassive submission to another's version of the one true way. Consider a rush of fear about not getting in too deep, about never scratching the surface; learning as a contest as opposed to just getting all wet; overcompliance; personal compromise rationalized as spiritual sacrifice; the need to breathe on your own once in a while.

"An automobile caravan" (20 Virgo)
and "A table set for an evening meal" (20 Pisces)

Aspect: Quintile.
Quality: Creative genius.
Shared motifs: 'Self-mastered internal power,'
'in line for ambition or reward.'

"An automobile caravan" is an image of self-powered vehicles traveling together. "Caravan" derives from the Persian *karwan,* referring to a train of camels traveling across the desert in single file. An "automobile" is a relatively recent invention consisting of usually four wheels and a self-contained source of power and fuel. The key feature of the automobile is that it can easily be driven by a single person behind the wheel. Powered by an internal combustion engine, one that contains and channels explosive energy through a system of transmission gears and drive shaft, the automobile places the individual *autos,* self, behind the driver's wheel in full command of his mobility: Latin *mobilis.*

"A table set for an evening meal" is an image of preparedness for sharing the fruits of the day's labors. The "evening meal" is symbolic of both the time of day and the season of reaping the rewards of human endeavor and industry. Families gather to enjoy the fruits of the day's labors at the evening mealtime. Associated with the direction west, the evening meal is a time of relaxed, smiling joy. "A table set" is a table all in readiness for the meal to begin, suggesting a gathering or company of people who will come to enjoy the meal together.

Think of the significance of the single-owner, internal combustion–powered automobile. Few inventions have empowered the individual more over the last century. Driving one's own car allows for a great range of freedom and a sense of relative ease regarding mobility. Driving in a caravan suggests joining with other drivers with a common destination in mind: harnessing personal power in a common direction with others who also command their own selves. The caravan suggests a level of self-mastery. The table set suggests rewards that lie ahead, a well-earned meal after graduating from school, or successfully mastering the graceful movements of swimming.

Apply this degree-pair with a mind to the authentic genius of one's own power; the rewards laid out ready in wait after long efforts of appropriating one's sense of self. Watch for the tendency to line up with others despite having come into one's own; the tendency to accept an easy spread of self-deserving rewards. Be alert to these questions: If you have mastered your own power, why follow others? If you have mastered your own power, why not join with others so that even more can be accomplished? Consider taking a well-deserved break; a future setup for either comforts or ambitions; mastery of the wild man within: orange rust turns to gold; untamed power meets graceful self-expression.

"A girls' basketball team" (21 Virgo) and "A little white lamb, a child, and a Chinese servant" (21 Pisces)

Aspect: Conjunction.
Quality: Focus.
Shared motifs: 'Pulling disparate parts together,'
'the issue of identity in group cooperation.'

"A girls' basketball team" is an image of a group organization that brings people with a common interest together through team-oriented goals. A "basketball team" is a group organized for cooperatively expressed achievement within a well-defined contest. "Basketball" is a game played within a zoned oblong court, the object of which is to throw a ball into the goal or basket of the opposing team. Basketball teams have equal numbers of players on the court at all times, suggesting a fairness to the contested result. A "team" is a group that harnesses collective abilities for the same goal. "Team" derives from the yoking of beasts of burden such that their combined strengths are directed toward a common purpose, and is akin to "teem," to produce offspring, suggesting abundance and overflowing resources.

"A little lamb, a child, and a Chinese servant" is an image of three seemingly disparate life presences gathered into a single glimpse of life. A "lamb" is a symbol of innocence, one that would immediately attract the affections of a young, also innocent, girl. A "Chinese servant" brings a different perspective with elements of hired service, a foreign culture, age, and experience. The path of service is one of the great paths in life recognized by all world religions as intrinsically rooted in a regard for the well-being of others. A hired servant may take on service duties as honorable work, the responsibilities of which are happily accepted and appreciated for their spiritual merits; or take on service as a job, a temporary means to other goals.

Imagine a girls' basketball team practicing set plays that may be ineffective, awkward motions or potent drills that lift the team to game readiness. Not everyone on a team is of equal skill or ability. Some may be more concerned about themselves than the team goal: their own play, their own appearance. Others may have their mind on other things: talking about boyfriends, the upcoming dance. There may be discontent on the team: naive arguments about details of the game, calling for a need to work things out. The girl may be embracing the young lamb. The servant may embrace the innocence of the child and lamb from the perspective of years of experience and service; that is, the servant's regard is conditioned by personal, social, and cultural realities in contrast with the child's naive innocence. The Chinese servant may have a stilted view of the innocent hope of youth, or of the inequities of social position and cultural privilege.

Apply this degree-pair with a mind to the awareness of differences within so-called level playing fields; personal concerns within a cooperative setting. Think of personal sacrifice for the benefit of the collective goal; watchful stewarding of nascent potentials; the temptation to be self-serving to the detriment of the team. Watch for the wise eye of experience that watches over the naive; disgruntled attitudes that can barely hide contempt; feelings of "What about me?"; warm eyes that embrace the innocence of youth. Consider feeling strange about having to learn foreign moves in order to reach one's goal; enormous patience while coaching others; improving; honing; carrying the ball.

"A royal coat of arms" (22 Virgo)
and "A man bringing down the new law from Mount Sinai" (22 Pisces)

Aspect: Opposition.
Quality: Awareness of.
Shared motifs: 'Might is right,' 'all authority goes to blazes.'

"A royal coat of arms" is an image of a representation emblematic of tradition, heritage, position, and privilege. "A coat of arms" is a tabard or other coat blazoned with armorial bearings, proclaiming a heritage of accomplishment, position, and privilege. The bearer of a coat of arms announces stewardship of a trail that has been blazed; like blazing a trail through the woods, the armorial bearings at once proclaim and show the way. Being "royal," the coat of arms claims a mandate for position: to lead the way; and privilege: all the benefits and honor such leadership may garner. "Blazing" suggests brilliance and outstanding marks of distinction that function like a guiding light for others and call for loyalty to the standard-bearer.

"A man bringing down the new law from Mount Sinai" is an image of elevated ordination that divines a mandate from higher authority. A single individual coming down from a sacred mountain, the peak of which touches a divine unearthly perspective, carries the weight of authority. "Bringing down the new law" suggests a connection with a higher sense of reality and the ability to formulate, even innovate, a new law that addresses civilization and its discontents. "Sinai" is the sacred mountain on which Moses received the Torah, the commandments prescribed by God. The implication is that there is no human hand in the writing of the laws. Moses had an incendiary relationship with the divine: his call to the Lord was a burning bush; the "fire of the Lord" consumed disgruntled Israelites at a place Moses called "Taberah," echoic of the tabard worn by knights of arms.

Laws are necessary to give order and direction for the community of mankind. All laws are based upon a sense of authority, like an official insignia announcing the right of mandate. Historically, the proof of right authority often invoked a test by fire. Imagine two knights of old riding toward one another, their armorial bearings emblazoned upon their tabards announcing differing camps of authority. The knights may charge at one another with the full force of arms to establish whose cause is more just: might is right. It's a hot burning issue over which many an innocent victim has fallen: a regal bearing worth fighting for; a heavenly mandate over which not even kings and queens have superseding authority.

Apply this degree-pair with a mind to the awareness of prevailing standards of privilege and power; justifications that can really burn you up. Think of tendencies to spiritually rationalize actions and one's own position of authority; to pontificate from an out-of-touch vantage point; intense feelings about being the chosen one; passions that champion divine rule. Watch for wearing authority on one's sleeve; official uniforms; badges; the smarts to see trouble coming; readiness to take up the fight.

"An animal trainer" (23 Virgo)
and "Spiritist phenomena" (23 Pisces)

Aspect: Trine.
Quality: Maintaining.
Shared motifs: 'Taming intangible matters of spirit,'
'harnessing energies.'

"An animal trainer" is an image of managing wild, dangerous instincts for tame expressions. "Animals" possess socialized traits inherited through the family to which they belong. When different animal families encounter one another, the result is usually a fierce row or show of strength. Animals, therefore, are not considered to possess civilized traits, but rather operate entirely out of fight-or-flight responses. "An animal trainer" is one who tames wild instincts such that they are manageable in the human world. "Taming" is derived from *tractus,* to draw along, to harness. One might put a leash on an animal or tame a wild mind or spirit through meditation. While "tame" is often associated with lacking spirit, dull insipid demeanors, it is also an amenable nature for cooperation.

Spiritist phenomena" is an image of manifestations of nonphysical, nonmaterial energy. "Spirit" derives from the Latin *spirare,* to breathe, and is echoic of *anima,* soul, hence divine spirit. "Phenomena" derives from the Greek *phainomai,* appear or show, and is akin to "phantasm," meaning an illusion or a phantom. Matters of spirit that show themselves in immaterial ways are illusive, hard to harness, and therefore difficult to prove with hard evidence. A show of spirit can be an inspiring experience, or it can be a troubling manifestation of wild, untamed energy. The goal of harnessing spiritual energies is not to render one listless and broken, but to contain in manageable ways that ultimately, on the human and physical level, do no harm.

A spirited horse is thought to be a good horse, although one whose wild nature needs to be tamed. Taming horses is known as breaking horses, which when applied too vigorously can break the spirit: do more harm than intended. Taming through gentleness, with a firm yet mindful attitude, is proving to be the only way to work with wild and frightened horses: the horse whisperers. The paradox regarding spiritualist phenomena lies in spirit, life-breath, being associated with disembodied, dead spirits. The identity of the spirit communicated with has been, historically, a contentious issue, often resulting in inflammable disputes. It is, therefore, understandable that one might wish to rein in the whole matter.

Apply this degree-pair with a mind to the reigning need to tame matters of spirit; to harness a connection with life-giving energy from a nonmaterial realm. Think of gentle approaches to wild energies: mindful, disciplined repetition with a soft touch. Be alert for the struggle to overcome baser instincts; the strength to wrestle with the lion within; a submissive manner as opposed to ruling with the rod; civilized refinements of noble human instincts, i.e., to be of good heart. Consider a knack for communing with the intangible; manifestations of passionate certainty that eventually fade away; fine-tuning one's reception and impressions.

"Mary and her white lamb" (24 Virgo) and "Tiny inhabited island" (24 Pisces)

Aspect: Square.
Quality: Challenge.
Shared motifs: 'The miracle of childlike innocence,'
'the influence of a light touch.'

"Mary and her white lamb" is an image of innocence free of tendencies to manipulate or engineer reality. The "white lamb" and "Mary," mother of Jesus, speak to an innocence, receptivity, even naiveté, regarding how one walks out into the world. "Mary had a little lamb" is a nursery rhyme familiar to all. The lamb passively follows wherever Mary goes, however both Mary and the lamb are not immune to the harsh realities of authority: taking a lamb to school is against the rules. An innocent and naive approach to life and the world, even when appearing to be folly or outside the rules and norms of conventional society, often successfully finds its way. Like the "fool" who steps into dangerous territory yet is unharmed, Mary brings a freshness and youthfulness to her vision of the world.

The "tiny inhabited island" is an image of an isolated manifestation of civilization: creating one's own world. An inhabited island carries a special flavor of community, an inward-looking social focus that, in distinction from global affairs, is villagelike. While this does not necessarily have to imply being cut off from the rest of the world, social insulation is ever a possibility. Islands are discrete land masses unto themselves that can provide a basis for building and creating a world based on the shared vision of the inhabitants. Isolated from the rest of mankind by broad expanses of sea, a tiny island may appeal as a destination suitable for getting away from it all.

Imagine the innocence of youth brushing up against the harsh realities of the social, political, and spiritual human world. It may inspire an attempt to escape the machinations of civilization in favor of a simpler, back-to-nature lifestyle. There still may be tiny isolated communities that exist unknown to the outside world. Such communities fascinate the so-called civilized world with wonder regarding the pure, unsullied naturalness of peoples who are often highly attuned to nature and spirit. It is somewhat of a paradox: a lion can be tamed, but a lamb cannot be brought to school; you can lead a horse to water, but you can't make it drink; you can run, but you cannot hide.

Apply this degree-pair with a mind to the tensions that develop when innocence meets hard realities; idealism meets realistic pragmatics; innovations in their infancy run up against established rule. Think of sweet natures that can get away with breaking the rules; small conceptions that take on a life of their own; innocuous suggestions, comments, actions that make a world of difference. Watch for youthful folly; naive good luck; dreams of a reclusive life, a return to nature. Consider sublime innocence; issues of purity; puritanical pursuits; being out of touch with reality; the lion laying beside the lamb; a knack for influencing others through gentleness and loving kindness.

"Flag at half-mast" (25 Virgo)
and "A purging of the priesthood" (25 Pisces)

Aspect: Quintile.
Quality: creative genius.
Shared motifs: 'Transition times of creative renewal,'
'perspective regarding change is everything.'

"A flag at half-mast" is an image of a public show and recognition of a time of mourning. The flag flies for all to see as a marker for universal respect. Being half-mast is, like in the nursery rhyme the Grand Old Duke of York marching his ten thousand men up and down the hill, saying, "When you are only halfway up, you are neither up nor down." Perception may be everything, alerting us to the question: Is the glass half-empty, or half-full? An emblem of social, national, or religious identity emblazoned on a flag both calls for and is a show of respect within the public arena. The colors one flies may be a well-balanced show of personal and public respect, or an overblown show that is not all it proclaims to be by half.

"A purging of the priesthood" is an image of cleansing an order of elders who serve as divine mediators. The "priesthood" is a contained organization of consecrated service, members of which have been ordained to serve a community of worshippers as divine intermediaries. In the early Christian church, priests were called "Presbyters," or ruling elders. "Purging" is an action of cleansing that removes impurities. In Roman Catholicism, "purgatory" is a temporary intermediate state or condition of being where the soul is cleansed and made fit for heaven. Like the sweat lodge of North American Indians, cleansing is a practice common to all spiritual traditions. It calls the individual, or institution, to renewal, to reinvigoration.

Imagine a self-contained, insular organization that, like the tiny inhabited island, over time loses touch with the world at large. Perhaps Mary and her little white lamb come along and spur on a fresh sense of renewal, inspire an open-hearted return to innocence. All things in the phenomenal world are subject to impermanence. Changing orders of institutions or changing times of an individual's position in life are not punishments, but rather times of reorganization: neither up nor down. It is possible to become overly serious about purges, times of mourning for old ways; however, the inherent genius of this degree-pair lies in a creative appreciation that at all times, the times are changing: that which is sacred cannot be destroyed nor damaged.

Apply this degree-pair with a mind to the genius of tender appreciation of the changing nature of reality; that the old is ever renewed; intermediate times and spaces. Think of confidence and trust that whatever the external changes, the sacred temple within can never be destroyed; that every potently creative time is tinged with a touch of sadness. Be alert for compulsive tendencies to cleanse; purge the stomach of food; purge the bowels; to stand transfixed in fear on threshold points. Watch for creative perspectives that are calmly centered with respect, trust, honor; celebrate transient moments of renewal.

"A boy with a censer" (26 Virgo) and "A new moon divides its influence" (26 Pisces)

Aspect: Conjunction.
Quality: Focus.
Shared motifs: 'The deep influence of glowing embers,'
'smoldering pervasive issues of perspective.'

"A boy with a censer" is an image of a youth carrying a vessel that burns incense to purify the air, evoking an atmosphere readied for divine presence. A "censer" is a vessel common in church settings, used to burn incense. The aromatic impact awakens the sense of smell, the sensory capacity associated with memory and motivational urges. In ritual process, incense is used to purify the air, to evoke a special atmosphere, to inflame an awareness open for divine presence. "Incense" also means to inflame, as in to be incensed with anger; however, the burning of incense is more a slow smoldering of glowing embers controlled and contained within a censer.

"A new moon divides its influence" is an image of different perspectives and impressions of a celestial orb at its moment of glowing the least. The "new moon" occurs when the moon passes between the earth and the sun, creating an appearance of only a sliver of moonlight. New moon phases are associated with beginnings, times of planting seeds, times that initiate an ascendancy of light and promise. A "divided influence" suggests that such times are not perceived in the same way by everyone. "Influence" is a power to produce effects, or to affect others, suggesting a significant degree of control or direction.

Imagine a young boy swinging a censer in a church ceremony. He may turn his nose up at the unfamiliar pungent fragrance because, since it is new to him, having no stirring effect on his memory, it just stinks. Imagine differing influences of the new moon phase: lovers may see the ascendancy of their love, the waxing growth of their family; gardeners might be out planting seeds in harmony with a lunar suggestion of the peak moment of fertility; a scientist might scoff at the gardener's superstition and reason away the faint glow of the moon as mere reflected light of the sun at its predictable low point in the lunar cycle. These are not intensely inflammable issues, yet the glowing, smoldering fragrance and light have a power that can hold sway over one's path in life.

Apply this degree-pair with a mind to the focus on motivational factors from seemingly insignificant influences; divergent interpretations of the most innocuous of events; discriminating awareness of exacting detail or overall influence. Think of a parting of the ways: the scientist from the romantic; the ordained priesthood from the passionate pagan; using formulated fertilizers rather than using the moon to fertilize the garden. Watch for powerful responses to smells, fragrances, odors; swaying motions like sowing seeds or swinging a censer. Consider pervasive influences that freshen stale air; that imbue an archaic feel for the novice; slivers of hope; preserved embers for future fires; being moved in a definite direction.

**"Grande dames at tea" (27 Virgo)
and "A harvest moon" (27 Pisces)**

Aspect: Opposition.
Quality: Awareness of.
Shared motifs: 'Distinction and refined details,'
'breaking through the surface sense of harvest.'

"Grande dames at tea" is an image of ladies of high rank or social stature at a social, secular ceremony. "Grande dame" is a French expression for a great lady. "Dame" is a mature woman and, in Great Britain, an honorific title equivalent to a knight. "Tea" is a secular tradition, in Britain for example, at a time of day marked for a re-laxing break and a refreshing drink. The name "tea" derives from the Chinese *ch'a,* *chia,* or *char.* A "charwoman" might break from household chores for a spot of "tay," the common pronunciation of "tea" into the nineteenth century. One can al-most hear the echo, feel the warmth, of charcoal embers slowly burning.

"A harvest moon" is an image of the lunar full moon phase near the time of the autumnal equinox. "Harvest" means to reap and gather, as in harvesting grain at the end of summer. The ancient term "harvest" was interchangeable with "autumn" and is the root word for many modern terms. Grain was crushed under a heavy mill wheel, called in ancient Rome the *tribulum,* hence tribulation, to be under great pres-sure, and paying tribute as with a portion of the harvest given over to the ruling lord and lady. "Defalcation" is to misappropriate funds, deriving from the Latin *de* plus *falcere,* to cut down someone else's possession, as a farmer with a sickle mows down crops, perhaps belonging to the great lady or appropriated by her from another's hard labor. "Aftermath" derives from after-*mowth,* meaning the return of new growth after mowing down the first crop.

These meanings may seem far-fetched, or perhaps sound far afield, unless one re-members that "to char" something is really just to burn the surface, the way fields are sometimes cleared for cultivation with small controlled fires. Field workers and titled society all enjoy their tea. "Tea time" cuts across social boundaries, mowing down the differences. "High tea" is a more formalized ceremony often involving pre-pared food and requiring proper dress. Like the Japanese tea ceremony, matters of detail and refinement are strictly observed in order to enhance the uplifting experience of tea. For most tea lovers it is a smoldering issue: drinking tea as opposed to the full experience of a proper cup of tea.

Apply this degree-pair with a mind to the awareness of secular rituals that unite peasant and lord, charwoman and lady; the far-reaching implications of harvest: cutting down, gathering, grinding, apportioning allotments. Watch for formalized ceremonies; hats and gloves; refinement of manners and preparation know-how; reaping from what others have sown; paying tribute and respect. Consider smoldering issues of social inequities; a taste for things slightly burnt; refreshing, uplifting qualities; precise attention to detail; inflating the importance of minor details.

"A bald-headed man " (28 Virgo)
and "A fertile garden under the full moon" (28 Pisces)

Aspect: Trine.
Quality: Maintaining.
Shared motifs: 'The glowing awareness of a calm, fertile mind,'
'hair and personal power.'

"A bald-headed man" is an image of a man with no covering on his head. "Bald" is to be without hair, with little hair, or without adornment or disguise: forthright, clear. A "bald mountain" is a snow-capped mountain or one that rises high above the tree line. The phrase "a bald-headed man" can refer to a man in haste, running off to do something without his cap. The "head" is the dome of intellect and awareness: a glowing crown of self-realization. The slang phrase "a chrome dome" suggests a silver glow or glare of reflected light, like the light reflected from a full moon. "Dome" derives from the rounded shape that covers a house or building, but is echoic of dominion and domination.

"A fertile garden under the full moon" is an image of potential abundance softly illuminated in the glowing light of a full moon. "Fertility" derives from the Latin *fertilis*, to bear: the capacity to produce associated with abundant offspring, inventive ideas, crops or vegetation. A "barren field" is the opposite of a fertile field since to be barren is to be sterile or incapable of producing. A fertile garden at the peak of fruition displays an overabundance of growth, but during the aftermath of harvest appears barren, its potency for organic growth hidden for the time being. A field or garden after being mowed or cut down appears free of growth, yet like the full moon that shines down upon it, bears a promise for the next season of growth.

Imagine Samson from the biblical story. His strength was said to lay in his luxuriant head of hair. Once his hair was cut, by deceit, conniving, and treachery, as the story goes, Samson lost all his strength. The betrayal backfired when his hair grew back. The cutting of hair is closely linked to the harvesting of crops. In Celtic lore, to have one's hair cut by the king or lord of the domain signaled a time of passage into full manhood, culminating in proving oneself in a way that was patently, baldly apparent to all. Recognition of manhood was synonymous with the regrowth of one's hair. In contemplative traditions, the head is often shaved as a signal of withdrawing from the world, but more importantly, as a gesture of recognizing the illumined mind of awareness free from obscurations: potent illumination and baldness growing and glowing together.

Apply this degree-pair with a mind to the maintenance of hair; of awareness; of an inner glowing sense of the seasonal cycles of growth and potency. Watch for thick, luxuriant heads of hair; baldness; intense issues about the cutting of hair. Think of the shining dome of awareness, which, like the full moon, quietly illuminates. Be alert for fertility stories; the return of strength and power; overconcern for the hairy details; glowing natures that delight in all life potentials. Consider distinctive appearances that dominate within a crowd; domineering natures; undeniable accomplishments.

"A man gaining secret knowledge from a paper he is reading" (29 Virgo) and "A prism" (29 Pisces)

Aspect: Square.
Quality: Challenge.
Shared motifs: 'Synthesis and analysis,'
'finding the missing puzzle piece.'

"A man gaining secret knowledge from a paper he is reading" is an image of finding the one scrap of knowledge that reveals deeper mysteries. "Secret knowledge" is knowledge that is not readily apparent to all, hidden and imbued with mystery. "Reading" is an action of apprehending the meaning of something, deciphering something written. "Paper" is a sheet of material made from the pulp of scraps of cloth, wood, or bark. "Pulp" is a liquid mash of such materials, suggesting a mishmash that sticks together. "Gaining secret knowledge" from something that essentially comes from a confused, condensed hodgepodge of things is a rare revelation. Just as a sheet of paper brings a mash of pulp into a single piece, one bit of knowledge can bring several bits of information into a unified whole.

"A prism" is an image of a transparent object used to refract light into a spectrum of colors. The "prism" itself does not act upon light, but rather passively receives light in such a way as to unlock the color within. "Prism" derives from the Greek *prixein*, to saw, cut into pieces, hence any object that resolves a substance into its elements. "Sawing" is related to "saga," a long story cut up into parts, and akin to the Latin *secula,* a sickle with which one cuts down the crops at harvest time. After crops are cut, they are gathered into bundles, stacks, separated by kind, quantity, and quality.

Imagine finding the one piece that ties a puzzle together into a comprehensive understanding of a deeper meaning. Imagine pure white light being broken up into a full spectrum of hidden colors. The prism reveals by separating; the piece of paper reveals by pulling together through apprehended understanding. One might be fascinated with the elements that make up a long story, perhaps dwelling on a particular section at the expense of the whole. One may be more inclined to the overview, the one thing that ties the whole together. A little bit of knowledge can be a dangerous thing, just as seeing the whole can sometimes be too superficial to count for anything.

Apply this degree-pair with a mind to the challenge of apprehending the deeper meaning of things through the processes of gathering and separating. Think of secrets locked within what appears to be a unified whole; secrets obscured by an overwhelming disarray of information. Watch for the ability to read a situation; knowing which color to show; discriminating between appearance and vibrant inner sense. Consider a receptive mind; piercing apprehension; gleaning insight in the aftermath of discovery; shreds of paper or information that make all the difference; an ability for clear-cut analysis; solving puzzles; clarity born out of a mishmash of ideas.

"A false call unheard in attention to immediate service" (30 Virgo) and "The Great Stone Face" (30 Pisces)

Aspect: Quintile.
Quality: Creative genius.
Shared motifs: 'Knowing when to call a bluff,'
'character, integrity, and selective inattention.'

"A false call unheard in attention to immediate service" is an image of an astute sense of priority rising above the clamor of unimportant issues. A "false call" is a summons that bears no weight or merit: a bluff for attention. A call or an utterance is "unheard" when it is not audible, for example, when it is too far away to be heard. "Hearing" differs from "listening." One can hear another's words, but not listen to what is said. "Attention to immediate service" implies a focus of concentration in the present moment to something that requires the benefit of personal assistance. Think of a parent ignoring a child's cry for attention while preparing the evening meal. Exercising selective inattention sets a nourishing meal above nonessential distraction.

"The Great Stone Face" is an image of a stern regard expressing little emotion. "The Great Stone Face" recalls the Nathaniel Hawthorne story of a boy who lives under and looks up to a mountain formation resembling the face of a man. "Stone" is hard and enduring, suggesting qualities of a character that withstands hardship throughout life. The projection of self culminates in an expression that seems to transcend the temporal existence of the individual, echoing for the ages, the face of mankind.

Imagine a poker game. Several astute players play their cards with an intense focus on the immediate hand at stake. One may smile or attempt to throw his opponents off with casual or humorous remarks; another may have a poker face, not revealing the slightest hint of the cards he holds. Bluffing is a common ploy: attempting to dominate a game with confident play despite holding a weak hand; attempting to disguise a very strong hand in order to encourage others to increase confidence in their own chances of winning. Sorting out what is important takes a bit of genius. If everyone runs when a boy cries "Wolf!" only to discover a childish prank, they may be reluctant to come when a wolf is actually among their flocks. A strong show of integrity, character, and honesty goes a long way to create and encourage trust.

Apply this degree-pair with a mind to the genius for knowing what is of immediate importance; letting trivial matters go by; promoting standards of enduring trust. Watch for stern poker faces; sage expressions that don't give much away; cold manners that seem to look beyond everyday concerns. Think of a readiness to drop everything at an emergency call; a capacity to listen intently when it is important to do so; a dismissive manner that doesn't seem to hear anything. Consider tired faces of those run ragged in service to the slightest call from others; monumental stoicism; uncompromising integrity and honesty; being totally absorbed in what calls one's attention; being lost in one's work; finding oneself in higher service to all mankind.

---

1. In his book *The Sabian Symbols in Astrology,* Marc Edmund Jones rewrote the notecard version of "A chocolate child playing with whites" to read: "A colored child playing with white children," cf. Diana E. Roche, *The Sabian Symbols: A Screen of Prophecy* (Victoria, B.C.: Trafford, 1998) p. 184.

APPENDIX I

KEYWORDS FROM MARC EDMUND JONES'
"THE SABIAN SYMBOLS IN ASTROLOGY"

Listed here are all of the Sabian Symbols together with the "keywords" Marc Edmund Jones wrote for each in his book *The Sabian Symbols in Astrology*. Jones' keywords are an extraordinary augmentation for understanding the Sabian Symbols. Their genius is especially evident in the divinatory use of the Sabian Symbols. In some instances, however, the keywords are words not commonly used today nor readily understood. Following each keyword below, I have appended a word or phrase in order to expand on the meaning or facilitate understanding of the keywords. The reader is referred to Diana E. Roche's book *The Sabian Symbols: A Screen of Prophecy*, where a generous exploration of each keyword is found in the "Stepping Stones" sections of each entry.

Aries 1 "A woman rises out water, a seal rises and embraces her": REALIZATION (initiating awareness).

Libra 1 "A butterfly made perfect by a dart through it": ARTICULATION (pinpoint).

Aries 2 "A comedian entertains a group": RELEASE (free from inhibition).

Libra 2 "The light of the sixth race transmuted to the seventh": THRESHOLD (uplifting).

Aries 3 "A cameo profile of a man in the outline of his country": EXPLOITATION (profile, façade).

Libra 3 "Dawn of a new day, everything changed": INNOVATION (fresh start).

Aries 4 "Two lovers strolling through a secluded walk": ENJOYMENT (shared privacy).

Libra 4 "A group around a campfire": AMIABILITY (social circle).

Aries 5 "A triangle with wings": ZEAL (visionary ideals).

Libra 5 "A man teaching the true inner knowledge": AFFINITY (shared realization).

Aries 6 "A square brightly lighted on one side": SET (facet).

Libra 6 "The ideals of a man abundantly crystalized": PERSONIFICATION (personal accentuation).

Aries 7 "A man successfully expressing himself in two realms at once": PROFICIENCY (a living metaphor).

Libra 7 "A woman feeding chickens and protecting them from the hawks": SHREWDNESS (vigilant awareness).

Aries 8 "A large hat with streamers flying, facing east": EXCITATION (anticipating change).

Libra 8 "A blazing fireplace in a deserted home": GUARDIANSHIP (hearth).

Aries 9 "A crystal gazer": ACUTENESS (prophetic).

Libra 9 "Three old masters hanging in an art gallery": ACCORD (exemplification of being ahead of the times).

Aries 10 "A man teaching new forms for old symbols": INTERPRETATION (reviving archaic sense).

Libra 10 "A canoe approaching safety through dangerous waters": COMPETENCY (navigating).

Aries 11 "The president of the country": IDEALIZATION (overseeing).

Libra 11 "A professor peering over his glasses": SPECIALIZATION (preoccupation).

Aries 12 "A flock of white geese": INSOUCIANCE (carefree).[1]

Libra 12 "Miners emerge from a mine": ESCAPE (finding the way out).

Aries 13 "An unsuccessful bomb explosion": IMPETUOUSNESS (make a mountain out of a molehill).

Libra 13 "Children blowing soap bubbles": ENCHANTMENT (effervescence).

Aries 14 "A serpent coiling near a man and a woman": REVELATION (integration, coming together).

Libra 14 "A noon siesta": RECUPERATION (peak time for refreshment).

Aries 15 "An Indian weaving a blanket": DILIGENCE (pulling it all together).

Libra 15 "Circular paths": CONGRUITY (coming full circle, completion).

Aries 16 "Brownies dancing in the setting sun": INVIGORATION (dancing into the setting sun).

Libra 16 "A boat landing washed away": RESPITE (rest, repair).

Aries 17 "Two prim spinsters": DIVORCEMENT (silent web).

Libra 17 "A retired sea captain": RELAXATION (stories respun).

Aries 18 "An empty hammock": REMINATION (suspended reminiscence).

Libra 18 "Two men placed under arrest": CONSEQUENCE (temporary suspension of activity).

Aries 19 "The magic carpet": PANORAMA (getting above it all).

Libra 19 "A gang of robbers in hiding": DIVERGENCE (covert, cloaked activity).

Aries 20 "A young girl feeding birds in winter": HOSPITALITY (generosity, compassion).

Libra 20 "A Jewish rabbi": HERITAGE (handing down).

Aries 21 "A pugilist entering the ring": EXERTION (arena of contest).

Libra 21 "A crowd upon the beach": EXHILARATION (one's place in a crowd).

Aries 22 "The gate to the garden of desire": PROSPECT (The grass is always greener).

Libra 22 "A child giving birds a drink at a fountain": SOLICITUDE (an invitation out of concern).

Aries 23 "A woman in pastel colors carrying a heavy and valuable but veiled load": RETICENCE (discretion).

Libra 23 "Chanticleer": FERVOR (pride).

Aries 24 "An open window and a net blowing into a cornucopia": MUNIFICENCE (allure of abundance).

Libra 24 "A third wing on the left side of a butterfly": DISTINCTIVENESS (distinguishing leanings).

Aries 25 "A double promise": SENSIBILITY (affording to go beyond self-concern).

Libra 25 "Information in the symbol of an autumn leaf": TACT (future considerations).

Aries 26 "A man possessed of more gifts than he can hold": EQUIPMENT (overwhelmed with potentials which run away).

Libra 26 "An eagle and a large white dove turning one into the other": ADEPTNESS (changeability).

Aries 27 "Lost opportunity regained in the imagination": REFORMULATION (reclamation).

Libra 27 "An airplane hovering overhead": REFLECTION (transcendence).

Aries 28 "A large disappointed audience": DISJUNCTION (expectations, getting ahead of oneself).

Libra 28 "A man in the midst of brightening influences": RESPONSIVENESS (grace).

Aries 29 "A celestial choir singing": VENERATION (intimations of the divine).

Libra 29 "Humanity seeking to span the bridge of knowledge": RATIONALITY (bridging).

Aries 30 "A duck pond and its brood": RELIABILITY (in accordance).

Libra 30 "Three mounds of knowledge on a philosopher's head": PRESCIENCE (harmony surpassing understanding).

Taurus 1 "A clear mountain stream": RESOURCEFULNESS (naturalness).

Scorpio 1 "A sight-seeing bus": FRIENDLINESS (tourist).

Taurus 2 "An electrical storm": TRANSFORMATION (discharge).

Scorpio 2 "A broken bottle and spilled perfume": PERMEATION (release of memories).

Taurus 3 "Steps up to a lawn blooming with clover": HOPEFULNESS (the uplifting path).

Scorpio 3 "A house-raising": HELPFULNESS (cooperation).

Taurus 4 "The rainbow's pot of gold": FAITH (inner faith and resource).

Scorpio 4 "A youth holding a lighted candle": RELIANCE (the quiet glow of inner spirit).

Taurus 5 "A widow at an open grave": REORIENTATION (accepting impermanence).

Scorpio 5 "A massive rocky shore": STABILIZATION (enduring realities).

Taurus 6 "A bridge being built across a gorge": CHANNELSHIP (solutions).

Scorpio 6 "A gold rush": AMBITION (excitation).

Taurus 7 "A woman of Samaria": AWAKENING (truthing).

Scorpio 7 "Deep-sea divers": INVOLVEMENT (lifeline).

Taurus 8 "A sleigh without snow": SUSTAINMENT (biding one's time).

Scorpio 8 "The moon shining across a lake": RAPPORT (guile).

Taurus 9 "A Christmas tree decorated": SYMBOLIZATION (unconditional giving).

Scorpio 9 "Dental work": PRACTICALITY (cutting one's teeth).

Taurus 10 "A Red Cross nurse": ENLISTMENT (applied compassion).

Scorpio 10 "A fellowship supper": FRATERNITY (tears of fellowship).

Taurus 11 "A woman sprinkling flowers": CARE (nurturing).

Scorpio 11 "A drowning man rescued": SAFETY (rescue).

Taurus 12 "Window-shoppers": VISUALIZATION (invisible barriers).

Scorpio 12 "An embassy ball": DISPLAY (elite standards).

Taurus 13 "A man handling baggage": INDUSTRY (the load bearer).

Scorpio 13 "An inventor experimenting": CLEVERNESS (the tinkerer).

Taurus 14 "Shellfish groping and children playing": EMERGENCE (attachment).

Scorpio 14 "Telephone linemen at work": ATTACHMENT (connection).

Taurus 15 "A man muffled up, with a rakish silk hat": SOPHISTICATION (poised inclinations).

Scorpio 15 "Children playing around five mounds of sand": NAIVETE (free play).

Taurus 16 "An old man attempting vainly to reveal the Mysteries": PERTINACITY (tenacious persistence).

Scorpio 16 "A girl's face breaking into a smile": ACQUIESCENCE (the levity of seriousness).

Taurus 17 "A battle between the swords and the torches": RESOLUTION (not twisting the issue).

Scorpio 17 "A woman the father of her own child": NUCLEATION (inner dynamics of self-integration).

Taurus 18 "A woman holding a bag out of a window": FACILITATION (receptive enhancements).

Scorpio 18 "A woods rich in autumn coloring": FULFILLMENT (exfoliate).

Taurus 19 "A newly formed continent": ORIGINALITY (breakaway innovation).

Scorpio 19 "A parrot listening and then talking": CONVENTIONALITY (repetition).

Taurus 20 "Wind, clouds and haste": EXALTATION (quickening).

Scorpio 20 "A woman drawing two dark curtains aside": DARING (revealing the unknown).

Taurus 21 "A finger pointing in an open book": CONFIRMATION (citation).

Scorpio 21 "A soldier derelict in duty": DEVIATION (uncompromising character).

Taurus 22 "White dove over troubled waters": GUIDANCE (peace beyond conflict).

Scorpio 22 "Hunters starting out for ducks": ENTERPRISE (expedition).

Taurus 23 "A jewelry shop": PRESERVATION (enchanting beauty).

Scorpio 23 "A bunny metamorphosed into a fairy": TRANSITION (the allure of fantasy).

Taurus 24 "A mounted Indian with scalp locks": COMMAND (credentials).

Scorpio 24 "Crowds coming down the mountain to listen to one man": APPEAL (rising above condescension; paying one's dues).

Taurus 25 "A large well-kept public park": RECREATION (behind-the-scenes cooperation).

Scorpio 25 "An X-ray": INVESTIGATION (penetrating awareness).

Taurus 26 "A Spaniard serenading his senorita": CONSTANCY (courtship).

Scorpio 26 "Indians making camp": EXTEMPORIZATION (resourceful improvisation).

Taurus 27 "A squaw selling beads": DETACHMENT (dignity in displaced circumstances).

Scorpio 27 "A military band on the march": INTREPIDITY (keeping in step).

Taurus 28 "A woman pursued by mature romance": PERSUASION (ripening with age).

Scorpio 28 "The king of the fairies approaching his domain": ALLEGIANCE (coming into one's own).

Taurus 29 "Two cobblers working at a table": CAPABILITY (making it work).

Scorpio 29 "An Indian squaw pleading to the chief for the lives of her children": EFFECTIVENESS (entreaty).

Taurus 30 "A peacock parading on an ancient lawn": ALOOFNESS (pride).

Scorpio 30 "A Halloween jester": SPONTANEOUSNESS (self-deprecating humor).

Gemini 1 "A glass-bottomed boat in still water": CURIOSITY (a degree of separation of emotion from intellect).

Sagittarius 1 "A Grand Army of the Republic campfire": REMINISCENCE (the spirit of common interest kept alive).

Gemini 2 "Santa Claus filling stockings furtively": PRODIGALITY (lavish).

Sagittarius 2 "The ocean covered with whitecaps": IRREPRESSIBILITY (the tip of the iceberg).

Gemini 3 "The garden of the Tuileries": LUXURY (revolutionary allegiances).

Sagittarius 3 "Two men playing chess": ABILITY (strategic checkmate).

Gemini 4 "Holly and mistletoe": RITUALIZATION (tapping into old protective resources).

Sagittarius 4 "A little child learning to walk": INDIVIDUALITY (standing on one's own two feet).

Gemini 5 "A radical magazine": TANGENCY (divergent branches of power).

Sagittarius 5 "An old owl up in a tree": NORMALITY (patient observation).

Gemini 6 "Drilling for oil": SPECULATION (penetrating industry).

Sagittarius 6 "A game of cricket": SPORTSMANSHIP (rules at the crux of the matter).

Gemini 7 "An old-fashioned well": RECOMPENSE (one's relationship to the deep source of life).

Sagittarius 7 "Cupid knocking at the door": ALLUREMENT (emotion within stirred from without).

Gemini 8 "An industrial strike": PROTEST (the alchemy of inequities).

Sagittarius 8 "Rocks and things forming therein": COMPOSITION (formation by pressure).

Gemini 9 "A quiver filled with arrows": PREPARATION (choosing from potentials).

Sagittarius 9 "A mother with her children on the stairs": EDUCATION (a helping hand where it counts most).

Gemini 10 "An aeroplane falling": CRISIS (crisis management).

Sagittarius 10 "A golden-haired goddess of opportunity": REWARD (the knack of good fortune).

Gemini 11 "A new path of realism in experience": IDENTIFICATION (practical benefit).

Sagittarius 11 "The lamp of physical enlightenment in the left temple": RECONCILIATION (the path less traveled).

Gemini 12 "A topsy saucily asserting herself": GROWTH (self-assertion).

Sagittarius 12 "A flag that turns into an eagle that crows": ADJUSTMENT (animating the issue; getting to the point).

Gemini 13 "A great musician at his piano": ACHIEVEMENT (command of a symphony of emotions).

Sagittarius 13 "A widow's past is brought to light": RECTIFICATION (pathos which cannot be hidden).

Gemini 14 "A conversation by telepathy": INTIMATION (mysterious intimacy).

Sagittarius 14 "The Pyramids and the Sphinx": CERTIFICATION (enigma; inscrutability).

Gemini 15 "Two Dutch children talking": CLARIFICATION (double meanings).

Sagittarius 15 "The groundhog looking for its shadow": REASSURANCE (hidden assumptions).

Gemini 16 "A woman suffragist orating": INDIGNATION (exhortation; an entreaty for support).[2]

Sagittarius 16 "Seagulls watching a ship": ALERTNESS (vigilant opportunism).

Gemini 17 "The head of health dissolved into the head of mentality": DEVELOPMENT (positive disintegration).

Sagittarius 17 "An Easter sunrise service": REBIRTH (renewal).[3]

Gemini 18 "Two Chinese men talk Chinese": DIFFERENCE (the protective veil of a common language).

Sagittarius 18 "Tiny children in sunbonnets": INNOCENCE (safeguarding).

Gemini 19 "A large archaic volume": BACKGROUND (tradition; heritage).

Sagittarius 19 "Pelicans moving their habitat": FRONTIER (social assimilation).

Gemini 20 "A cafeteria": SUPPLY (shared diversity).

Sagittarius 20 "Men cutting through ice": PROCUREMENT (creative thought for the future).

Gemini 21 "A labor demonstration": REPRESENTATION (magnifying one's views).

Sagittarius 21 "A child and a dog with borrowed eyeglasses": EXAMINATION (new, unfamiliar perspectives).

Gemini 22 "A barn dance": GREGARIOUSNESS (cue the gaiety).

Sagittarius 22 "A Chinese laundry": SECLUSION (social footholds).

Gemini 23 "Three fledglings in a nest high in a tree": ELEVATION (trepidatious beginnings).

Sagittarius 23 "Immigrants entering": ENTRANCE (anticipation of something new).

Gemini 24 "Children skating on ice": FUN (pushing off).

Sagittarius 24 "A bluebird standing at the door of the house": FORTUNE (opportunity beckons).

Gemini 25 "A man trimming palms": ENHANCEMENT (fine flourish).

Sagittarius 25 "A chubby boy on a hobbyhorse": EMULATION (envisioning victory).

Gemini 26 "Winter frost in the woods": SPLENDOR (frosty enchantment).

Sagittarius 26 "A flag bearer": NOBILITY (standard bearer).

Gemini 27 "A gypsy coming out of the forest": EXPENDITURE (test of character).

Sagittarius 27 "A sculptor": IMMORTALIZATION (leaving one's mark).

Gemini 28 "A man declared bankrupt": DELIVERANCE (starting anew).

Sagittarius 28 "An old bridge over a beautiful stream": CONSERVATION (overarching structures, principles).

Gemini 29 "The first mockingbird in spring": QUICKENING (harbinger).

Sagittarius 29 "A fat boy mowing the lawn": PARTICIPATION (rewards for efforts).

Gemini 30 "Bathing beauties": CHARM (being seen, blessed).

Sagittarius 30 "The Pope": SANCTITY (giving audience).

Cancer 1 "A furled and unfurled flag displayed from a vessel": ADAPTABILITY (transitions).

Capricorn 1 "An Indian chief demanding recognition": INFLEXIBILITY (claiming one's own power).

Cancer 2 "A man suspended over a vast level place": CONTEMPLATION (raising questions).

Capricorn 2 "Three stained-glass windows, one damaged by bombardment": COMMEMORATION (surviving the fray).

Cancer 3 "A man all bundled up in fur leading a shaggy deer": INDOMITABILITY (rugged spirit).

Capricorn 3 "The human soul receptive to growth and understanding": AVIDITY (eagerness).

Cancer 4 "A cat arguing with a mouse": JUSTIFICATION (argument; catechism).

Capricorn 4 "A party entering a large canoe": ORDERING (cooperatively taking one's place).

Cancer 5 "An automobile wrecked by a train": DISPERSION (individuality versus collective forces).[4]

Capricorn 5 "Indians rowing a canoe and dancing a war dance": MOBILIZATION (pumping up team spirit).

Cancer 6 "Game birds feathering their nest": METICULOUSNESS (comforting reassurance).

Capricorn 6 "A dark archway and ten logs at the bottom": THOROUGHNESS (the way into the unknown).

Cancer 7 "Two fairies on a moonlit night": ASCENDANCY (a reality twice removed).

Capricorn 7 "A veiled prophet of power": SUPREMACY (seeing through an invisible veil).

Cancer 8 "Rabbits dressed in clothes and on parade": APPROPRIATION (appearances).

Capricorn 8 "Birds in the house singing happily": ESTABLISHMENT (cheerfully domesticated).

Cancer 9 "A tiny nude miss reaching in the water for a fish": INCLINATION (innocent curiosity).

Capricorn 9 "An angel carrying a harp": ATTUNEMENT (pluck).

Cancer 10 "A large diamond not completely carved": LATENCY (hidden potential).[5]

Capricorn 10 "An albatross feeding from the hand": NURTURE (graceful generosity).

Cancer 11 "A clown making grimaces": INIMITABILITY (impossible to imitate).

Capricorn 11 "A large group of pheasants": ILLIMITABILITY (social pretense).

Cancer 12 "A Chinese woman nursing a baby with a message": MATERIALIZATION (messages from an unexpected source).

Capricorn 12 "A student of nature lecturing": EXPLANATION (fresh interpretation).

Cancer 13 "One hand slightly flexed with a very prominent thumb": DETERMINATION (taking a definite stand).

Capricorn 13 "A fire worshipper": MAGIC (emphatic devotions).

Cancer 14 "A very old man facing a vast dark space to the northeast": SANCTION (inner stillness).

Capricorn 14 "An ancient bas-relief carved in granite": FOUNDATION (salient features).

Cancer 15 "A group of people who have overeaten and enjoyed it": SATIETY (making the most of it while one can).

Capricorn 15 "Many toys in the children's ward of a hospital": ABUNDANCE (benevolent distraction).

Cancer 16 "A man before a square with a manuscript scroll before him": PROFUNDITY (decoding).

Capricorn 16 "Boys and girls in gymnasium suits": ANIMATION (natural enthusiasm).

Cancer 17 "The germ grows into knowledge and life": UNFOLDMENT (organic growth).

Capricorn 17 "A girl surreptitiously bathing in the nude": IMMERSION (tender beginnings).

Cancer 18 "A hen scratching for her chicks": PROVISION (instinctual transmission).

Capricorn 18 "The Union Jack": SUPERVISION (displaying one's stripes).

Cancer 19 "A priest performing a marriage ceremony": CONFORMITY (commitment responsibilities).

Capricorn 19 "A child of about five with a huge shopping bag": EXPECTATION (bearing loaded expectations).

Cancer 20 "Gondoliers in a serenade": SENTIMENT (courtship).

Capricorn 20 "A hidden choir singing": WORSHIP (uplifting background harmonies).

Cancer 21 "A prima donna singing": EXCELLENCE (center stage mastery).

Capricorn 21 "A relay race": FITNESS (excelling through teamwork).

Cancer 22 "A woman awaiting a sailboat": EQUANIMITY (quiet readiness to receive).

Capricorn 22 "A general accepting defeat gracefully": EXPEDIENCY (acceptance with dignity).

Cancer 23 "Meeting of a literary society": CRITICISM (special interests).

Capricorn 23 "Two awards for bravery in war": RECOGNITION (double-edged assessment).

Cancer 24 "A woman and two men on a bit of sunlit land facing south": INCEPTION (contemplating important choices).

Capricorn 24 "A woman entering a convent": CONSECRATION (retreat).

Cancer 25 "A dark shadow or mantle thrown suddenly over the right shoulder": DESTINY (taking a definite stance).

Capricorn 25 "An oriental-rug dealer": CONSIGNMENT (trading on a special orientation).

Cancer 26 "Contentment and happiness in luxury, people reading on davenports": REPOSE (lying in the bed of one's own choosing).

Capricorn 26 "A water sprite": RESTLESSNESS (awareness of intangible consequences).

Cancer 27 "A storm in a canyon": INTENSIFICATION (escalation dynamics).

Capricorn 27 "A mountain pilgrimage": PERSEVERANCE (intent on reaching the peak).

Cancer 28 "A modern Pocahontas": COMPATIBILITY (identity assimilation).

Capricorn 28 "A large aviary": COMMUNITY (birds of a feather flock together).

Cancer 29 "A muse weighing twins": VALUE (consideration).

Capricorn 29 "A woman reading tea leaves": SIGNATURE (deeper significance of ordinary events).

Cancer 30 "A daughter of the American Revolution": INHERITANCE (carrying tradition on).

Capricorn 30 "A secret business conference": OPPORTUNITY (setting agendas).

Leo 1 "A case of apoplexy": IRRESISTIBILITY (flushed with enthusiasm).

Aquarius 1 "An old adobe mission": DURABILITY (establishing new roots).

Leo 2 "An epidemic of mumps": INFECTION (infectious growth).

Aquarius 2 "An unexpected thunderstorm": ACCIDENT (sudden unforeseen developments).

Leo 3 "A woman having her hair bobbed": DECISION (bouncing back; a refreshing change).

Aquarius 3 "A deserter from the navy": DEFIANCE (willingness to start again).

Leo 4 "A formally dressed man and a deer with its horns folded": MORALE (show of credentials).

Aquarius 4 "A Hindu healer": THERAPY (healing misnomers).

Leo 5 "Rock formations at the edge of a precipice": ENDURANCE (life as "on the edge").

Aquarius 5 "A council of ancestors": ANTECEDENCE (wisdom of those who have gone before).

Leo 6 "An old-fashioned woman and a flapper": CONTRAST (generation gap).[6]

Aquarius 6 "A performance of a mystery play": SUBTLETY (new barn, same hay).[7]

Leo 7 "The constellations in the sky": SURETY (pattern recognition).

Aquarius 7 "A child born of an eggshell": ESSENTIALITY (creative tension between the fleeting and fragile, and the eternal and indestructible).

Leo 8 "A Bolshevik propagandist": LEAVEN (fermentation).

Aquarius 8 "Beautifully gowned wax figures": IMPACT (modeling an ideal)

Leo 9 "Glass blowers": DEFTNESS (bringing new forms to life)

Aquarius 9 "A flag turned into an eagle": DRAMATIZATION (animating ideals).

Leo 10 "Early morning dew": REJUVENATION (refreshing manifestation).

Aquarius 10 "A popularity that proves ephemeral": APPROBATION (fleeting approval).

Leo 11 "Children on a swing in a huge oak tree": DELIGHT (delight under the umbrella of a sturdy support).

Aquarius 11 "Man tête-à-tête with his inspiration": ECSTASY (divine influence through a meeting of the minds.

Leo 12 "An evening lawn party": COMPANIONSHIP (association).

Aquarius 12 "People on stairs graduated upwards": PROGRESSION (social steps).

Leo 13 "An old sea captain rocking": RETROSPECT (past experience).

Aquarius 13 "A barometer": INDICATION (forecasting).

Leo 14 "The human soul awaiting opportunity for expression": INGENUOUSNESS (prenatal innocence).

Aquarius 14 "A train entering a tunnel": COURTESY (on track).

Leo 15 "A pageant": DEMONSTRATION (procession).

Aquarius 15 "Two lovebirds sitting on a fence": AFFIRMATION (glad tidings).[8]

Leo 16 "Sunshine just after a storm": RECOVERY (a restoring breakthrough).

Aquarius 16 "A big businessman at his desk": ACCOMPLISHMENT (influence).

Leo 17 "A non-vested church choir": COMMUNION (informal harmonies).

Aquarius 17 "A watchdog standing guard": PROBITY (faithful vigilance).

Leo 18 "A teacher of chemistry": INSTRUCTION (transmitting inner arrangements).

Aquarius 18 "A man unmasked": ANALYSIS (uncovering).

Leo 19 "A houseboat party": CONGENIALITY (social gathering).

Aquarius 19 "A forest fire quenched": CONCERN (calming circumstances).

Leo 20 "The Zuni sun worshippers": FIDELITY (veneration for life).

Aquarius 20 "A big white dove, a message bearer": CONVICTION (divine guidance).

Leo 21 "Chickens intoxicated": ACCENTUATION (uncommon excitement).

Aquarius 21 "A woman disappointed and disillusioned": CLEARANCE (seeing things as they are).

Leo 22 "A carrier pigeon": ENLIGHTENMENT (expanding horizons).

Aquarius 22 "A rug placed on a floor for children to play": REFINEMENT (playfulness and well-defined boundaries).

Leo 23 "A bareback rider": AUDACITY (daring without a saddle).

Aquarius 23 "A big bear sitting down and waving all its paws": APTITUDE (mastering strength).

Leo 24 "An untidy, unkempt man": IMPERTURBABILITY (unselfconscious).

Aquarius 24 "A man turning his back on his passions and teaching from experience": SERENITY (mastering passions).

Leo 25 "A large camel crossing the desert": ADEQUACY (well-balanced capacity).

Aquarius 25 "A butterfly with the right wing more perfectly formed": UNIQUENESS (subtle perfections).

Leo 26 "A rainbow": SIGNIFICANCE (buoyant hopes).

Aquarius 26 "A hydrometer": EFFICIENCY (controlling the variables).

Leo 27 "Daybreak": GENESIS (spreading luminosity).

Aquarius 27 "An ancient pottery bowl filled with violets": TRADITION (modest adornment of traditional roots).

Leo 28 "Many little birds on the limb of a tree": RAMIFICATION (overtones and connotations).

Aquarius 28 "A tree felled and sawed": IMMEDIACY (thought for the future).

Leo 29 "A mermaid": IMPORTUNITY (the imperative of longing).

Aquarius 29 "Butterfly emerging from chrysalis": EMANATION (natural metamorphosis).

Leo 30 "An unsealed letter": CONFIDENCE (a trusting availability).

Aquarius 30 "The field of Ardath in bloom": CONTINUITY (blessings fulfilled).

Virgo 1 "A man's head": CHARACTER (stamp of identity).

Pisces 1 "A public market": COMMERCE (the field of common commerce).

Virgo 2 "A large white cross upraised": GLORIFICATION (crossroad).

Pisces 2 "A squirrel hiding from hunters": CAUTION (wariness).

Virgo 3 "Two angels bringing protection": SECURITY (invisible assurance).

Pisces 3 "Petrified forest": SURVIVAL (enduring principles).

Virgo 4 "A colored child playing with white children": INTIMACY (natural acceptance).[9]

Pisces 4 "Heavy traffic on a narrow isthmus": CONVERGENCE (bottleneck).

Virgo 5 "A man dreaming of fairies": OUTLOOK (reverie).

Pisces 5 "A church bazaar": BENEFIT (welcoming).

Virgo 6 "A merry-go-round": DIVERSION (cyclic ups and downs).

Pisces 6 "Officers on dress parade": DISCIPLINE (rank and file).

Virgo 7 "A harem": RESTRAINT (comfortable confines).

Pisces 7 "A cross lying on the rocks": CONSCIENCE (a path without compromise).

Virgo 8 "First dancing instruction": ASSISTANCE (social primer).

Pisces 8 "A girl blowing a bugle": SUMMONS (call to action).

Virgo 9 "A man making a futuristic drawing": EXPERIMENT (personal innovation).

Pisces 9 "A jockey": PRACTICE (go for broke).

Virgo 10 "Two heads looking out and beyond the shadows": INTELLIGENCE (searching ahead).

Pisces 10 "An aviator in the clouds": OBSERVATION (feeling one's way).

Virgo 11 "A boy molded in his mother's aspirations for him": EXACTION (projection).

Pisces 11 "Men seeking illumination": DEDICATION (seekers).

Virgo 12 "A bride with her veil snatched away": INVITATION (uncovering).

Pisces 12 "An examination of initiates": QUALIFICATION (affirmation test).

Virgo 13 "A strong hand supplanting political hysteria": POWER (calming control).

Pisces 13 "A sword in a museum": EXAMPLE (inner power).

Virgo 14 "A family tree": GENTILITY (noble ancestry).

Pisces 14 "Lady in a fox fur": TASTEFULNESS (wrapped with cunning).

Virgo 15 "An ornamental handkerchief": GRACEFULNESS (uplifting refinements).

Pisces 15 "An officer preparing to drill his men": PRECISENESS (impeccability).

Virgo 16 "An orangutan": DEXTERITY (instinctual power).

Pisces 16 "The flow of inspiration": INGENUITY (inner resource).

Virgo 17 "A volcano in eruption": EXPLOSION (breaking out).

Pisces 17 "An Easter promenade": CELEBRATION (a spring in one's step).

Virgo 18 "A ouija board": ACUMEN (optimism).

Pisces 18 "A gigantic tent": APPORTIONMENT (rare occasion).

Virgo 19 "A swimming race": ELIMINATION (keeping the head above water).

Pisces 19 "A master instructing his pupil": ELUCIDATION (channeling knowledge).

Virgo 20 "An automobile caravan": VARIETY (in line for a destination).

Pisces 20 "A table set for an evening meal": FAMILIARITY (fruits of one's labors).

Virgo 21 "A girls' basketball team": EXPRESSION (team effort).

Pisces 21 "A little white lamb, a child, and a Chinese servant": TALENT (perspective differentials).

Virgo 22 "A royal coat of arms": PREROGATIVE (right).

Pisces 22 "A man bringing down the new law from Mount Sinai": MANDATE (higher authority).

Virgo 23 "An animal trainer": RESOLUTENESS (harnessing).

Pisces 23 "Spiritist phenomena": SENSITIVITY (the intangible touch).

Virgo 24 "Mary and her white lamb": ARTLESSNESS (innocent attitude).

Pisces 24 "Tiny inhabited island": CULTIVATION (the insulated world).

Virgo 25 "Flag at half-mast": RESPECT (perception of transitions).

Pisces 25 "A purging of the priesthood": REFORMATION (clearing the way for the new).

Virgo 26 "A boy with a censer": RAPTURE (a new pervasive atmosphere).

Pisces 26 "A new moon divides its influence": FINESSE (smoldering issues).

Virgo 27 "Grande dames at tea": APLOMB (poise).

Pisces 27 "A harvest moon": BENEDICTION (aftermath).

Virgo 28 "A bald-headed man": DOMINANCE (personal power).

Pisces 28 "A fertile garden under the full moon": ULTIMACY (latent abundance).

Virgo 29 "A man gaining secret knowledge from a paper he is reading": DISCOVERY (comprehension).

Pisces 29 "A prism": VALIDATION (analysis of the whole through parts).

Virgo 30 "A false call unheard in attention to immediate service": SAFEGUARD (prioritizing).

Pisces 30 "The Great Stone Face": DISCERNMENT (stoic).

---

1. In his book *The Sabian Symbols in Astrology,* Marc Edmund Jones replaced the original word on the notecard, "white," with "wild," cf. Diana E. Roche, *The Sabian Symbols: A Screen of Prophecy* (Victoria, B.C.: Trafford, 1998) p. 43.

2. M. E. Jones replaced the original word on the notecard, "orating," with "haranguing," cf. Roche, p. 107.

3. The notecard reads "An Easter service," with "early A.M." circled in the margin note. M. E. Jones later changed "early A.M." to "sunrise," cf. Roche, p. 291.

4. M. E. Jones replaced the word "auto" with "automobile," cf. Roche, p. 125.

5. M. E. Jones replaced the word "carved" with "cut," cf. Roche, p. 340.

6. M. E. Jones replaced the word "flapper" with "an up-to-date girl," cf. Roche, p. 156.

7. M. E. Jones replaced the word "performance" with "performer," cf. Roche, p. 340.

8. M. E. Jones replaced the word "singing" with "sitting," cf. Roche, p. 349.

9. M. E. Jones rewrote the notecard version of "A chocolate child playing with whites" to read: "A colored child playing with white children," cf. Roche, p. 184.

APPENDIX II

sabian symbol quick reference guide

ARIES

1. A woman rises out of water, a seal rises and embraces her

2. A comedian entertains a group

3. A cameo profile of a man in the outline of his country

4. Two lovers strolling through a secluded walk

5. A triangle with wings

6. A square brightly lighted on one side

7. A man successfully expressing himself in two realms at once

8. A large hat with streamers flying, facing east

9. A crystal gazer

10. A man teaching new forms for old symbols

11. The president of the country

12. A flock of white geese

13. An unsuccessful bomb explosion

14. A serpent coiling near a man and a woman

15. An Indian weaving a blanket

LIBRA

A butterfly made perfect by a dart through it

The light of the sixth race transmuted to the seventh

Dawn of a new day, everything changed

A group around a campfire

A man teaching the true inner knowledge

The ideals of a man abundantly crystalized

A woman feeding chickens and protecting them from the hawks

A blazing fireplace in a deserted home

Three old masters hanging in an art gallery

A canoe approaching safety through dangerous waters

A professor peering over his glasses

Miners emerge from a mine

Children blowing soap bubbles

A noon siesta

Circular paths

ARIES

16. Brownies dancing in the setting sun
17. Two prim spinsters
18. An empty hammock
19. The magic carpet
20. A young girl feeding birds in winter
21. A pugilist entering the ring
22. The gate to the garden of desire
23. A woman in pastel colors carrying a heavy and valuable but veiled load
24. An open window and a net curtain blowing into a cornucopia
25. A double promise
26. A man possessed of more gifts than he can hold
27. Lost opportunity regained in the imagination
28. A large disappointed audience
29. A celestial choir singing
30. A duck pond and its brood

LIBRA

A boat landing washed away

A retired sea captain

Two men placed under arrest

A gang of robbers in hiding

A Jewish rabbi

A crowd upon the beach

A child giving birds a drink at a fountain

Chanticleer

A third wing on the left side of a butterfly

Information in the symbol of an autumn leaf

An eagle and a large white dove turning one into the other

An airplane hovering overhead

A man in the midst of brightening influences

Humanity seeking to span the bridge of knowledge

Three mounds of knowledge on a philosopher's head

TAURUS

1. A clear mountain stream
2. An electrical storm
3. Steps up to a lawn blooming with clover
4. The rainbow's pot of gold
5. A widow at an open grave
6. A bridge being built across a gorge
7. A woman of Samaria
8. A sleigh without snow
9. A Christmas tree decorated
10. A Red Cross nurse
11. A woman sprinkling flowers
12. Window-shoppers
13. A man handling baggage
14. Shellfish groping and children playing
15. A man muffled up, with a rakish silk hat

SCORPIO

A sight-seeing bus

A broken bottle and spilled perfume

A house-raising

A youth holding a lighted candle

A massive rocky shore

A gold rush

Deep-sea divers

The moon shining across a lake

Dental work

A fellowship supper

A drowning man rescued

An embassy ball

An inventor experimenting

Telephone linemen at work

Children playing around five mounds of sand

TAURUS

16. An old man attempting vainly to reveal the Mysteries
17. A battle between the swords and the torches
18. A woman holding a bag out of a window
19. A newly formed continent
20. Wind, clouds and haste
21. A finger pointing in an open book
22. White dove over troubled waters
23. A jewelry shop
24. A mounted Indian with scalp locks
25. A large well-kept public park
26. A Spaniard serenading his senorita
27. A squaw selling beads
28. A woman pursued by mature romance
29. Two cobblers working at a table
30. A peacock parading on an ancient lawn

SCORPIO

A girl's face breaking into a smile

A woman the father of her own child

A woods rich in autumn coloring

A parrot listening and then talking

A woman drawing two dark curtains aside

A soldier derelict in duty

Hunters starting out for ducks

A bunny metamorphosed into a fairy

Crowds coming down the mountain to listen to one man

An X-ray

Indians making camp

A military band on the march

The king of the fairies approaching his domain

An Indian squaw pleading to the chief for the lives of her children

A Halloween jester

GEMINI

1. A glass-bottomed boat in still water
2. Santa Claus filling stockings furtively
3. The garden of the Tuileries
4. Holly and mistletoe
5. A radical magazine
6. Drilling for oil
7. An old-fashioned well
8. An industrial strike
9. A quiver filled with arrows
10. An aeroplane falling
11. A new path of realism in experience
12. A topsy saucily asserting herself
13. A great musician at his piano
14. A conversation by telepathy
15. Two Dutch children talking

SAGITTARIUS

A Grand Army of the Republic campfire

The ocean covered with whitecaps

Two men playing chess

A little child learning to walk

An old owl up in a tree

A game of cricket

Cupid knocking at the door

Rocks and things forming therein

A mother with her children on the stairs

A golden-haired goddess of opportunity

The lamp of physical enlightenment in the left temple

A flag that turns into an eagle that crows

A widow's past is brought to light

The Pyramids and the Sphinx

The groundhog looking for its shadow

GEMINI

16. A woman suffragist orating
17. The head of health dissolved into the head of mentality
18. Two Chinese men talk Chinese
19. A large archaic volume
20. A cafeteria
21. A labor demonstration
22. A barn dance
23. Three fledglings in a nest high in a tree
24. Children skating on ice
25. A man trimming palms
26. Winter frost in the woods
27. A gypsy coming out of the forest
28. A man declared bankrupt
29. The first mockingbird in spring
30. Bathing beauties

SAGITTARIUS

Seagulls watching a ship
An Easter sunrise service

Tiny children in sunbonnets
Pelicans moving their habitat
Men cutting through ice
A child and a dog with borrowed eyeglasses
A Chinese laundry
Immigrants entering

A bluebird standing at the door of the house
A chubby boy on a hobbyhorse
A flag bearer
A sculptor
An old bridge over a beautiful stream
A fat boy mowing the lawn
The Pope

CANCER

1. A furled and unfurled flag displayed from a vessel
2. A man suspended over a vast level place
3. A man all bundled up in fur leading a shaggy deer
4. A cat arguing with a mouse
5. An auto wrecked by a train
6. Game birds feathering their nests
7. Two fairies on a moonlit night
8. Rabbits dressed in clothes and on parade
9. A tiny nude miss reaching in the water for a fish
10. A large diamond not completely carved
11. A clown making grimaces
12. A Chinese woman nursing a baby with a message
13. One hand slightly flexed with a very prominent thumb
14. A very old man facing a vast dark space to the northeast
15. A group of people who have overeaten and enjoyed it

CAPRICORN

An Indian chief demanding recognition

Three stained-glass windows, one damaged by bombardment

The human soul receptive to growth and understanding

A party entering a large canoe

Indians rowing a canoe and dancing a war dance

A dark archway and ten logs at the bottom

A veiled prophet of power

Birds in the house singing happily

An angel carrying a harp

An albatross feeding from the hand

A large group of pheasants

A student of nature lecturing

A fire worshipper

An ancient bas-relief carved in granite

Many toys in the children's ward of a hospital

CANCER

16. A man before a square with a manuscript scroll before him

17. The germ grows into knowledge and life

18. A hen scratching for her chicks

19. A priest performing a marriage ceremony

20. Gondoliers in a serenade

21. A prima donna singing

22. A woman awaiting a sailboat

23. Meeting of a literary society

24. A woman and two men on a bit of sunlit land facing south

25. A dark shadow or mantle thrown suddenly over the right shoulder

26. Contentment and happiness in luxury, people reading on davenports

27. A storm in a canyon

28. A modern Pocahontas

29. A muse weighing twins

30. A daughter of the American Revolution

CAPRICORN

Boys and girls in gymnasium suits

A girl surreptitiously bathing in the nude

The Union Jack

A child of about five with a huge shopping bag

A hidden choir singing

A relay race

A general accepting defeat gracefully

Two awards for bravery in war

A woman entering a convent

An oriental-rug dealer

A water sprite

A mountain pilgrimage

A large aviary

A woman reading tea leaves

A secret business conference

LEO

1. A case of apoplexy
2. An epidemic of mumps
3. A woman having her hair bobbed
4. A formally dressed man and a deer with its horns folded
5. Rock formations at the edge of a precipice
6. An old-fashioned woman and a flapper
7. The constellations in the sky
8. A Bolshevik propagandist
9. Glass blowers
10. Early morning dew
11. Children on a swing in a huge oak tree
12. An evening lawn party
13. An old sea captain rocking
14. The human soul awaiting opportunity for expression
15. A pageant

AQUARIUS

An old adobe mission

An unexpected thunderstorm

A deserter from the navy

A Hindu healer

A council of ancestors

A performance of a mystery play

A child born of an eggshell

Beautifully gowned wax figures

A flag turned into an eagle

A popularity that proves ephemeral

Man tête-à-tête with his inspiration

People on stairs graduated upwards

A barometer

A train entering a tunnel

Two lovebirds singing on a fence

LEO

16. Sunshine just after a storm

17. A nonvested church choir

18. A teacher of chemistry

19. A houseboat party

20. The Zuni sun worshippers

21. Chickens intoxicated

22. A carrier pigeon

23. A bareback rider

24. An untidy, unkempt man

25. A large camel crossing the desert

26. A rainbow

27. Daybreak

28. Many little birds on the limb of a tree

29. A mermaid

30. An unsealed letter

AQUARIUS

A big businessman at his desk

A watchdog standing guard

A man unmasked

A forest fire quenched

A big white dove, a message bearer

A woman disappointed and disillusioned

A rug placed on a floor for children to play

A big bear sitting down and waving all its paws

A man turning his back on his passions and teaching from experience

A butterfly with the right wing more perfectly formed

A hydrometer

An ancient pottery bowl filled with violets

A tree felled and sawed

Butterfly emerging from chrysalis

The field of Ardath in bloom

VIRGO

1. A man's head
2. A large white cross upraised
3. Two angels bringing protection
4. A colored child playing with white children
5. A man dreaming of fairies
6. A merry-go-round
7. A harem
8. First dancing instruction
9. A man making a futuristic drawing
10. Two heads looking out and beyond the shadows
11. A boy molded in his mother's aspirations for him
12. A bride with her veil snatched away
13. A strong hand supplanting political hysteria
14. A family tree
15. An ornamental handkerchief

PISCES

A public market

A squirrel hiding from hunters

Petrified forest

Heavy traffic on a narrow isthmus

A church bazaar

Officers on dress parade

A cross lying on the rocks

A girl blowing a bugle

A jockey

An aviator in the clouds

Men seeking illumination

An examination of initiates

A sword in a museum

Lady in a fox fur

An officer preparing to drill his men

VIRGO

16. An orangutan
17. A volcano in eruption
18. A ouija board
19. A swimming race
20. An automobile caravan
21. A girls' basketball team

22. A royal coat of arms

23. An animal trainer
24. Mary and her white lamb
25. Flag at half-mast
26. A boy with a censer
27. Grande dames at tea
28. A bald-headed man
29. A man gaining secret knowledge from a paper he is reading
30. A false call unheard in attention to immediate service

PISCES

The flow of inspiration

An Easter promenade

A gigantic tent

A master instructing his pupil

A table set for an evening meal

A little white lamb, a child, and a Chinese servant

A man bringing down the new law from Mount Sinai

Spiritist phenomena

Tiny inhabited island

A purging of the priesthood

A new moon that divides its influence

A harvest moon

A fertile garden under the full moon

A prism

The Great Stone Face

BIBLIOGRAPHY

Funk & Wagnall's Standard College Dictionary. Markham, Ontario: Fitzhenry & Whiteside Limited, 1976.

Graves, Robert. *The Greek Myths, Volumes 1 and 2*. First Folio Society, 2001.

Hendrickson, Robert. *The Facts on File Encyclopedia of Word and Phrase Origins*. Revised and expanded edition. New York: Checkmark Books, 2000.

Hill, Lynda. *The Sabian Symbols as an Oracle*. Avalon, Australia: White Horse Book, 2002.

Jones, Marc Edmund. *The Sabian Symbols in Astrology*. Santa Fe, NM: Aurora Press, 1993.

Partridge, Eric. *Origins: A Short Etymological Dictionary of Modern English*. New York: Greenwich House, 1983.

Pearsall, Judy, and Bill Trumble. *The Oxford English Reference Dictionary*. Second edition. Oxford: Oxford University Press, 2001.

Roche, Diana E. *The Sabian Symbols: A Screen of Prophecy*. Victoria, B.C.: Trafford Publications, 1998.

Room, Adrian. *Brewer's Dictionary of Phrase and Fable*. New York: Harper Collins, 1999.

Rudhyar, Dane. *An Astrological Mandala*. New York: Vintage Books, 1974.

Wilhelm, Richard, and Cary F. Baynes, trans. *The I Ching or Book of Changes*. Princeton, NJ: Princeton University Press, 1972.

ABOUT THE AUTHOR

BLAIN BOVEE (Ontario, Canada) is a practicing astrological and philosophic counselor. A highly regarded teacher in many disciplines—astrology, creative writing, mandala principle, I Ching, and meditation—Blain is known for his engaging and compelling writing style.